AF539189

RICE AND ITS RESPONSE TO WATER HYACINTH

RICE AND ITS RESPONSE TO WATER HYACINTH

By

Dr. Bhaskar Chandra Mohanty

M.Sc., M.Phil., Ph.D.

Sr. Lecturer in Botany

L.N. Mohavidyalaya, Kodala, (Ganjam)

Odisha (India)

DISCOVERY PUBLISHING HOUSE PVT. LTD.

NEW DELHI-110 002

Published by:
Tilak Wasan

DISCOVERY PUBLISHING HOUSE PVT. LTD.
4383/4B, Ansari Road, Darya Ganj
New Delhi-110 002 (India)
Phone : +91-11-23279245, 43596064-65
Fax : +91-11-23253475
E-mail : discoverypublishinghouse@gmail.com
sales@discoverypublishinggroup.com
web : www.discoverypublishinggroup.com

First Edition: 2015

ISBN: 978-93-5056-721-0

Rice and its Response to Water Hyacinth

Printed at:
Infinity Imaging Systems
Delhi

This Book is Dedicated
To
My Beloved Father

Preface

It is an open truth that all living organisms during their life time face to both biotic and abiotic factors of the environment. Among biotic factors, biochemical linteraction between plants, commonly known as "allelopathy", play a vital role on growth and development of plants. Allelopathy is an emerging branch of science which deals with the input of secondary metabolites of one plant, release from any part of plants either by means of leaching by rainwater, dew, fog or volatilization of volatile compounds or root exudates into the environment, on other plants. The interaction between crop plants and weeds, weeds and weeds, weeds and crops, trees and crops are common phenomena in the natural conditions.

Many crop plants thrive well in the water logging conditions where other aquatic weeds also grow. Though a lot of work has been done on the allelopathic effects of various weeds on several crops through out the globe, insufficient work has been done on allelopathic impact of *Eichhornia crassipes* on rice crops as both are water loving plants.

Data are available on allelopathic effect of water hyacinth *(E. crassipes)* on seed germination and seedling growth only on limited crop plants. Hence, this piece of work is aimed at to provide informations on the allelopathic impact of plant dust of water hyacinth (shoot and root separately) on seed germination, seedling growth, vegetative growth, yield and components of yield of four popular cultivars of rice widely cultivated by many cultivators of Odisha and other states and create awareness among farmers.

The book is divided into four chapters. A general introduction on aim and objective of the project is described in CHAPTER-1 under the heading Introduction. CHAPTER-2 deals with materials used and methods adopted to carry out the investigation, whereas CHAPTER-3 indicates about the results observed during experimentation supported by figures. A general discussion is presented in CHAPTER-4 followed by a brief summary of the work carried out.

I shall consider my efforts amply rewarded if the book effectively survey the need of those for whome it has been written. I trust this book will receive a warm response from my esteemed colleagues, beloved students and conscientious readers.

Suggestions for improvement of the quality of the book from all quarters will be highly appreciated. I bear the full responsibility for all errors and omissions found in this book since it may not come out in complete perfection in this addition.

Dr. Bhaskar Chandra Mohanty

Acknowledgements

I have many debts to acknowldge at the beginning I owe my deepest sense of gratitude and indebtedness to my esteemed teacher Prof. Bhaskar Padhy, Department of Botany, Berhampur University, for his valuable suggestions, constant inspiration, constructive criticism and tideless cooperation throughout this work.

I express my deepest thanks to all my beloved teachers, Department of Botany, Berhampur University, for their valuable advice.

I will fail in my duty, if I do not acknowldge my indebtedness to all the successive Heads of the Department of Botany, Berhampur University, for providing me necessary laboratory and departmental seminar facilities to carryout this piece of work in the department during my research period.

My work will be incomplete if I fail to acknowldge the indebtedness to Officer-in-charge, Regional Agricultural Research Station of Odisha University of Agriculture and Technology (OUAT), Berhampur for supplying pure line seeds of rice cultivars used in this piece of investigation.

I express my thanks to all my senior research scholars and co-scholars of plant physiology and biochemistry laboratory of Botany Department, Berhampur University and all well-wishers whose inspiration and cooperation helped me a lot to complete this work.

My hearty regards and thanks are due to my wife Smt. Surjyamani Mohanty whose love, affection, cooperation, undertook all responsibilities of my household during the period of my work and all sacrifices stand before me as a constant source of inspiration in every step of this work.

I am thankfull to Mr. E. Rama Chandra Patra, Principal, L.N. Mohavidyalaya, Kodala, Ganjam whose generous help, cooperation and encouragement stimulated me to acquire this work in the stipulated time.

Dr. Bishnu Narayana Sethi, HOD, Department of Economics, L N Degree College, Kodala has gone through the entire manuscript of this book. I record my deep sense of gratitude to him for this valuable comments that provide in improving the work.

I have taken months of time to complete this book during that period I receive encouraging and enquiries for this book from Sri H.K. Praharaj, Sri P.K. Majhi, Sri D.R. Bishoyi, Sri M.K. Pattnaik and other Lecturers of my college, space limitations keep me of mentioning them all individually. I am grateful to all of them for making them the dream a reality.

I shall commit a great mistake unless I express my thanks to my loving son **Ashis**, and daughter **Charchika** for their undisturbed cooperation and sacrifices during the course of my research work.

Last but not least I have no words to express my gratitude to Sri Tilak Wassan of Discovery Publication (P) Ltd., New Delhi without his kind help this book could not have seen the light of the day.

B.C. Mohanty

List of Symbols and Abbreviations

a.i	=	Active ingredients
°C	=	Degree Celsius
@	=	At the rate of
cc	=	Cubic centimetre
Chl.	=	Chlorophyll
cm.	=	Centimetre
Conc.	=	Concentration
cv	=	Cultivar
DAS	=	Days after soaking
Dry wt.	=	Dry weight
Fig.	=	Figure
fr.wt.	=	Fresh weight
g	=	Gram
h	=	Hour
K.lux	=	Kelo lux
m.h.	=	Million hectare
mg.	=	Milligram
mg./g.	=	Milligram per gram
ml./l.	=	Millilitre per litre
nm	=	Nanometer
O.D.	=	Optical density

q/h = Quintal per hectare

pH = Hydrogen ion concentration

SE = Standard Error

V = Volume

v/v = Volume/volume

Var. = Variety

± = More or less

/ = Per

% = Per cent

> = More than

< = Less than

: = Is to

Contents

1

Introduction

There are three main components of the environment, such as (a) biotic that includes flora and fauna of the earth, (b) abiotic that includes climatic (temperature, humidity, rain fall, cloudiness etc.) and adaphic (soil and soil characters) and (c) energy compounds such as geothermal energy, thermo-electrical energy, hydro electrical energy and nuclear or atomic energy which directly or indirectly control the nature.

The biotic components, which constitute the biosphere and play an important role on the earth, are present in three main segments of the environment such as atmosphere, hydrosphere and lithosphere. The hydrosphere consists of oceans, seas, streams, rivers, lakes, ponds, polar ice caps, glaceries and groundwater. The hydrosphere ecosystem is further divided into two groups such as fresh water and marine water. The fresh water ecosystems play important roles on growth and sustainable development of flora and fauna of the earth. The fresh water that lodge on the earth create ponds, lakes, wetlands besides seas and oceans. Major flora and fauna of the earth are fresh water habitats. Most of the flora of aquatic habitats including wetlands are weeds.

WETLAND

Wetlands are biologically diverse, hydrologically disperse and ecologically vibrant land scaps of the world embracing soils, water, plants, animals and human begins. These are shallow seasonally or permanently water-lodged areas that normally support hydrophytic vegetation. A wetland has atleast one of the following attributes:

(*a*) Atleast periodically the land supports predominantly hydrophytes,

(*b*) the substrate is predominantly undrained hydric-soil and

(*c*) the substrate is non-soil and is saturated with water or covered by shallow water at some time during the growing season of each year.

Wetlands, present in all climatic and topographic settings around the world, relatively common in tropical and temperate lowlands, are estimated to cover about 6% of the earth's surface out of which 5.7 million km^2 are fresh water wetland.

India possesses about 7.6 million hectare wetlands excluding paddy fields, river and canals out of which 3.6 and 4.6 million ha are inland and costal respectively. India presently has 25 sites designated as wetlands of international importance.

Out of 30 districts of Odisha, South Odisha consists of seven districts (Gajapati, Ganjam, Kandhamala, Koraput, Malkangiri, Nawarangapur and Rayagada) possess about 49,528 hectare in post-monsoon and 36,965 hectare in pre-monsoon period constituting 14% and 12% respectively of the total wetland areas of the State (Misra and Panda, 2008).

The major flora of wetlands are generally weeds which has economic importance in nature.

WEEDS

Robbins *et al.* (1942) termed those obnoxious plants as weeds which are "unwanted, unuseful often prolific and persistent, interfere with agricultural operations, increase labour, add to cost and reduce yields". Weeds vary in size, form and behaviour having many striking features. According to Muenscher (1946) "weeds are those plants with harmful or objectionable habits or characteristics, which grow where they are not wanted, usually in places where it is desired that something else should grow." Whether a plant is considered a weed depends not only on its characters and habit but also its relative position with reference to other plants and human beings. These are classified by grouping together whose similarities are greater than their differences such as terrestrial and aquatic, woody and herbaceous or trees and shrubs. Basing on their life cycle, they may be annual, binneal or perennial. Gupta and Lamba (1978) classified weeds according to (i) ontogeny, (ii) cotyledon characters, (iii) nature of stem, (iv) nature of soil and (viii) climatic types.

About Water-Hyacinth Weed

Among fresh water aquatic weeds (*Eichhornia crassipes*) commonly known as water hyacinth or water orchid, distributed throughout the world. It belongs to family Pontederiaceae of the order Liliales *E. crassipes* (Mart.) Solm syn *E. pesciosa* Kunth., the dominant species is native to Amazon basin of Brazil has been introduced to tropical and subtropical regions around the world (Langeland and Burks, 1998). Holm *et. al.* (1977) reported that this weed was found in 56 countries including USA as noxious weeds. Ramey (2001) reported that *E. crassipes* was a dominate flora in Virginia, Texas (Alice Baytown, Deer Park, Port Neches, Santo Fe, Spring branch, Sugar land etc.), California (Clayton, Merced, Sacramento, San Francisco), Florida (Deland, Hollywood, Lutz, North Fort Myers, Orange Spring, Rockledge), Georgia (Atlanta, Hinesville), North Carollina (Jacksonville), Umberland of Mary Land and Hawaii but now they are irradicated in those locations. This plant was introduced into Australia in 1930. It was also spread to a number of water sources in Africa in 1950 where it was popularly known as "Florida Devil". During 1957 it became an acute problem in Zaira and in subsequent years it gained increase in dimension in Sudan and Central America. In Bangladesh this weed is recognized as "German weed" due to its appearance during first world war in undivided India.

Water-hyacinth made its entry into India from Brazil via Bengal in 1986 in form of an ornamental free floating pond plant. It is recognized as "Blue Devil" in Bengal and popularly known as "Bengal Terror".

Now these plants profusely grow throughout India in fresh water ponds, pools, tanks, reservoirs, irrigation channel and paddy fields mainly in States/UT like Andhra Pradesh, West Bengal, Bihar, Chandigarh, Kerala, Tamil Nadu etc.

In Odisha (Latitude 17° 40°-22° 33′ N and Longitude 81° 24′-87° 26′ E), water hyacinth is found to grow profusely in fresh water habitats and commonly known as "*Bilati Dal*" due to its migration from eastern countries. "*Jala Kumbhi*" or "*Samudra Sokh*" are vernacular names of this weed. The former relates to its morphology (Plants with Kumba - "Pitcher like" swollen petiole floating on the surface water) while latter signifies its power to absorb large quantities of water from a water body rendering the same to dry.

Habit and Description of Plant

Water-hyacinth is a free floating and / or rotted hydrophyte grows upto 0.5-1.0 meter. It thrives well where the annual temperature ranges from 20 to 30°C, annual precipitation from 8.0 to 27.0 dm, pH ranging from 5.0 to 7.5 and salinity of water lesser than 50% of sea water (Gopal, 1987). It grows very fast by releasing high amount of Vanillic, p-hydroxy benzoic, ferulic, *cis*-and *trans-p*-coumaric acids and by conserving dihydroxy phenolic compounds such as protocatechuic, chlorogenic, genetisic, caffeic acids and gibberllin like substance (Chetty, 1988). Due to its tremendous growth potential and wide range of adoptability potential and tolerance to various conditions of the nature, this weed enables to respect and occupy vast areas, where water facilities are available.

Several features make this plant easy to recognize including rosettes of rounded and leathery, waxy, glossy green leaves attached to thick, spongy (often bulbus or inflated for floating) petiole, dark, feathery roots, typically hang suspended in the water below the floating plant, and attractive Lavender flowers when the plants are in bloom. The inflorescence is a distinct aereal spike growing up to 30 cm, the flowers have six stamens and fruit is a three chambered seed capsule.

Plate 1: A bloom of habit of water hyacinth

Plate 2: A flowering plant of water hyacinth

Plate 3: An inflorecence of water hyacinth

Plate 4: A flower of water hyacinth

Economic Importance

Water-hyacinths possess both harmful as well as beneficial importances. It is considered as the worst aquatic plant of the world. Since past few decades this weed has been creating problems in the environment in almost all developing countries of the world by blocking irrigation and drainage channels, irrigation sumps, suppressing the primary production of submerged and bottom dwelling autotrophs, depriving of obtaining oxygen from atmosphere for aquatic life setting of huge amount of dead organic matter of the weed, providing breeding facilities and good in habitable conditions for mosquitoes and other organisms like insects and snails and causing fish mortality. Though attempts are being taken to overcome these hazardous affects throughout the world by means of application of various growth inhibitors (2,4-D, Triazole, Thiadiazole etc.), allelochemicals such as sesquiterpens, lactones etc. leach-out of the plants. Parthenium hystorophorus, Lantana camera etc., the results are not up to the mark (Narasaiash *et al*, 1989; Gopal and Goyel, 1993).

Besides these harmful effects, these weeds are being used in agriculture as green manure. As the leaves contain goods amount of protein (80% on dry wt. basis) and vitamin-A, it can be used as supplementary protein food source for human nutrition. The plant can be used in preparation of food stuffs such as hyacinths curry, biscuits, cakes, suji etc. Some tribals in Bangladesh eat the flowers, young pedancles and petioles of the plant fried or cooked in oil (Srivastava, 1990). Microcrystalline cellulose (MCC) prepared from water hyacinth is found to be acceptable anti-caking agent and thickening agent for food formulation and is comparable to commercial MCC in almost all respects. (Gaonkar and Kulkarni, 1987). Residues of pressed bulbs and leaves free for potassium and SiO_2 are suitable for prominent feed. Green plants, after chopping can be existed by mixing with chopped wheat or paddy straw and molasses in the ratio of 7:2:1 in a silo for 8 to 10 weeks and could be fed to cattle and buffaloes as a source of energy (Kibria *et al.*, 1990; Poddar *et al.*, 1991; Chakraborty *et al.*, 1991; Kumar, 1992). Compost mulch or ash of water hyacinth has been reported to have a positive effect on the soil water balance, increase the yields of wheat, sesame, onion, carrot, cow-bean etc. and was found to be a good substitute for cow manure and when composted exhibited batter result than it (Majid et. al, 1992). Water-hyacinth can be successfully used for biogas production due to its high moisture content that advantages for fermentation in biogas production. Fermentation not only provides sufficient amount of biogas but also the slurry are useful as organic fertilizer. The water-hyacinth can be used a source to remove the minerals, nutrient organic substances and even heavy metals such as Cd, Cr, Cu, Zn and Ni, present as pollutants received from domestic or industrial effluents. This plant can be used for the treatment of low level liquid radioactive wastes and mercurial waste water. The root exudates of this plant containing aromatic amines (N-Pheny-1-naphthylamine and N-Phenyl-2-naphthylamine) show antialgal activity and are 2.5 times as inhibitory as $CuSO_4$, a commonly used algaecide (Sukla and Tripathy, 1989, 1990; Law and Lee, 1990; Dai *et al.*, 1992). Jamil *et al.*, (1988) and Toki *et al.*, (1994) reported that petroleum ether extract of the plant was found to be a source of potential juvenile hormone mimic against insect pests such as *Dysdercus cingulatus* Fabr. and *Tribolium castaneum* Herbst. The sterol present in extract also show inhibitory activity against rice weevil (*Corcyra cephalonica*) a serious pest on stored products (Sharma and Habib, 1994).

From the above facts it is found that water hyacinth is more beneficial than harmful in agricultural point of view.

FOOD SECURITY AND ATTEMPTS TO INCREASE FOOD PRODUCTION

At present over 840 million people most of them in Africa, South Africa and Latin America, do not get enough food to meet the basic needs for energy and nutrition. More than two billion people don't get proper diet as well as essential vitamins and minerals required for their normal growth and development. Most of the people live in the world with persistent hunger and wide spread under-nourishment. One of the reason of food scarcity is over population of the world.

India is one of the most malnourished nations on the earth with galloping population that tops 800 millions. Our population is growing at an increasing rate of 1.8% per year. If this trend continues, our population will be doubled within few years (Ninawe, 1997). In order to irradicate hunger and to face the food scarcity, persistent attempts are to be carried out through agricultural and horticulture researches (Sen,1999). Green revolution partially, if not fully, has solved the above problems by releasing high-yielding variety (HYV) seeds through hybridization, mutation and green manipulation. In order to have more production from HYV seeds, application of chemical fertilizers, biofertilizers, pesticides and insecticides have been reached at the peak as a result the earth directly or indirected faces environmental hazards.

ABOUT RICE

The evolutionary trends of rice, its importance, its scenario in India and Odisha and production constrains are briefly described below.

Evolutionary Trends

Rice belongs to family Poaceae, tribe *Oryzae* with eleven genera. The genus *Oryza* has two cultivated and 22 wild species. The two cultivated species are *Oryza sativa* and *Oryza glaberrima* among which *O. sativa* is the Asian rice grown world-wide while *O. glaberima* is the African rice cultivated on a limited scale in West Africa. The progenitor of *O. sativa* is a common wild rice *O. rufipogon* / *O.perennis* (perennial form) as well as *O.nivara* the annual type. The progenitor of *O. glaberrima* is *O. longistaminata* with *O. breviligulata* as the annual form illustrated below in Fig. 1.1.

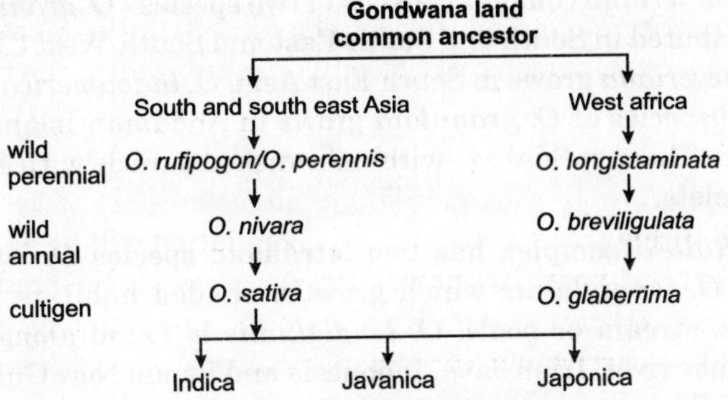

Fig 1.1 : A Evolutionary roots of two cultivated rice species (Adapted from Chang,1976)

The genus *Oryza* has been divided into four species complexes viz. The *sativa* complex, The *Officinalis* complex, The *Meyeriana* complex and the *Ridleyi* complex. The wild species *O. brachyantha* and *O. schlechteri* cannot be placed in any of these groups. (Vaughan, 1989)

Sen *et al.* (2010) reviewed the exploitation of secondary and tertiary gene pool in the genus *oryza. Sativa* complex consists of two cultivated species and six wild taxa. The weedy type species are named as *"fatua"* and *"spontanea"* in Asia and *O. stapfii* in Africa. These weedy forms usually have "red rice" and may be more closely related to *O. rufipogon* and *O. nivara* in Asia and *O. longistaminata* or *O. breviligulata* in Africa. Another species *O. meridionalis* is distributed in tropical Australia.

Officinalis complex consists of nine species and also known as *Oryza latifolia* complex. The tetraploid species *O. minuta* is sympatric with *O. officinalis* distributed in the Central Philippines. *O. rhizomatis* is a species from Srilanka and another species *O. eichingeri* grows in forest shade of Uganda and Sri Lanka. *O. punctata* is distributed in Africa. *O. latifolia, O. alta, O. grandiglumis* are tetraploids. *O. latifolia* is widely distributed in Central and South America and Caribbean islands, whereas *O. australiensis,* a diploid species occurs in Northern Australia.

Meyeriana complex consists of two species - *O. granulata* distributed in South and South-East and South-West China. *O. meyeriana* grows in South East Asia. *O. indoamericana* is a subspecies of *O. granulata* grows in Andaman Islands,in India. These species are with unbranched panicle with small spikelets.

Ridleyi complex has two tetraploid species *O. ridleyi* and *O. iongiglumis* which grow in shaded habitats near river, stream or pools. *O. longiglumis* is found along the Koembe river, Irian Java, Indonesia and Papua New Guinea. *O. ridleyi* grows across South East Asia and Papua New Guinea.

O.. brachyantha is a diploid species widely distributed in East Africa. *O. schlechteri* a tetraploid species found in North-East New Guiana. It is a tufted perennial with 4-5 cm panicles and small awnless spikelets. Besides *Oryza,* the tribe *Oryzae* has ten other genera, namely: *Chikusiochloa, Hygroryza, Leersia, Luziola, Prosphytochoa, Rhynchoryza, Zizania, Zizaniopsis, Porteresia and Potamophila.*

Wild species of *Oryza* are important reservoir of useful traits i.e. resistant to major diseases and insect pests tolerance to several a biotic stresses and also a good source of cytoplasmic male sterility. Even though resistant sources are available in cultivated rice germplasm, the resistant varieties are becoming susceptible to pest and diseases due to change in insect biotypes and pathogen races. In order to overcome these problems researches at molecular and sub-moleular levels are being carried out to produce high yielding varied seeds (HYVS).

Importance of Rice

Rice is one of the most staple cereal food crops of nearly more than half of the world's population. Rice consumption is highest in Asia where average per capita consummation is higher than 50 kg/year. In India and other subtropical countries the per capita consumption average is between 30 to 60 kg/person/year. People in developed western countries of Europe, U.S.A. etc. consume less than 10 kg/ person/year. In addition to consumption of rice as cereal food, rice is also used for commercial application such as beer production. India is the second highest rice consuming country after China. The consumption of rice is increasing year after year. A comparatively statement on consumption of rice by different countries mentioned in Table-1.1 indicates the importance of rice. Increase in day by day worldwide consumption of rice is alarming the whole world as well as India that there is an increase in food scarcity.

Table 1.1: Consumption of Rice in Different Countries During the Year 2003-04

Name of the Country	Rice Consumption in Million Metric Tons
China	135
India	125
Egypt	39
Indonesia	37
Bangladesh	26
Brazil	24
Vietnam	10
Thailand	10
Myanmar	10
Philippines	9.7
Japan	8.7
Mexico	7.3
South Korea	5.0
United States	3.9
Malaysia	2.7

Source: United States Department of Agriculture.

In order to overcome rice scarcity, it is grown over an average of about 137 million hectares in the tropical and sub-tropical parts of the world. It covers more than 750,000 hectares in India largely in Southern areas and to some extant in Western and Eastern parts of the country (Sundaram and Bentur, 2006).

There is a sharp decline in the overall growth rate of food production from 4.23% during 1967-1978 to 3.77% during 1979-1991 and 2.96% during 2000-2005 (Paroda, 2006).

The usefulness of rice is, indeed, universal because men get benefit not only for its starch grains for high caloric food but also make use of other parts of the plant. The total yield of milled rice of home rice varies from 67-72% and the energy of 100 g of milled kernels equals to 359 calories. The dry matter of milled rice contains 80% starch (basically amylase and amylo-pectin), 6-8% protein, 0.5% fat and 0.5% sugar. The byproducts of rice hull and polish that include bran, aleuronic layer etc. are used in pharmaceutical industry for the production of phytin and Vit.-B (Thiamin, Riboflavin and Niacin). The germ in rice, in fact, being a good sources of butter and rice-oil, is used in the manufacture of soap and candlesticks. Rice bran and polish are fed to farm animals and also used for the production of high quality rice-oil used in medicine. Broken rice or second head rice are used by canning industries for human food and for making alcoholic beverages, rice-wine and beer specialties (brewer's rice). The broken and screening rice, good sources of starch (85-95% rice-starch) are also used in face powders (Kolykhamatov, 1985).

Over 30 different useful articles and materials can be made from rice chaff. For example (a) the feed-grade yeast is the most valuable product for livestock, (b) chemical processing of rice chaff gives furfural which is a basic raw material for the manufacture of plastic, (c) cardboards processed from rice chaff is a fairly good construction material, (d) chaff char is an indispensable substitute for bone char in sugar refining, etc. (Koly-Khamatov, 1985).

Although the rice straw is very coarse and inferior in palatability, its nutritive value is much superior to the straw of other grain crops. Processed and flavoured with other grain flours, rice straw which contains 1% protein, 0.5% fat and 30% carbohydrate may be fed to farm animals. Straw of the rice combining with straw of other grain- yielding plants and green peas of alfalfa are prepared as fairly good feed of cattle. Rice straw is a valuable raw material for the manufacture of high quality paper. Other products are also made from rice straw such as cardboards, ropes, packing materials, rayon, linoleum, handbags, floor-mats, rugs, hats, sandals, sacks, baskets, brooms and many other household articles in various parts of the world. In Asia, especially in India, rice straw are used for thatching roofs, fuel, soil mulches and cattle feeds due to its appreciable nitrogen (8 kg / ton), phosphorus (1 kg/ ton) and potassium (12 kg /ton) content. These are also used as fertilizer. Besides the above usefulness, rice is cultivated throughout the world for its grain yield and food value (Koly-Khamatov, 1985).

Rice Scenario in India

Rice (*Oryza sativa L.)* one of the most important cheap crops in many countries throughout the world in variable areas is influenced by the climatic conditions of that locality. It is often considered to be a tropical crop although it is cultivated in the temperate zones in Asia, North and South America and Southern part of Europe and Africa. About 91% of the word's rice crop is being grown in Asia, 5.8% in the two Americas 2.8% in Africa and 0.4% in Europe (Koly-Khamatov, 1985). In Asia, India has the largest area under rice cultivation (44.8 million ha) in the world and ranks 2nd in production next to China (84.74 million tons) (Mohanty and Nagaraju, 2003). It is cultivated world wise in diverse ecological and agro-climatic conditions like rain-fed upland (7.1 million ha), irrigated (17.7 million ha), favourable low-land (10.0 million ha) unfavourable low-land (6.0 million ha). and deep water (1.5 million ha). Out of 44.8 million ha rice-cultivated areas of the country, eastern India comprising Assam, West Bengal, Odisha, Jharkhand, eastern U.P. and eastern M.P. (Chattishgarh) accounts for 27.8 million ha out of this area, 53 and 19.8% are rain-fed low land and upland areas respectively (Mohapatro, 2002).

Rice Scenario in Odisha

Rice is the major dominate crop of Odisha. Out of 85 lakh hectares of cultivated area about 64 lakh hectares are under foodgrain production. Rice is cultivated in 53% of the total area under cultivation and 70% of the total area under food-grains. In Odisha the total rice production was 5.2 million tones out of 4.6 million hectares of area under rice during the year 1999-2000. The productivity of rice in Odisha was 11.0 q/ha as against all India average of 19.7 q/ha. During past 10 years ending (1990-2000) the area under rice has increased by 2 lakh hectares. The area under high-yielding variety during the same period has increased from 22.6 lakh hectares to 34.3 lakh hectares. The rice-cultivated area, production and yield rate in different growing seasons in Odisha from 1990 to 2002 as reported by Mohapatra (2002) is given in Table – B.

Table 1.2: Rice-cultivated Areas, Production and Yield Rate in Odisha during the Period 1990-2002

Year	Area under cultivated (in lakh ha)			Production (million tons)			Yield rate (tons per ha)		
	Autumn	Winter	Summer	Autumn	Winter	Summer	Autumn	Winter	Summer
90-91	41.9	2.1	44.0	48.0	4.3	52.7	1156	2019	1198
91-92	42.6	2.9	45.5	60.3	6.3	66.6	1416	2176	1464
92-93	42.3	2.1	44.4	49.8	4.1	53.9	1176	1939	1213
93-94	42.3	2.4	45.5	61.5	5.2	66.2	1415	2109	1452
94-95	41.9	2.7	44.6	58.3	5.2	63.5	1393	1944	1426
95-96	42.5	2.8	45.3	56.5	5.8	62.3	1327	2103	1375
96-97	42.0	2.7	44.7	38.3	6.1	44.4	912	2267	993
97-98	42.6	2.4	45.0	57.5	4.5	62.0	1350	1924	1380
98-98	41.8	2.7	45.5	48.9	5.0	53.9	1169	1889	1212
99-00	42.2	3.8	46.0	42.8	9.1	51.9	1013	2389	1127
00-01	42.3	2.0	44.3	41.7	4.4	46.1	987	2136	1041
01-02	42.3	2.7	45.0	65.7	5.8	71.5	1554	2127	1589

Source: *Oryza*, Vol. 39 (1-4), 2002, page 22.

In spite of all the increased inputs, the productivity of rice per hectare has stagnated and is far below the national rice productivity. Even though natural calamities such as drought, flood and cyclone are partly responsible for this lower productivity of rice in Odisha compared to national average, there are other factors affecting the productivity such as climate, soil, inadequate crop management, late land preparation, delayed planting, inadequate plant population, old seedlings, non-availability of fertilizers inputs in the right time and quality, non-synchronous credit, input and technology deliver system to the small and marginal farmers etc.

Rice Production Constraints

Rice production is, generally, affected by various constraints in India in general and Odisha in particular. Theses constraints are broadly divided into four major categories.

Socio-economic constraints

It includes the following factors:

- High cost of cultivation compare to value of the products.
- Distress sale of rice /non-remunerative prices.
- Poor storage and marketing facilities at farm level.
- No institutional support.
- Lack of transport facilities.
- Inadequate credit facilitates.
- Lack of consolidation of holdings.
- Small and scattered holdings.
- Stray cattle menace.
- Lack of resources of the farmers.
- Low literacy level of the farmers.
- Non-availability of labour for timely operations.

- Social taboos.
- Near absence of single delivery system of credit, inputs and technology.
- Non-existence of custom hire services at Panchayat level.
- Incomplete crop insurance cover.

Extension Services

It includes the following events :

- Inadequate research-extension linkage.
- Inadequate extension literature.
- Non-functional village extension agents.
- Absence of mini but many small demonstrations nearby the farmers.
- Single factor demonstration instead of multi factor demonstration.
- Lack of proper extension agents with commitments.
- Lack of feedback to the research scientists by the extension workers.
- Non-existence of diagnostic survey by the team of competent scientists.
- Lack of mobility of the research scientists and extension workers.

Biophysical Constraints

It has mainly two factors such as:

(i) **Climate:** Cyclone, tornado, drought, erratic rainfall, distribution and intensity of light, temperature, humidity etc.

(ii) **Water:** High rates of infiltration/percolation in uplands, Water stagnation in lowlands, poor drainage, flash folds in early and mid-season, lack of adequate irrigation in rabi season etc.

Technical Constraints

These include pests, diseases and weeds:

(i) **Insects:** Yellow stem borer, gall midge, gundhi bug, green leaf hopper, army worm leaf folder, plant hopers, whorl maggot etc.

(ii) **Diseases:** Bacterial leaf blight, blast, brown spot, sheath blight, sheath rot, false smut, bacterial leaf steak, tungro virus etc.

(iii) **Weeds:** Heavy weed infestation in direct seeded rice field, sedges, broad leaved weeds in upland, grasses, sedges, relatively low weed infestation in transplanted rice as compared to direct seeded rice in low land rice field etc.

Cultural Practice

It includes:

(i) **Land Preparation:** Inadequate land preparation, low plant population, late planting, old seedling, absence of timely gap filling, late weeding, deep transplanting, poor blustering operations, unscientific cropping systems.

(ii) **Rice Varieties:** Use of traditional low yielding varieties with low response to inputs especially in lowlands (rainfed) and deep-water conditions, lack of rice varieties resistant to pests and diseases and low seed replacement by the farmers.

(iii) **Soils:** Shifting cultivation in sloppy lands without soil and water conservation measures, improper watershed management, low water holding capacity in sandy soils, high soil acidity, soil salinity, soil alkalinity, absence of use of soil amendments, formation of hard pan below plough layer in rice-rice rotation.

(iv) **Manures and fertilizers:** Lack of farm yard manurc (F.Y.M.) and compost, low organic matter or low organic carbon content, near absence of green manuring practice, inadequate / imbalanced fertilizers use, late top dressing of fertilizers, decline in response of rice to fertilizer nutrients (factor productivity), non-availability of inputs in time.

(*v*) **Nutritional disorders:** Deficiency of nitrogen, phosphorus, potassium, calcium, sulphur, zinc; Iron chlorosis in alkaline soils, iron toxicity in acid soils and almunium toxicity in uplands.

Farm Machinery and Equipments

It include the followings:

- Lack of improved farm implements at farmers level.
- Lack of efficient bullock drawn field equipments for upland preparation and seedling at panchayat level.
- Lack of inadequate intercultural operation, tractor ploughing is costly and hence extensive use of tillers by the farmers.
- Maintenance of bullocks are costly.
- Near absence of mechanical transplanting and harvesting operations.
- Inordinate delay in farm operations result in poor yields.
- Lack of custom hire services for tractor drawn implements.
- Lack of mechanically operated electrical and diesel operated pumps.
- Lack of manually operated sprayers and dusters.
- Lack of transport facilities for taking the produce from the field to the threshing floor and from farm house to market center.
- Near absence of mechanical threshing and drying.

To meet the demand of the burgeoning population, it is of paramount important that a second breakthrough in food grain production and productive advance is to be achieved in the country.

ALLELOPATHY AND ALLELOCHEMICLAS

In natural condition, both abiotic and biotic factors play important role on the growth and development of phytocommunitites. The biotic factors include the influence of living organisms and/or their products on the other living beings. The various influences or interactions of biotic factors are generally (i) interaction among plants, (ii) interaction between plants and animals and (iii) interaction between plants and micro-organisms present in soil, water and air. In case of plant – plant interaction, competition for light, space, water and nutrients are the major factors. Besides this "allelopathy", the chemical influence of one plants on the other or "chemical interactions among plants", play a major role on growth and development of plants. Through there are various definitions for allelopathy (Molish, 1937; Bonner, 1950; Martin and Rademacher, 1960; Muller, 1969; Lodhi, 1970; Del Moral and Cates, 1971; Bokhari, 1978, Stowe 1979; Kid and Yim, 1983; Rice, 1984 and Putnam, 1985), the International Alleloathy Society (IAS) suggested the following definitions to include in the IAS constitution which need further comments. Allelopathy may be defined as (a) any process involves in secondary metabolites produced by plants and microorganism that influences the growth and development of agricultural and biological systems and (b) a study of the function of secondary metabolites, their significance in biological organizations, their evolutionary origin and elucidation to the mechanism involving plant-plant, plants-micro organisms, plant-viruses, plants-insects etc. (Waller, 1998).

Generally, all plants have capacity to produce and store large number of secondary metabolites such as alkaloids, essential oils, phenolic compounds, steroids, terpenoids, coumarins, flavonoids, cyanohydrins, phytohormones, etc. which vary in their biosynthetic pathways, concentrations and localization from species to specie (Levin, 1976).

The chemicals which involve in allelopathy are commonly known as allelochemicals, botanicals, phytochemicals or natural products are non-nutritional chemicals produced by on organism that affect the growth, health and behavior or population biology or other species (Reese, 1979). These substances are synthesized in living organisms from the metabolism or carbohydrates, fats, and amino acids and arise from acetate or the shikimic acid pathways (Robinson, 1963) as indicated in Fig. 1.2.

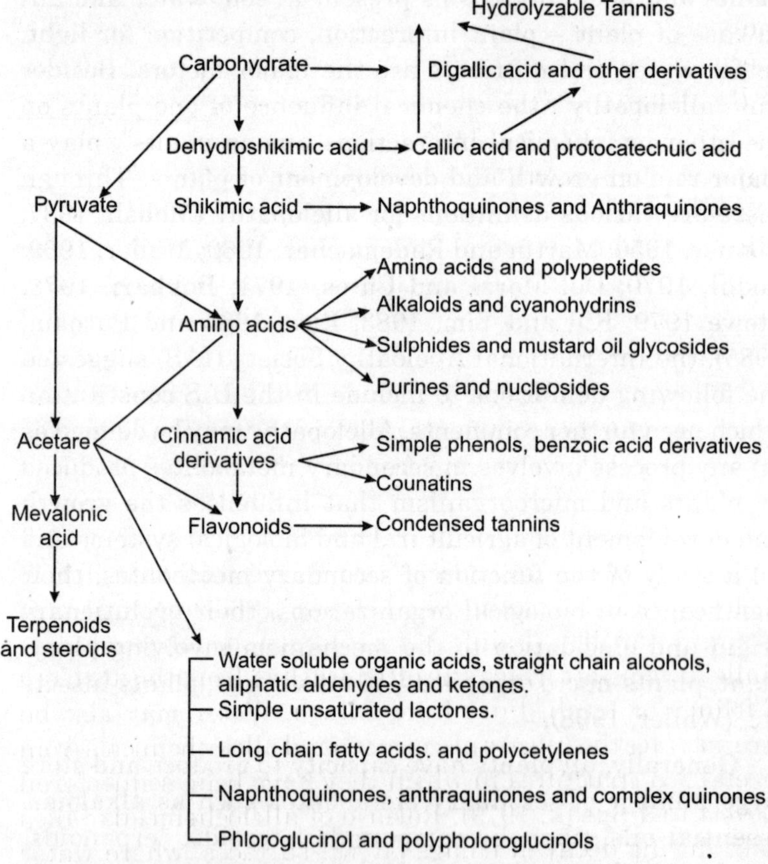

Fig. 1.2: Probable major biosynthetic pathways leading to production of the various categories of allelopathic agents

Mode of Release of Allelochemicals

Plant parts known to contain allelochemcials are roots and rhizomes, stems, leaves, flowers, inflorescence, pollens, fruits and seeds. Allelochemicals can be transferred from a donor plant to a recipient plant. The donor plants which release these chemicals generally store them in the plant cells in bound forms, such as water-soluble glycosides, polymers including tannins, lignins and salts. It has been reported that upon cleavage by plant enzymes or environmental stresses, the toxic chemicals are released into the environment from special glands present in stems or leaves (Putnam and Duke, 1978; Fisher, 1979; Einhelling, 1985).

In higher plants allelochmicals are released from plans through (a) volatilization (b) leaf or stem leachates, (c) root exudates and (d) decomposition of plants residues (Rice, 1984 and Putnam, 1985). The terpenoids such as α-pinene, β-pinene, cineole and camphor are released to the environment through volatilization which is noticeable under drought conditions. The water soluble phenolics and alkaloids are moved out by rainfall through leaching. Phytotoxic aglycones such as phenolics are produced during the decomposition of plant residues in soil. Many secondary metabolites such as scopoletin and hydroquinones are released to the surrounding soil through root exudates.

Role of water is critical to release and transfer of allelochemicals. Grummer and Bayer (1960) reported that natural of artificial rainfall is necessary for foliar transfer of allelochemcials which are often washed from the surfaces of foliage or leached out from foliage. Water may also be necessary for the release of concentrated allelochemicals from specialized structures in which they have been sequestered (Lovett and Speak, 1979). Release of allelochemcials takes place during decay of foliage on soil surfaces, where water act as an essential factor for bacterial activity (Lovett, 1982). Winter (1961) reported that phytotoxins produced from plants residues move readily from soli surfaces into the soil and, subsequently, into roots from which they were translocated. Such transfer and translocation as well as transfers of root exudates must also be facilitated by the presence of water.

It is generally assumed that allelcohemcials are not toxic to the donor plants. Once the chemicals are released from the donor plants into the environment, they may be either degraded or transformed into other forms. The resultant stage of these chemicals may also be toxic to the host plant.

Mode of Action of Allelochemcials

Winter (1961) suggested that readily visible effects of chemicals interchanged between plants are only secondary sings of primary changes. Effects on crop growth and development such as delayed or inhibited germination, stimulation or inhibition of root or shoot growth must, therefore, be interpreted in terms of effects upon basic plant processes.

The claimed mechanisms of direct action of allelochemcials have been summarized by Rice (1979) under the following categories :

- Effects on cell elongation and ultra structure of root tips, including inhibition of cell division.
- Effects on hormone-induced growth.
- Inhibition of protein synthesis and changes in lipid and organic acid metabolism.
- Inhibition or stimulation or specific enzymes. Effects on membrane permeability.
- Effects on stomatal opening and on photosynthesis.
- Effect on respiration.
- Corking and clogging of xylem elements and stem conductance of water.
- Effects on mineral uptake.
- Effects on easily available phosphorus and potassium on soils.

ALLELOCHEMCIALS STUDIES ON EICHHORNIA

Weed species like *Eichhornia, Pistia, Hydrilla, Typha* etc. grow on water logging and wet fields since ancient times which become harmful or beneficial to certain crops. It has been reported that root extracts of *Eichhornia crassipes* contain considerable amount of growth regulating substances which affect seed germination and seedling growth of rice varieties (Sircar and Kundu, 1959, 1960), pea (Ganguly and Sircar, 1954), jute (Sircar and Chakravorty, 1961) of West Bengal (Mohanty (1995), observed that the aqueous leachates of shoot and root of water hyacinth reported to contain GA_3 and IAA-like substances respectively (Sircar *et al.,* 1973) and water soluble phytochemcals which enhanced seed germination and seeding growth in both shoot and root of rice (*O. sativa* L. cv. CR-1014), ragi (*E. coracana* Geartn. cv. AKP-2), green gram (*P. aureus* Roxb. CV. K-851), black gram (*P radiatus* L.cv. T-2), mustard (*B. juncea* L. cv. M-27), and til (*S. orientalae* L. cv. SL-14) at lower concentrations (0.05 to 0.25%). Yang *et al* (1992) and Feng-min *et al.,* (2005) reported antialgal actionvity of ethyl ether fraction of an extract from *E. crassipes.* Wu *et al.* (1991) isolated and identified steroids from *E. crassipes* weed in China. Hence, it is presumed that the phytochemcals of water hyacinth weed might be regulating the plant growth and development in its habitat.

AIM OF PRESENT WORK

Since no considerable and quantitative information on the allelopathic affects of weed on crop plants are available, the present investigations are undertaken to find out allelopathic effect of *Eichhornia crassipes,* if any, on seed germination, growth and yield response of some rice cultivars of Odisha.

2 Materials and Methods

In the present piece of investigation pure line seeds of four cultivars of rice (*Oryza sativa* L.cvs. Swarna mahsuri, Samba mahsuri, Pratikshya and Vijetha), procured from regional agriculture research station of Odisha University of Agriculture and Technology (OUAT) located at Ratnapur, 8 km away from Berhampur city, are being commonly cultivated by most of the farmers of Odisha for their high yielding and other important agronomical characteristics features. Some of such characters of each cultivar are described below (Table 2.1).

Table 2.1: Some Agronomical Characters of Four Test Cultivars of Rice used in this Investigation

Agronomical characters	Swarna mahsuri (MTU-7029)	Samba mahsuri (BPT-5204)	Pratikshya (ORS-2015)	Vijetha (MTU-1001)
Paratage	Vasista × Mahsuri	GEP 24 × T.N. Mahsuri	Swarna × IR -64	MTU-5249 X MTU-7014
Seed to seed duration	150-155	140-145	140-145	Kharif-140-145
Plant Height (cm)	95-100	90-100	100-105	105-110
Vegetative characters	Semi-dwarf plant with professed tillering, non-lodging, dark green foliage, medium long panicle	Dwarf medium tall erect, short leaf, non-lodging	Semi dwarf plant with low tillering short stem, resistant to lodging, suitable to late sown condition	Erect plant with medium tellering, dark green foliage, non – lodging

Agronomical characters	Swarna mahsuri (MTU-7029)	Samba mahsuri (BPT-5204)	Pratikshya (ORS-2015)	Vijetha (MTU-1001)
Grain type	Short slender bold, white Kernal	Medium Slender	Medium slender, golden coluor a whole with white kernal	Medium slender gain
Yield rate (Qtl./ hectare)	60 – 70	55 – 60	70 – 75	Kharif- 60-62 Rabi- 62-65
Cooking quality	Very good	Excellent	Good	Good
Required land type	Medium and low land	Medium land	Medium land	Medium land
Photoperio-dism	Long day	Long day	Short day	Day neutral
Sensitivity	Photo and thermo-sensitive	Photo and thermo-sensitive	Photo-sensitive	Photo-insensitive
Resistant to	Leaf blight, sheath blight, suseptivble to BPH and galmidg	Brown spot, leaf blight, sheath light, suseptivble to BPH and GLH	Brown spot, sheath blight, suseptivble to Stem bores, leaf bores and WBPH	Blast, suseptivble to gal midg, stem borer and leaf border

Source: Mannual on Agricultural Production Technology (Kharif-2008). Directorate of Agriculture and Food Production, Odisha, Bhubaneswar. pp-141-142.

COLLECTION OF WATER HYACINTH AND PREPARATION OF DUST

Healthy plant of water hyacinth (*Eichhornia crassipes*) were collected at pre-flowering stage from an undisturbed pond located at notified area of council (NAC) of Kodala town (Longitude: 84° 92' 72" to 84° 96' 28" E, Latitude : 19° 61' 98" to 19° 62' 20" N) of Ganjam district of Odisha. Then the plants were thoroughly washed with water in order to remove the dust particles and other sticky particles from the surface of the plants. Thereafter the plants were separated in to shoot and root, again washed thoroughly, soaked on blotting paper and allowed to air dry under shade. After complete dried, the root and shoot parts of plants were ground separately with the help of grinder. The dust so obtained were further dried in an incubator maintained at 40 ± 1°C and then kept in closed and lebelled polythene bags for further use.

Plate 5: Collection of Water Hyacinth

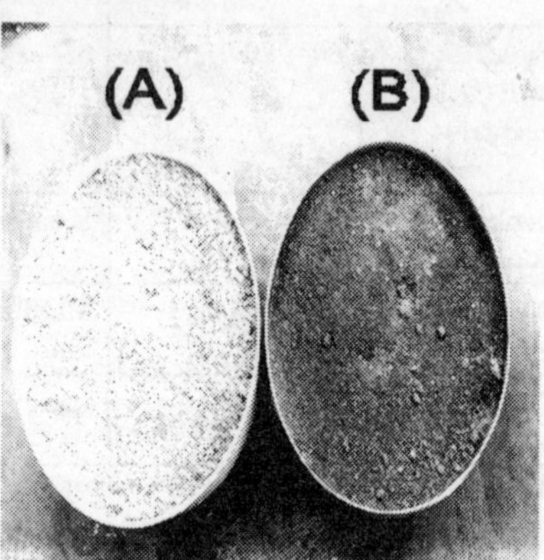

Plate 6: Powder of Water Hyacinth (A)

COLLECTION AND SELECTION OF RICE SEEDS

The procured seeds of rice cultivars were visually selected for their uniform size, colour and healthiness and then surface sterilised with 0.03% (v/v) formalin solution for 20 minutes followed by thoroughly washing with distilled water prior to commencement of experiments.

EXPERIMENTAL SCHEDULES

The following experiments were performed in this piece of investigation whose detailed procedures are given below:

Seed Germination and Seedling Growth

Fine river sands were collected and gravels, soil granules and other particles were separated through a fine sieve. Then such sands were washed thoroughly with running water in order to remove soil dust particles, water soluble chemicals and then sun-dried followed by to complete dryness in an incubator set at 55 ± 2°C. Thereafter such sterilized sands were kept in a closed polythene bags for further use.

Clean and dry plastic trays (5 × 10 × 15 cm size) were filled with equal quantity (150 g) of cleaned and dried sands described above. The trays were divided in to 12 sets (6 for shoot dust and 6 for root dust) for each cultivar of rice with 5 trays in each set.

In first set no dust of shoot and root were mixed which served as control set. Trays of 2nd, 3rd, 4th, 5th and 6th sets were thoroughly mixed with previously prepared shoot and root dust of water hyacinths in order to get 5, 10, 15, 20 and 25 per cent (w/w) concentrations of dust in sand respectively.

Visually selected and surface-sterilized seeds of four test cultivars of rice were sown one cm below the sand surface in each tray of respective sets @ 20 seeds per tray. Equal volume of water were supplied into each tray in order to make the sand dust mixture wet. The trays were kept in dark in a B.O.D. incubator maintained at room temperature (30 ± 2° C). Periodically equal amount of water were supplied to each tray in order to maintain the wetness of sand dust mixture. Emergence of coleoptiles from seeds was considered as onset of germination. The rate of seed germination in trays of each set was recorded from 3 days after sowing (DAS), at an interval of one day, till cent per cent germination observed in control set.

After germination, all the trays containing germinated seeds kept in B.O.D. incubator maintained at 30 ± 2°C were provided with continuous light illumination of 2.5 ± 0.5 K Lux light intensity from florescent tube lights fitted in B.O.D. incubator. Care was taken to provide equal volume of water into each tray to keep the seedling alive.

In order to study seedling growth, the seedling from each tray of both control and treated sets were collected at the rate of two seedlings from each tray of all sets at random at an interval of two days from 6 DAS till 12 DAS, gently washed with water to remove sand particles, soaked on blotting paper and shoot and root lengths were measured with help of centimetre scale. Then the shoot and root portions were separated from the seed and their fresh weights were measured with help of an electrically operated balance. Then the weighed shoot and root mistrials of both control and treated rice seedlings were kept in an incubator maintained at 40 ± 2° C for 24 hours for the measurement of dry weights.

Vegetative Growth

In order to study the vegetative growth of test cultivars of rice influenced by different concentrations of shoot and root dust of water hyacinth, pot culture method was adopted.

A mixture of sandy loam soil and composted cow-dung manure in a ratio of 8:1 was prepared, dried manually powered, gravels and other stony particles were removed and used for pot culture.

Earthenware pots (30 × 30 cm size) were taken and filled with prepared soil manure mixture as described above at the rate of 5 kg/pot.

The pots were divided into 12 sets (6 for shoot dust and 6 for root dust) for each cultivar with five pots in each set. In pots of first set no dust of shoot and root were applied which served as control whereas pots of 2nd, 3rd, 4th, 5th and 6th sets were provided with dust of shoot or root (as per experimental design) in order to get 5, 10, 15, 20 and 25 per cent concentrations (w/w) respectively. Prior to transplantation of rice seedlings, the soil manure mixture and the shoot or root dusts of test weed were thoroughly mixed, puddled and allowed to settle down.

The seedlings of test rice cultivars raised from visually selected and surface sterilized seeds in plastic trays lined with two layers of blotting paper soaked with distilled water and kept in germinating chamber separately were transferred to seedling growth chamber kept in the laboratory at 30 ± 2° C and provided with illumination of ca 2.0 ± 0.5 K Lux light intensity from florescent tube lights. Thereafter twenty days old rice seedlings were transplanted in to pots containing puddle soil manure mixture along with or without shoot or root dust of test weeds @ 10 seedlings/pot. The pots were kept in the experimental filed. Periodically equal volume of water was provided to maintain the equal water level in pots. After 10 days of transplantation, the seedlings were thinned to have four healthy seedlings/pot. The vegetative growth parameters such as (a) number of green leaves on main shoot, (b) number of tillers/plant, (c) total number of green leaves / plant and (d) plant height from soil surface were measured at an interval of 10 days from 30 DAS till flowering following the method adopted by Padhy (1980). Appearance of tip of the spikelet through flag leaf was taken as the criterion of flowering.

Yield and Components of Yield

For this experiment, the plants grown in pots at field condition were allowed to flower and yield. Care was taken to maintained the water content in pots by providing equal quantity of water/pot. At the time of harvesting the following parameters were recorded following the methods adopted by Bhattacharjee *et al.*, 1973 as described below in order to study the influence of shoot and root dust of water hyacinth on yield and components of yield of test rice cultivars

(*a*) Total numbers of panicles per plant.

(*b*) Length of panicles.

(*c*) Number of spikelets per panicle.

(*d*) Number of fertile grains per panicle.

(*e*) Percentage of seed setting.

(*f*) Weight of 1000 grains.

(*g*) Grain yield per plant.

The detailed procedures for collecting data on above parameters

(*a*) **Number of panicles per plant:** The number of tillers bearing panicles in a hill (plant) was taken as number of panicles per plant and it was measured as per the following calculation.

No. of panicles per plant = P/N.

Where 'P' indicates the total number of panicles in all plant samples and the 'N' is the number of plants samples *i.e.* 20.

(*b*) **Length of panicle:** The measurement from the neck node to the tip of panicle was taken as the length of panicle and was expressed in cm.

(c) Number of spikelets per panicle: Total spikelets (filled and unfilled) of the top most panicle (1st panicle) were counted for each plant and summed them for 20 plants. It was calculated as follows:

Number of pikelets per panicle

$$= \frac{\text{Total No. of spikelets on panciles}}{\text{Total No. of panicles}}$$

(*d*) **Number of fertile grain per panicle:** The grains of the top most panicles (1st panicle) were thrashed from panicles of 20 plans and filled and unfilled grains were separated and then counted, for calculation of number of grains per panicle as per the following formula.

Number of fertile grains per panicle

$$= \frac{\text{Total No. of grains on panciles}}{\text{Total No. of panicles}}$$

(*e*) **Percentage of seed setting:** This represents the well filled spikelets (grains) in relation to unfilled (chaffy) and partially filled spikelets on per cent basis on each panicle. This was calculated as per the method adopted by Matsushima and Yamaguchi (1953).

Per cent of seed setting

$$= \frac{\text{Total No. of well filled grains per panciles} \times 100}{\text{Total spielets (partially filled + chafy + well filled grains)}}$$

(*f*) **Weight of 1000 grains:** This represents the weight of 1000 grains taken at random from the total yield from each plant and was calculated as below. The data are expressed in grams.

$$\text{Weight of 1000 grains} = \frac{\text{wt. of filled grains}}{\text{No. of filled grains}} \times 1000$$

(*g*) **Grain yield per plant:** Grain yield per plant was obtained by collecting the fertile grains of all panicles from each plant and their weights were taken and the calculation was made as per the following formula.

Grain yield/Plant

$$= \frac{\text{Total grains weight from harvested panciles per platne}}{\text{Total No. panicles developed per plant}}$$

The average of 20 plants was calculated and grain yield per plant is expressed in grams.

STATISTICAL ANALYSIS

All the data collected from seedling/plant of both control and treated sets in different experiments were subjected to statistical analysis to calculate standard error (S.E.)

PRESENTATION OF DATA

The data so obtained during different experiments were presented in form of both tables and figures. To avoid clumsiness in figures, the S.E. values were presented in tables only. The figures are placed at appropriate places in chapter-3 (Results) whereas tables are placed after summary at Annexure-I.

❑❑❑

3 Results

The results on effect of different connections of shoot and root dust of water hyacinth on seed germination, seedling growth, vegetative growth and yield and components of yield of four test cultivars of rice are described below in detail.

SEED GERMINATION

The ‹ffects of both shoot and root dust of water hyacinth on seed germination of *Swarna mahsuri*, *Samba mahsuri*, *Pratikshya* and *Vijetha* are described below:

Swarna Mahsuri

(*a*) Shoot Dust: It was observed that the percentage of germination influenced by 5% concentration of shoot dust on 6 days after sowing (DAS) was 99.00 $\pm$ 0.44 whereas it was only 20.00 $\pm$ 0.52 per cent influenced by 25% concentration of shoot dust. In control set the value was cent per cent during the same period of incubation. Other concentrations exhibited intermediate values (Table–Ia). The rate of germination exhibited positive corelation with increase of incubation period and negative corelation with increase of concentration of dust in sand of the trays except 5% concentration. The later concentration enhanced a higher rate of germination compared with control as well as other treated sets (Fig.3.1a).

(*b*) Root dust: The root dust also exhibited more or less similar values throughout the period of observation as was noticed in case of shoot dust. Maximum percentage of germination observed in seeds of control set on 6 DAS was 100

± 0.87 % while it was only 18.02 ± 0.91 % in seeds influenced by 25% dust concentration. Date of intermediate values were recorded at different DAS (Table-Ib).

Like the impact of shoot dust, the percentage of seed germination showed positive correlation with increase of incubation period and root dust concentrations expect 5% (Fig. 3.1b).

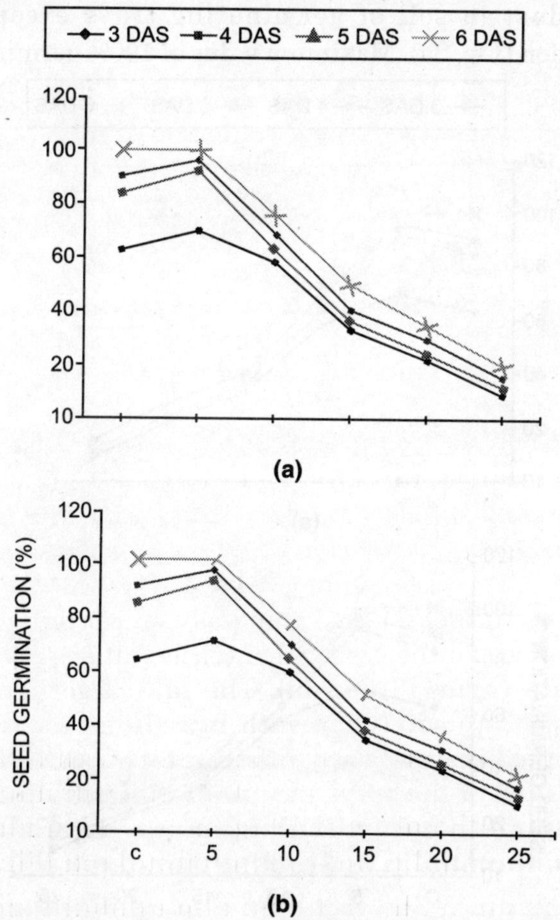

Fig. 3.1: Effect of different concentrations of shoot (a) and root (b) dust of water hyacinth *(E. crassipes)* on seed germination of *O. sativa* L.cv. Swarna mahsuri

Among the two hypes of dusts, shoot dust caused higher rate of seed germination compare to root dust.

Samba Mahsuri

(*a*) Shoot dust: In this cultivar, the rate of seed germination gradually increased with advance of incubation period and gradually decreased by the influence of higher concentration of shoot dust in soil of germinating trays except 5% concentration (Fig. 2a). Maximum value of 100% germination

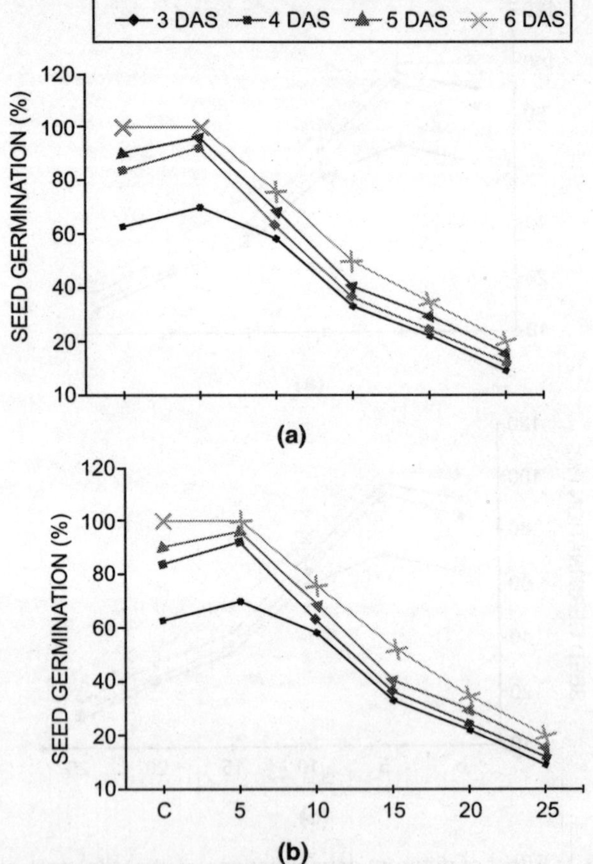

Fig. 3.2: Effect of different concentrations of shoot (a) and root (b) dust of water hyacinth *(E. crassipes)* on seed germination of *O. sativa* L.cv. Samba mahsuri

was noticed in seeds of control set on 6 DAS while it was only 25.60 ± 0.86% in seeds affected by 25% soot dust of water hyacinth recorded at different days during the period of observation (Table–II b).

***(b)* Root dust:** Like shoot dust effects, root dusts also exhibition more or less similar values (Table–II b) and trends (Fig.–2 b) as was noticed in case of influence of shoot dust of water hyacinth.

In this cultivar shoot dust exhibited slight higher rate of germination than the root dust.

Pratikshya

***(a)* Shoot dust:** Like other two cultivars, this cultivar also exhibited similar response to different concentration of dust of water hyacinth (Fig. 3.3a). The percentages of germination influenced by 5% and 25% concentrations of shot dust on 6 DAS were 97.80 ± 0.77 and 15.20 ± 0.56% respectively whereas in control set it was 100.0 ± 0.87% other concentrations of shoot dust caused germination of intermediate values during the period of observation (Table–III a).

***(b)* Root dust:** The different concentration of root dust of water hyacinth exhibited more or less similar values (Table-III b) and trends (Fig. 3.3b).

Amount the two types of dusts root dust were found to be more adversely affected the process of germination as a result lesser percentage of germination was observed.

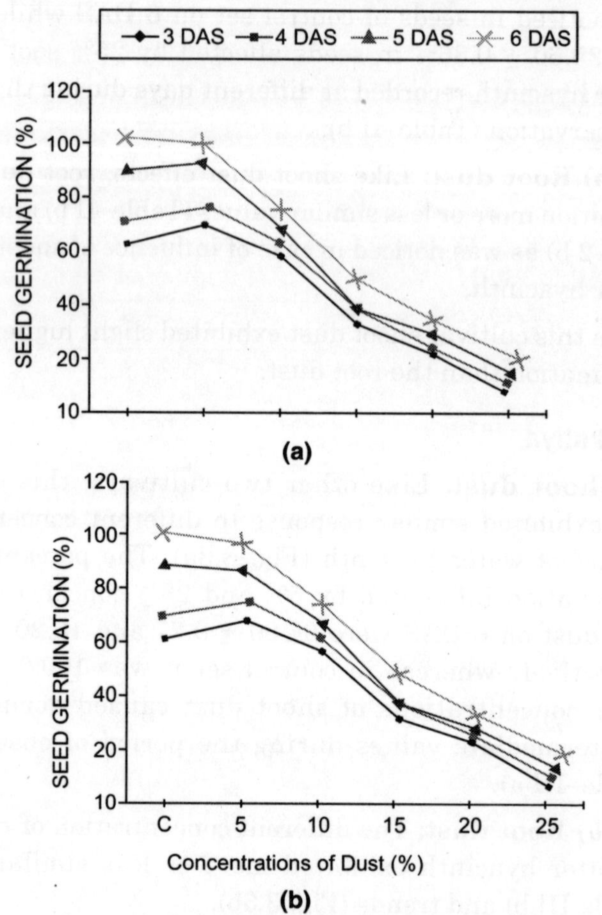

Fig. 3.3: Effect of different concentrations of shoot (a) and root (b) dust of water hyacinth *(E. crassipes)* on seed germination of *O. sativa* L.cv. Pratikshya

Vijetha

(*a*) Shoot dust: The percentage of germination in this cultivar influenced by 25% concentration of dust on 6 DAS was 22.80 ± 0.94 whereas by 5% concentration it was 100.00 ± 0.81% and equal to control value. Dust concentrations of 10.15 and 20% exhibited 78.40 ± 0.64, 51.8 ± 0.91 and 36.40 ± 0.66% of germination on 6 DAS respectively. Data of intermediate values were recorded on 3, 4 and 5 DAS (Table–IVa). The percentage of seed germination exhibited positive corelation with increase of incubation period and negative corelation with higher concentration of dust more than 5%. The later exhibited higher value than other concentrations and control too (Fig. 3.4a).

***(b)* Root dust:** Like other cultivars, this cultivar also exhibited similar response to root dust of water hyacinth.

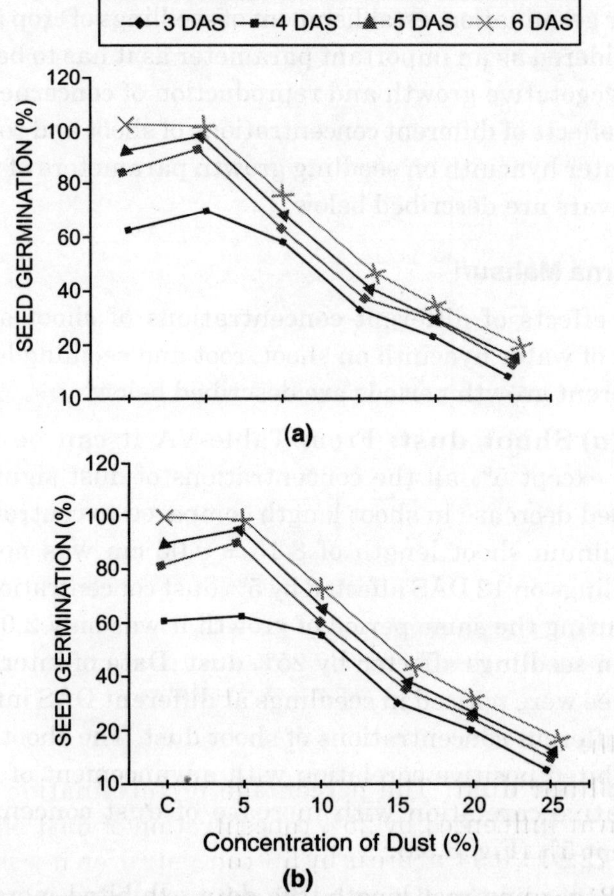

Fig. 3.4: Effect of different concentrations of shoot (a) and root (b) dust of water hyacinth *(E. crassipes)* on seed germination of *O. sativa* L.cv. Vijetha

The date so collected exhibited more or less similar values and same trends as was noticed in case of other cultivars. (Table-IVb and Fig. 3.4b).

Higher rate of germination was observed in this cultivar influenced by shoot dust than root dust.

SEEDING GROWTH

After germination, establishment of seedlings of crop plants is considered as an important parameter as it has to be control the vegetative growth and reproduction of concerned plant. The effects of different concentrations of shoot and root dusts of water hyacinth on seedling growth parameters of test rice cultivars are described below.

Swarna Mahsuri

The effects of different concentrations of shoot and root dust of water hyacinth on shoot, root and seedling length at different growth periods are described below.

(*a*) Shoot dust: From Table-VA it can be noticed that except 5% all the concentrations of dust significantly caused decrease in shoot length compared to control plants. Maximum shoot length of 8.15 ± 0.05 cm was noticed in seedlings on 12 DAS affected by 5% dust concentration where as during the same period of growth it was only 2.01 ± 0.04 cm in seedlings affected by 25% dust. Data of intermediate values were noticed in seedlings at different DAS influenced by different concentrations of shoot dust. The shoot lengths exhibited positive corelation with advancement of age and negative corelation with increase of dust concentrations except 5% (Fig. 3.5a).

Regarding root length, the data exhibited more or less same values and similar trends as were noticed in case of shoot length (Table–V A and Fig. 3.5b).

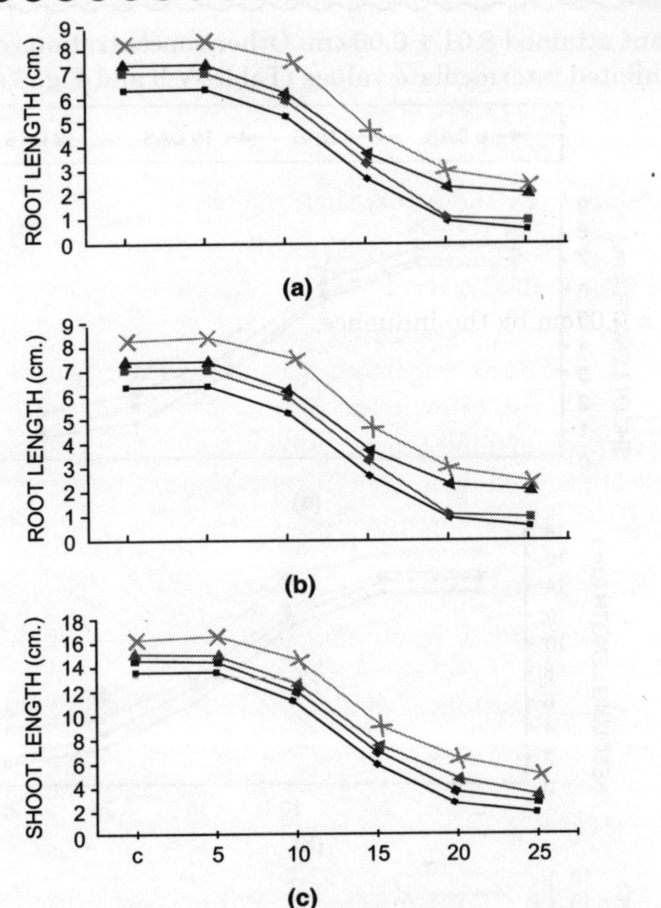

Fig. 3.5: Effect of different concentrations of shoot dust of water hyacinth *(E.crassipes)* on seedling growth of Swarna mahsuri cultivar

The total seedling lengths were also found to be decreased due to reduced shoot and root length of seedlings influenced by different concentration of shoot dust throughout the period of observation as evidenced from Table–V a and Fig.–5 c.

***(b)* Root dust:** The shoot lengths recorded in seedlings of this cultivars influenced by 5 and 25% concentrations of dust on 12 DAS were 8.06$\pm$ 0.04 and 2.00 $\pm$ 0.03 cm respectively. During the same period of growth the seedlings of control plant attained 8.01 ± 0.06 cm. Other concentrations of dust exhibited intermediate values (Table–V b and Fig. 3.6a).

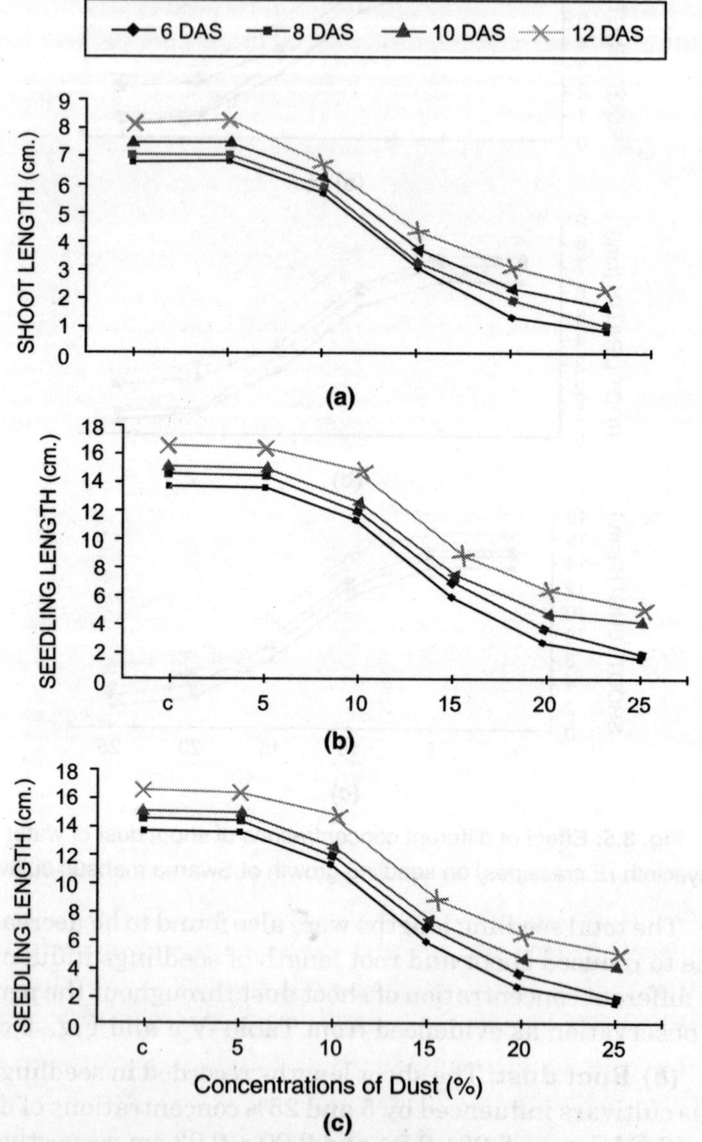

Fig. 3.6: Effect of different concentrations of root dust of water hyacinth *(E. crassipes)* on seedling growth of Swarna mahsuri cultivar

The root lengths of this cultivar of rice were found to be slightly higher compared with their shoot lengths. The root lengths were found to be slightly enhanced due to influence of different concentration of dust. The values varied from 2.22 ± 0.02 to 8.35 ± 0.03 cm in seedlings affected by 25 and 5% dust concentrations on 12 DAS respectively. Other concentrations showed intermediate values (Table–V b). The root lengths exhibited negative corrections with increase of dust concentrations except 5% and positive corlation with advancement of seedling age (Fig. 3.6b).

The total seedling lengths were found to be considerably reduced due to reduction in shoot and root length (Table–Vb). From Fig. 3.6c it can be noticed that the seedling growth exhibited negative corecation with increase of dust concentration in the soil (except 5%) and positive corelation with increase in the growth period.

Among shoot and root dust effects, shoot dust was found to be more effective than the later.

Samba Mahsuri

The effect of different concentrations of both shoot and root dusts on shoot, root and seedling lengths are described below.

(*a*) Shoot dust: The shoot lengths measured in seedlings on 12 DAS influenced by 5 and 25% concentrations of dust were 8.09 ± 0.07 and 1.52 ± 0.06 cm respectively while the value was 8.08 ± 0.04 cm in seedlings of control set. Data of intermediate values were recorded in seedlings affected by different dust concentrations at various growth periods (Table–VI a) the root lengths exhibited positive corelation with advancement of seedling age and negative corelations with increase of dust concentrations except 5% (Fig. 3.7a).

The root lengths influenced by different concentrations of dust considerably reduced the root length while it was enhanced by the increase of seedling age (Table–VI a and Fig. 3.7b).

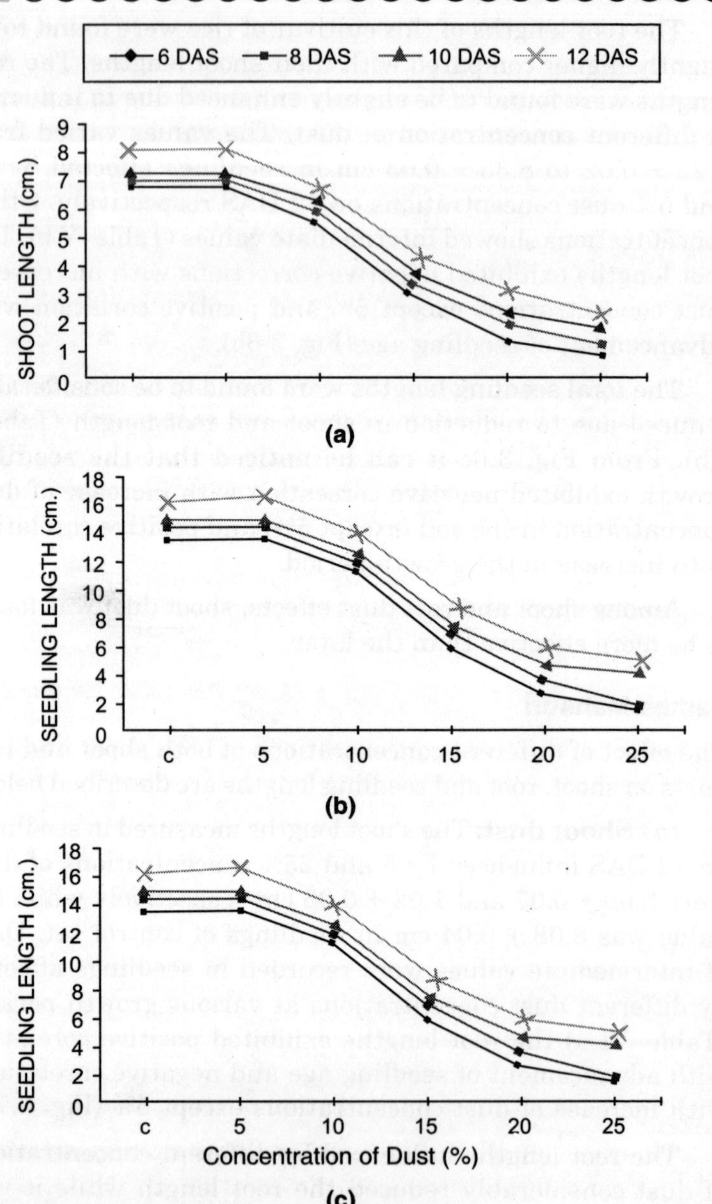

Fig. 3.7: Effect of different concentrations of shoot dust of water hyacinth *(E. crassipes)* on seedling growth of Samba mahsuri cultivar

The total seedling length were also reduced considerably due to decrease in shoot and root length of the seedlings. The data ranged from 3.88 $\pm$ 0.07 to 16.35 $\pm$ 0.03 cm in seedlings affected by 25 and 5% dust concentrations respectively on 12 DAS. Intermediate values were recorded in seedlings at different of dust in the soil of the tray (Table–VIa). Like shoot and root lengths, the seedlings lengths also exhibited similar trends and correlation with dust concentrations and seedling growth period (Fig. 3.7c).

***(b)* Root dust:** From Table-VI b it can be noticed that all the concentrations of dust except 5% considerably caused decrease in shoot, root and seedling length of this cultivar. The reduction in seedlings length was due to the decreased shoot and root growth influenced by different concentrations of root dust. Positive corelations were noticed between shoot length (Fig. 3.8 a) root length (Fig.-8 b) and seedling length (Fig.-8 c) with advancement of seedling growth period and negative corelation of growth parameters with increase of dust concentrations.

Among two types of dusts, shoot dusts were found to be favorable for seedling growth parameters of this cultivar.

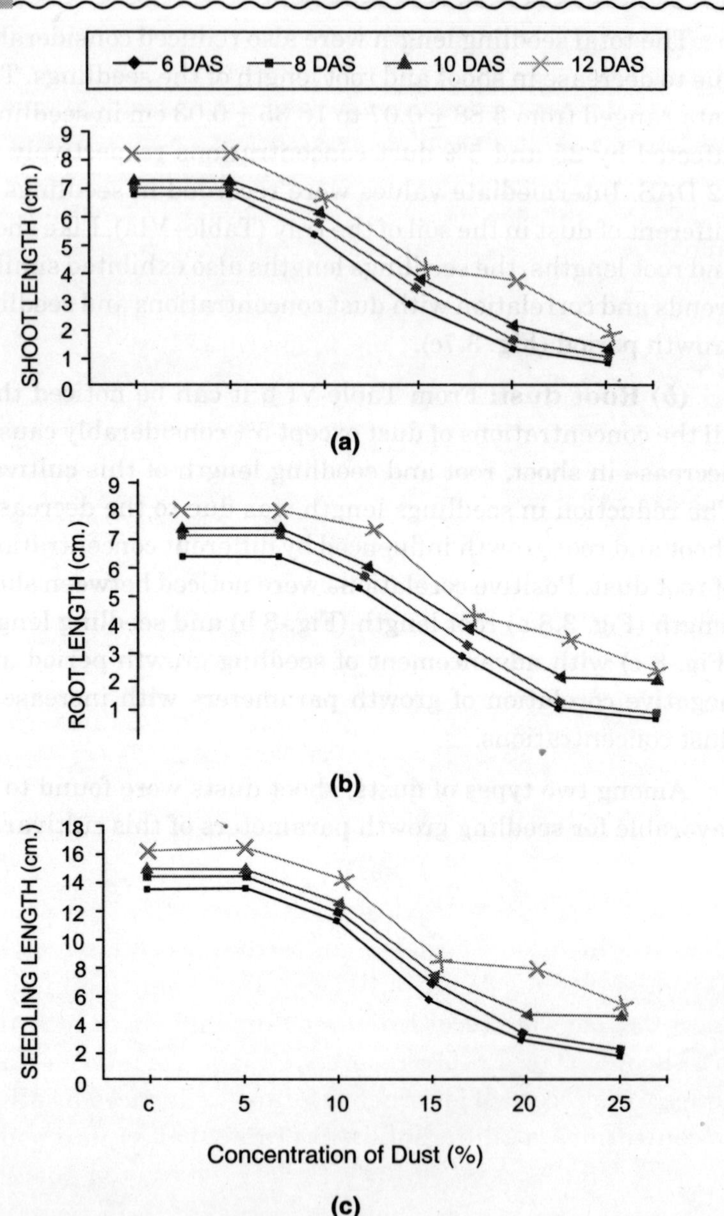

Fig. 3.8: Effect of different concentrations of root dust of water hyacinth *(E. crassipes)* on seedling growth of Samba mahsuri cultivar

Pratikshya

The seedling growth response of this cultivar to different dust consternations of shoot and root of water hyacinth is described below.

***(a)* Shoot dust:** The shoot length measured in seedlings of this cultivar on 6 DAS influenced by 5 and 25% concentrations of dust were 6.10 ± 0.05 and 0.66cm respectively, whereas the values were 8.31 ± 0.09 and 1.40 ± 0.07cm by the influence of 5 and 25% concentration of dust respectively on 12 DAS. Other concentrations showed intermediate values (Table–VII a). The shoot lengths exhibited positive corelation with increase of plant age and negative corelation with increase of dust concentration except 5% (Fig. 3.9a).

Similarly the root lengths, influenced by different concentrations of dust, were considerably deceased (expect 5%) in this cultivar of rice as evidenced from Table-VII a. Like shoot lengths, root lengths were also followed the same trend influenced by different concentrations of dust (Fig. 3.9 b).

The seedling growths of this cultivar were considerably decreased due to reduced shoot and root lengths influenced by different concentrations of dust. Among the five concentrations of dust tried, 5% of dust was found to be more effective which considerably enhanced the seedling growth. Maximum seedling length of 16.55 ± 0.02 cm and minimum of 3.58 ± 0.01cm were recorded in seedling influenced by 5 and 25% shoot dust on 12 DAS respectively. Data of intermediate values were recorded for other seedlings influenced by other concentrations at different DAS (Table–VII a) like shoot and root lengths, the seedlings lengths exhibited positive correlation with advancement of plant age and negative correlation with increase of dust concentration in the soil except 5% of dust (Fig. 3.9c).

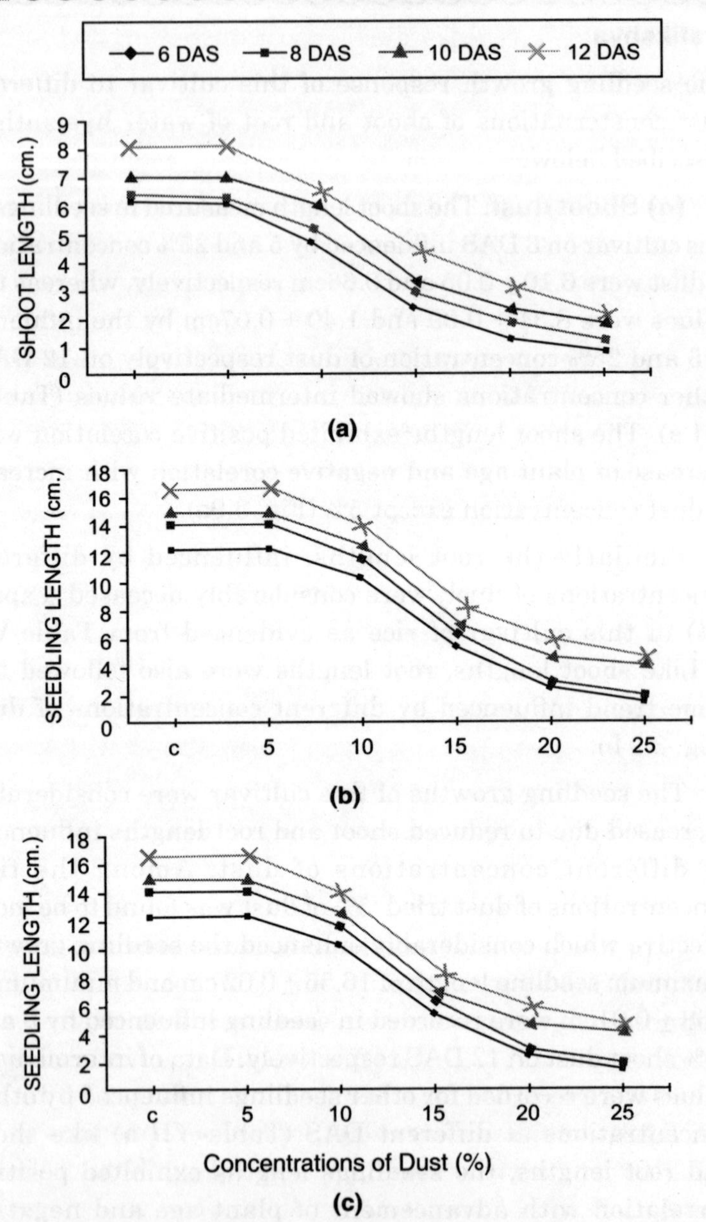

Fig. 3.9: Effect of different concentrations of shoot dust of water hyacinth *(E. crassipes)* on seedling growth of Pratikshya cultivar

Among two types of dusts, shoot dusts were found to be favorable for seedlings growth parameters of this cultivar.

(*b*) Root dust: The results noticed and recovered on seedlings growth influenced by different concentrations of root dust are described below.

The root lengths recorded in seedlings of this cultivar influenced by 5 and 25% of dust on 12 DAS were 8.22 $\pm$ 0.09 and 1.0 $\pm$ 0.07 cm respectively, whereas the value of control set was 7.99 $\pm$ 0.08 cm. Intermediate values between these two data were recorded for the seedlings influenced by other concentrations and at different DAS (Table-VIIb).Like other cultivars, the shoot length exhibited positive corelation with increase of growth period and negative corelation with increase of different dust concentrations except 5% (Fig. 3.10 a).

The root length of test cultivar of rice seedlings were found to be significantly reduced due to influence of different concentrations of root dust of water hyacinth. The data varied from 2.24 $\pm$ 0.03 to 8.27 $\pm$ 0.06 cm recorded in seedlings influenced by 25% and 5% on 12 DAS respectively (Table–VIIIb). Like shoot length, the root lengths exhibited positive corelation with increase of growth period and negative corelation with increase of dust concentration in the soil of the trays (Fig. 3.10 b).

The total seedling lengths were found to be considerably reduced due to reduction in shoot and root lengths. From Table–VIIb it can be noticed that seedling lengths were decreased from 16.49 $\pm$ 0.02cm (seedlings influenced by 5% dust) to 3.24 $\pm$ 0.01 cm (seedlings influenced by 25% dust) on 12 DAS. Other concentrations showed intermediate values at different growth periods. Fig. 3.10 c depict the corelations between seedling length and enhancement of growth periods as well as influence of different concentrations of root dust of water hyacinths.

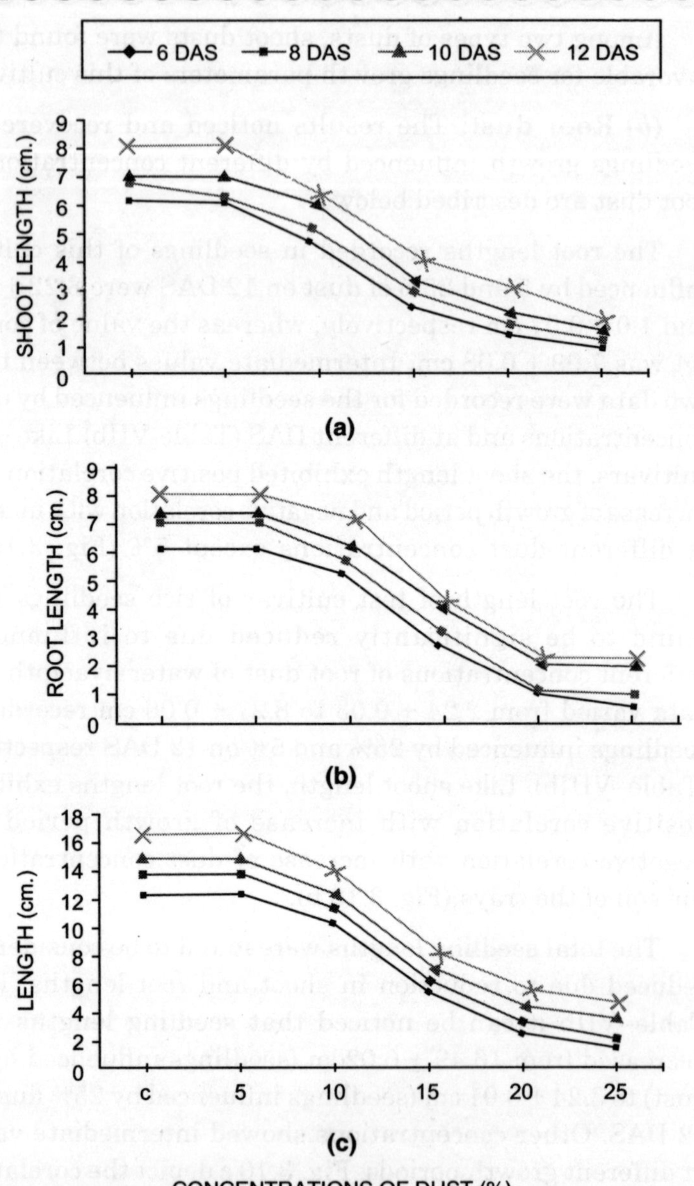

Fig. 3.10: Effect of different concentrations of root dust of water hyacinth *(E. crassipes)* on seedling growth of Pratikshya cultivar

Vijetha

(*a*) Shoot dust: From Table–VIIIa it can be noticed that except 5% all the concentrations of dust significantly caused decrease in shoot length compared to control plants. Maximum shoot length of 8.16 ± 0.07cm was noticed in seedlings on 12 DAS affected by 5% dust concentration whereas during the same period of growth it was only 2.31 ± 0.06 cm in seedlings affected by 25% dust. Data of intermediate values were noticed in seedlings at different DAS influenced by different concentrations of shoot dust. The shoot lengths exhibited positive corelation with advancement of age and negative corelation with increase of dust concentrations except 5% (Fig. 3.11a).

Regarding root length, the data exhibited more or less same values and similar trends as were noticed in case of shoot length (Table–VIII a and Fig. 3.11b).

The total seedling lengths were also found to be decreased due to reduced shoot and root length of seedlings influenced by different concentration of shoot dust throughout the period of observation as evidenced from Table–VIII a and Fig. 3.11c.

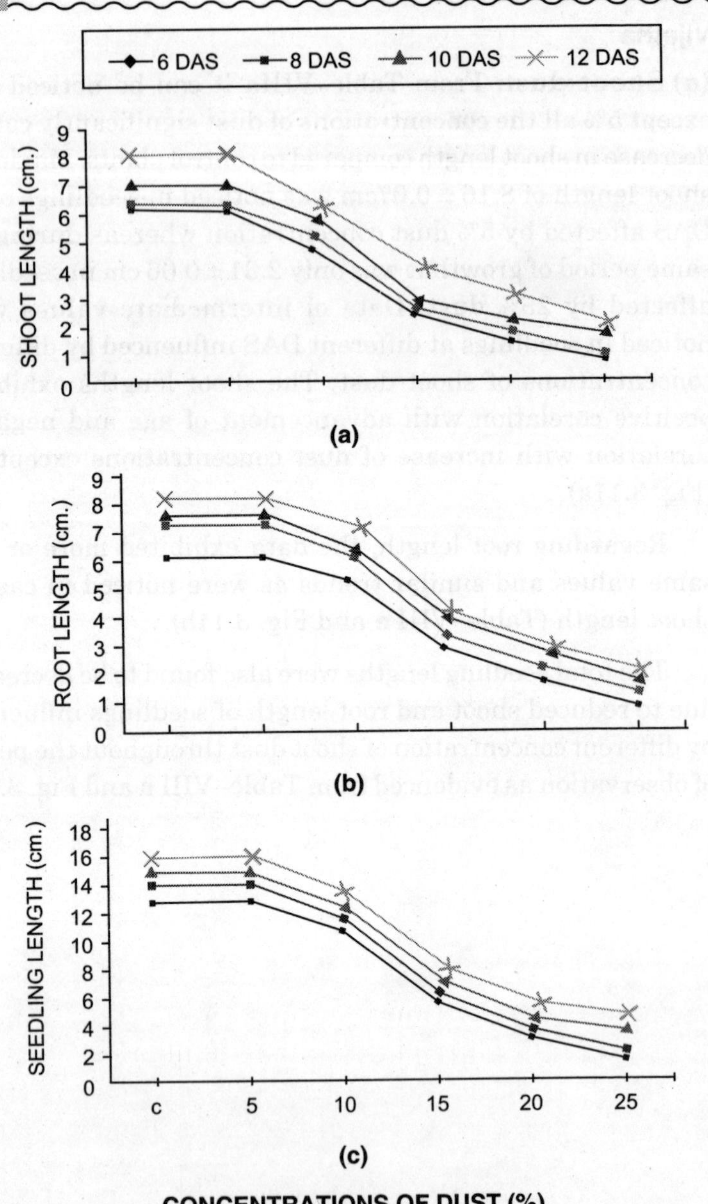

Fig. 3.11: Effect of different concentrations of shoot dust of water hyacinth *(E. crassipes)* on seedling growth of Vijetha cultivar

(*b*) **Root dust:** From Table–VIII b it can be noticed that all the concentrations of dust except 5% considerably caused

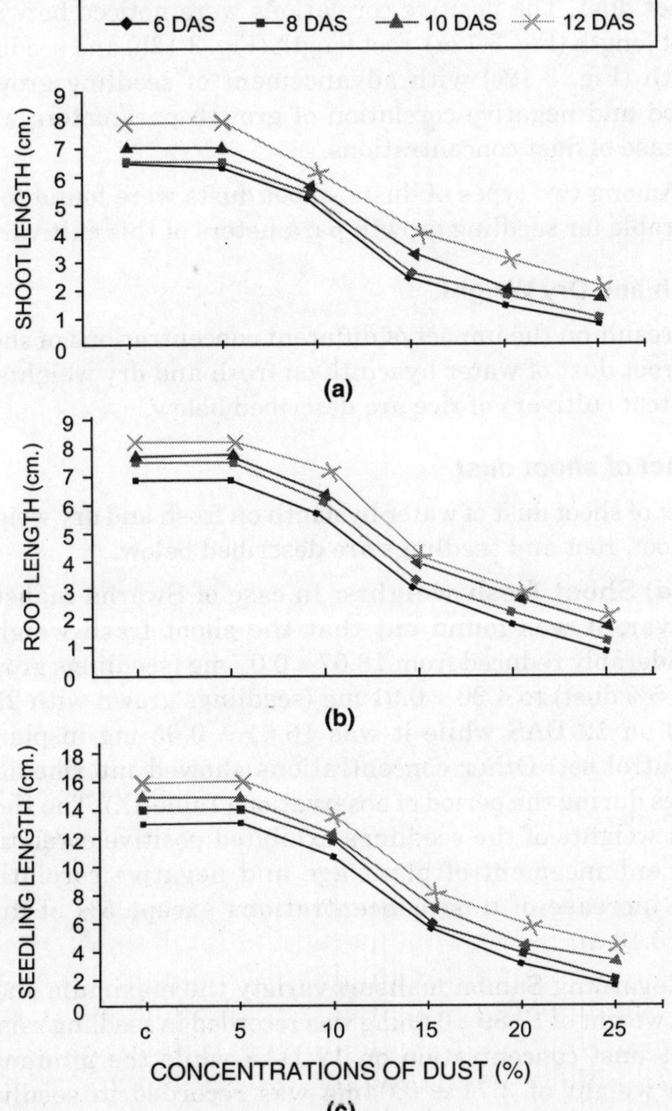

Fig. 3.12: Effect of different concentrations of root dust of water hyacinth *(E. crassipes)* on seedling growth of Vijetha cultivar

decrease in shoot, root and seedling length of this cultivar. The reduction in seedlings length was due to the decreased shoot and root growth influenced by different concentrations of root dust. The positive corelations were noticed between shoot length (Fig. 3.12a), root length (Fig. 3.12b) and seedling length (Fig. 3.12c) with advancement of seedling growth period and negative corelation of growth parameters with increase of dust concentrations.

Among two types of dusts, shoot dusts were found to be favorable for seedling growth parameters of this cultivar.

Fresh and Dry Weight

The result on the impact of different concentrations of shoot and root dust of water hyacinth on fresh and dry weights of four test cultivars of rice are described below.

Impact of shoot dust

Effect of shoot dust of water hyacinth on fresh and dry weight of shoot, root and seedlings are described below.

(*a*) Shoot fresh weights: In case of Swarna mahsuri cultivar, it was found out that the shoot fresh weights considerably reduced from 18.67 ± 0.07 mg (seedlings grown with 5% dust) to 4.30 ± 0.01 mg (seedlings grown with 25% dust) on 12 DAS while it was 16.61 ± 0.05 mg in plants of control set. Other concentrations showed intermediate values during the period of observation (Table-IX). The shoot fresh weights of the seedlings exhibited positive corelation with enhancement of plant age and negative corelation with increase of dust concentrations except 5% of dust (Fig. 3.13 a).

Regarding Samba mahsuri variety the maximum shoot fresh weight of 17.89 ± 0.05mg was recorded in seedling raised in 5% dust concentration on 12 DAS while the minimum fresh weight of 3.71 ± 0.04mg was recorded in seedling grown with 25% dust. The seedlings of control set exhibited 16.08. ± 0.05 mg of fresh weight during the same period of growth. Data of intermediate values were recorded in other seedlings influenced by different concentrations of shoot dust at varying period of growth (Table-X). Like Swarna mahsuri cultivar, this cultivar also exhibited similar trends for shoot fresh weight with growth period and dust concentration (Fig. 3.13 b).

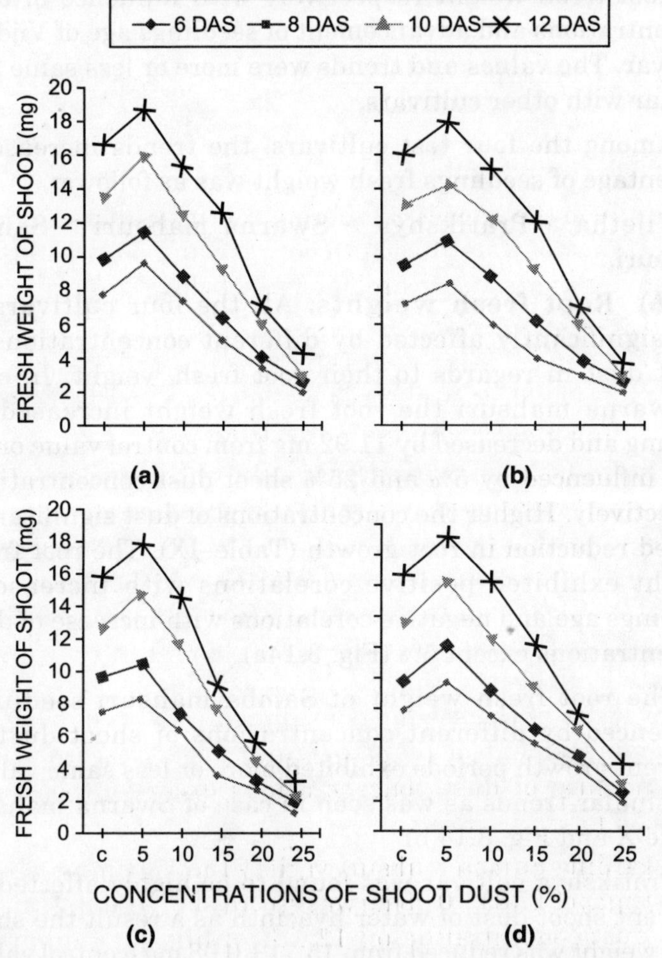

Fig. 3.13 : Impact of different concentrations of shoot dust of water hyacinth *(E. crassipes)* on shoot fresh weight of 4 test rice cultivars (a) Swarna mahsuri, (b) Samba mahsuri, (c) Pratikshya, (d) Vijetha

Pratikshya cultivar also exhibited more or less same value and similar trends in regards to fresh shoot weight with seedlings age and dust concentrations as was noticed in case of other two cultivars (Table-XI and Fig. 3.13c).

Table-XII and Fig. 3.13d indicate the values and trends of shoot fresh weight respectively with influence of dust concentrations and advancement of seedlings age of Vijetha cultivar. The values and trends were more or less same and similar with other cultivars.

Among the four test cultivars, the trends increase of percentage of seedlings fresh weight was as follows:

Vijetha > Pratikshya > Swarna mahsuri > Samba mahsuri.

***(b)* Root fresh weights:** All the four cultivars of rice significantly affected by different concentrations of shoot dust in regards to their root fresh weight. In case of Swarna mahsuri the root fresh weight increased by 2.80 mg and decreased by 11.92 mg from control value on 12 DAS influenced by 5% and 25% shoot dust concentrations respectively. Higher the concentrations of dust significantly caused reduction in root growth (Table–IX). The root fresh weight exhibited positive corelations with increase of seedlings age and negative corelations with increase of dust concentrations except 5% (Fig. 3.14a).

The root fresh weight of Samba mahsuri seedlings influenced by different concentrations of shoot dust at different growth periods exhibited more or less same values and similar trends as was seen in case of Swarna mahsuri (Table-X and Fig. 3.14 b).

Pratikshya cultivar was found to be highly affected by different shoot dust of water hyacinth as a result the shoot fresh weight was reduced from 15.71 ± 0.08 mg (control value) to 3.25 ± 0.04 mg (seedlings affected by 25% concentrations on 12 DAS. Concentration of 5% dust caused an increase of only 1.74 mg compared with control value on 12 DAS. Data of intermediate values were recorded for other concentrations at different DAS (Table-XI). Like other cultivars, the root fresh weight exhibited positive corelation with advancement seedling age negative corelatio with increase of shoot dust concentrations in the soil of the trays (Fig. 3.14c).

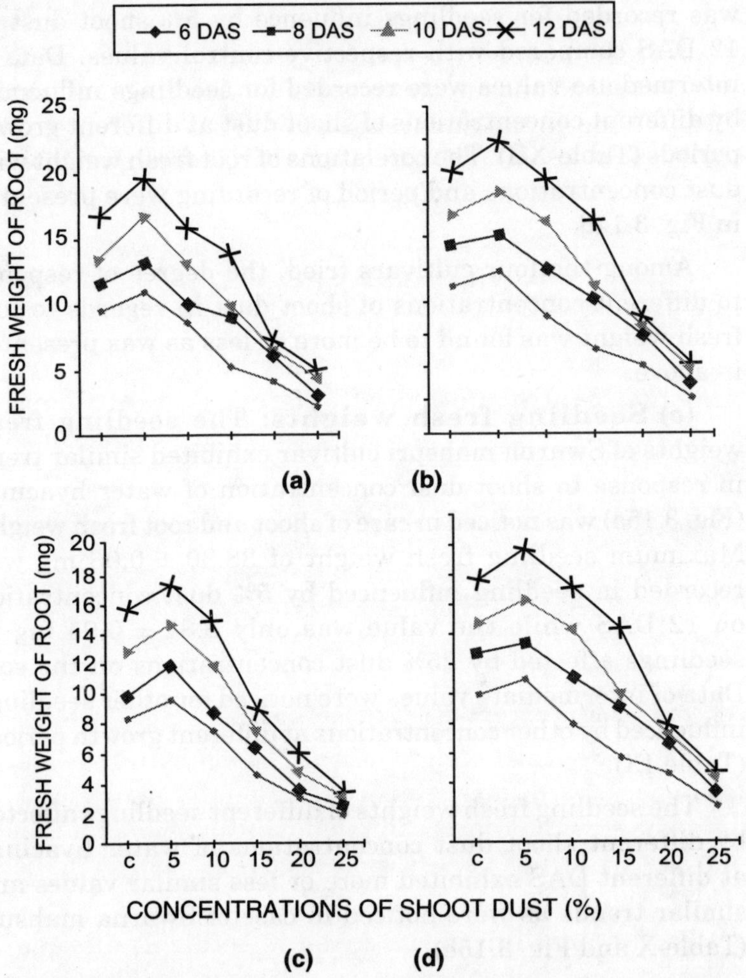

Fig. 3.14: Impact of different concentrations of shoot dust of water hyacinth *(E. crassipes)* on root fresh weight of 4 test rice cultivars (a) Swarna mahsuri, (b) Samba mahsuri, (c) Pratikshya, (d) Vijetha.

The seedlings of Vijetha cultivar were also more or less similarly affected by different concentrations of shoot dust as a result the shoot fresh weight reduced from 16.89 ± 0.02 mg (control value) to 4.81 ± 0.02 (seedlings affected by 25% dust) on 12 DAS. An increase of 3.02 mg of root fresh weight was recorded for seedlings influence by 5% shoot dust on 12 DAS compared with respective control values. Data of intermediate values were recorded for seedlings influenced by different concentrations of shoot dust at different growth periods (Table-XII). The corelations of root fresh weight with dust concentrations and period of recording were presented in Fig. 3.14d.

Among the four cultivars tried, the degree of response to different concentrations of shoot dust in regards to root fresh weight was found to be more or less as was presented in above.

(*c*) Seedling fresh weights: The seedling fresh weights of Swarna mahsuri cultivar exhibited similar trend in response to shoot dust concentration of water hyacinth (Fig. 3.15a) was noticed in case of shoot and root fresh weight. Maximum seedling fresh weight of 38.30 ± 0.06 mg was recorded in seedling influenced by 5% dust concentration on 12 DAS while the value was only 8.81 ± 0.04 mg in seedlings affected by 25% dust concentrations on the soil. Data of intermediate values were noticed for other seedlings influenced by other concentrations at different growth periods (Table-IX).

The seedling fresh weights of different seedlings affected by different shoot dust concentrations of water hyacinth at different DAS exhibited more or less similar values and similar trends as were noticed in case of Swarna mahsuri (Table-X and Fig. 3.15b).

Table-XI depicts the seedlings growth response in term of their fresh weight of Pratikshya cultivar to different concentrations of shoot dust at different DAS. Maximum seedling fresh weight of 34.34 ± 0.02 mg was recorded for seedlings influenced by 5% dust on 12 DAS while minimum weight of 6.25 ± 0.03 mg was recorded in seedlings influenced by 25% dust concentration. Data of intermediate values were noticed in other seedlings at different DAS. The seedlings fresh weight of this cultivar exhibited positive corelation

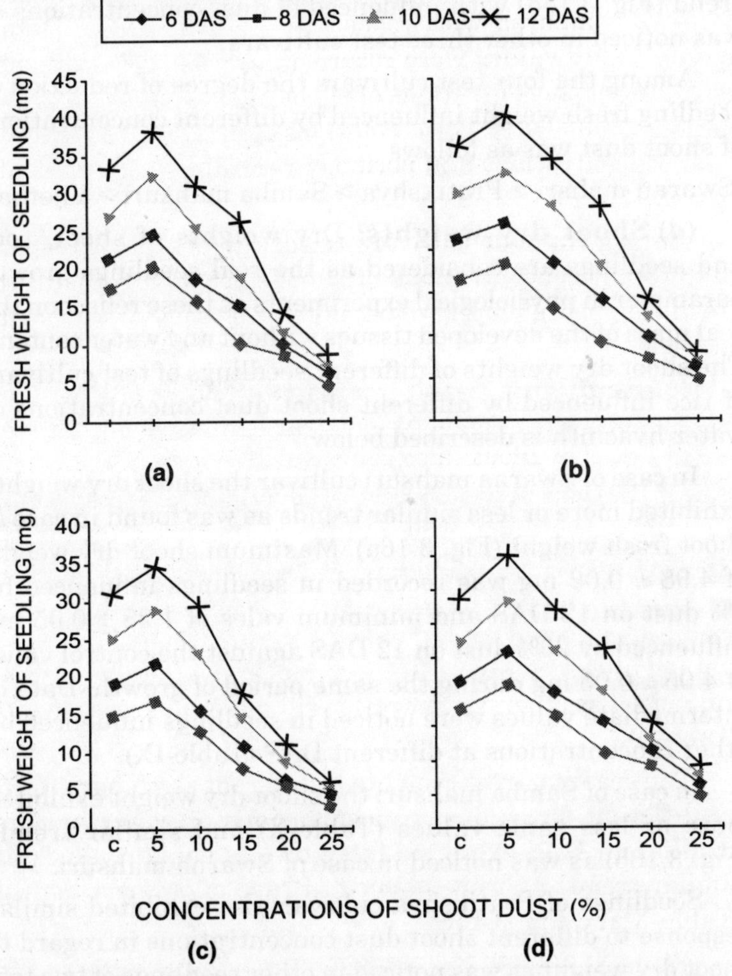

Fig. 3.15: Impact of different concentrations of shoot dust of water hyacinth *(E. crassipes)* on seedling fresh weight of 4 test rice cultivars (a) Swarna mahsuri, (b) Samba mahsuri, (c) Pratikshya, (d) Vijetha

with advancement of seedlings age and negative corelation with increase of dust concentrations except 5% at which the seedlings fresh weight were found to be maximum at all stages (Fig. 3.15c).

In case of Vijetha cultivar the seedlings fresh weight exhibited more or less same values (Table-XIII) and similar trend (Fig. 3.15d) with influenced of dust concentrations as was noticed in other three test cultivars.

Among the four test cultivars the degree of reduction of seedling fresh weight influenced by different concentrations of shoot dust was as follows.

Swaran mahsri > Pratikshya > Samba mahsuri > Vijetha.

(*d*) Shoot dry weights: Dry weights of shoot, root and seedlings are considered as the real seedlings growth parameter in physiological experiments as these reflect on the real mass of the developed tissues without any water content. The shoot dry weights of different seedlings of test cultivars of rice influenced by different shoot dust concentrations of water hyacinth is described below.

In case of Swarna mahsuri cultivar the shoot dry weights exhibited more or less similar trends as was found in case of shoot fresh weight (Fig. 3.16a). Maximum shoot dry weight of 4.98 ± 0.02 mg was recorded in seedlings influenced by 5% dust on 12 DAS and minimum vales of 1.28 ± 0.05 mg influenced by 25% dust on 12 DAS against the control value of 4.05 ± 0.05 mg during the same period of growth. Data of intermediate values were noticed in seedlings influenced by other concentrations at different DAS (Table-IX).

In case of Samba mahsuri the shoot dry weight exhibited more or less same values (Table-X) and similar trends (Fig. 3.16b) as was noticed in case of Swarna mahsuri.

Seedlings of Pratikshya cultivar also exhibited similar response to different shoot dust concentrations in regard to shoot dry weight as was noticed in other seedlings of two test cultivars. The data are presented in Table-XI and graphically expressed in Fig. 3.16c.

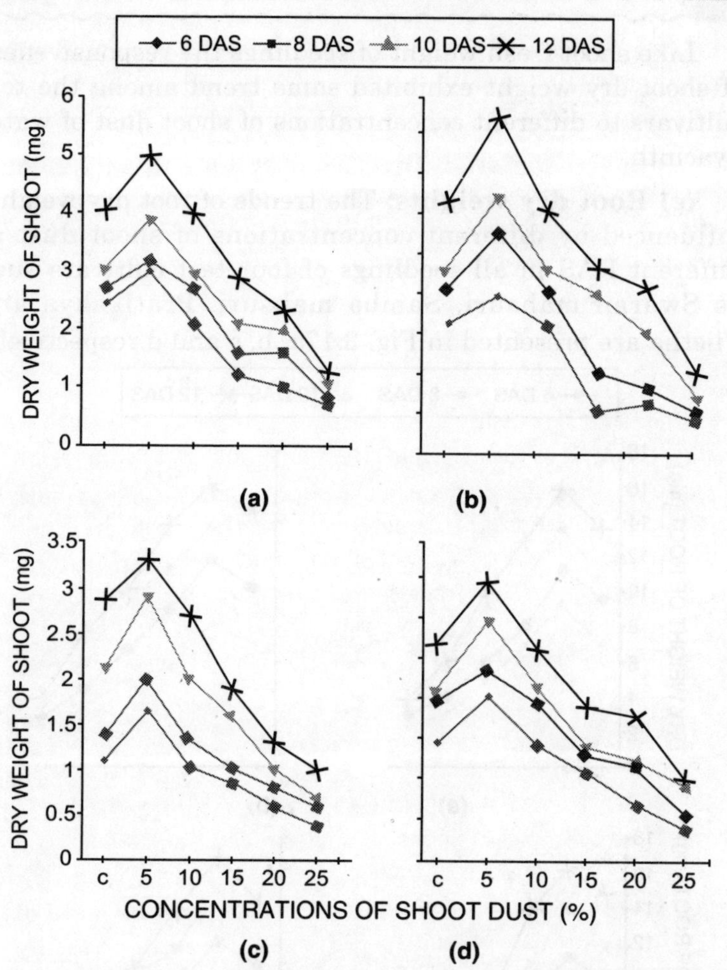

Fig. 3.16: Impact of different concentrations of shoot dust of water hyacinth *(E. crassipes)* on shoot dry weight of 4 test rice cultivars (a) Swarna mahsuri, (b) Samba mahsuri, (c) Pratikshya, (d) Vijetha

Shoot dry weight of the Vijetha cultivar also significantly reduced by the influence of different concentrations of shoot dust of water hyacinth at different DAS (Table-XII). The shoot dry weights exhibited positive corelation with advancement of growth period and negative correlation with increase of dust concentration except 5% (Fig. 3.16 d).

Like shoot fresh weight of seedlings the responsiveness of shoot dry weight exhibited same trend among the test cultivars to different concentrations of shoot dust of water hyacinth.

***(e)* Root dry weights:** The trends of root dry weights influenced by different concentrations of shoot dust at different DAS in all seedlings of four test cultivars such as Swaran mahsuri, Samba mahsuri, Pratikshya and Vijetha are presented in Fig. 3.17a, b, c and d respectively.

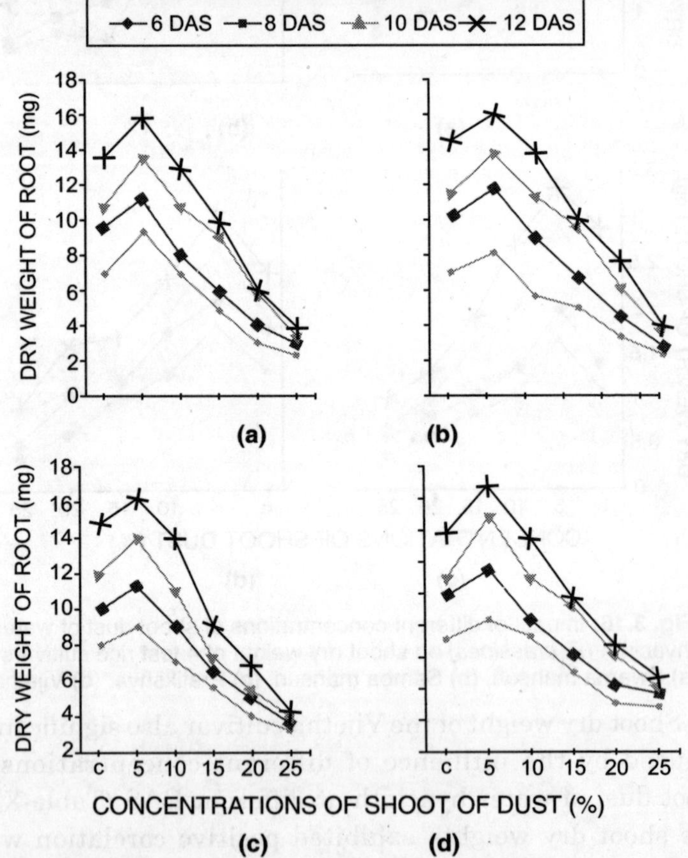

Fig. 3.17: Impact of different concentrations of shoot dust of water hyacinth *(E. crassipes)* on root dry weight of 4 test rice cultivars (a) Swarna mahsuri, (b) Samba mahsuri, (c) Pratikshya, (d) Vijetha

Concentrations of shoot dust of water hyacinth of Swarna mahsuri, Samba mahsuri, Pratikshya and Vijetha cultivars are presented in Tables-IX, X, XI and XII respectively.

The degree of responsiveness to different dust concentrations in relation to root dry weight reduction was found to be similar as was noticed incase of root fresh weight.

***(f)* Seedlings dry weights:** The seedling dry weights of four test cultivars of rice influenced by different

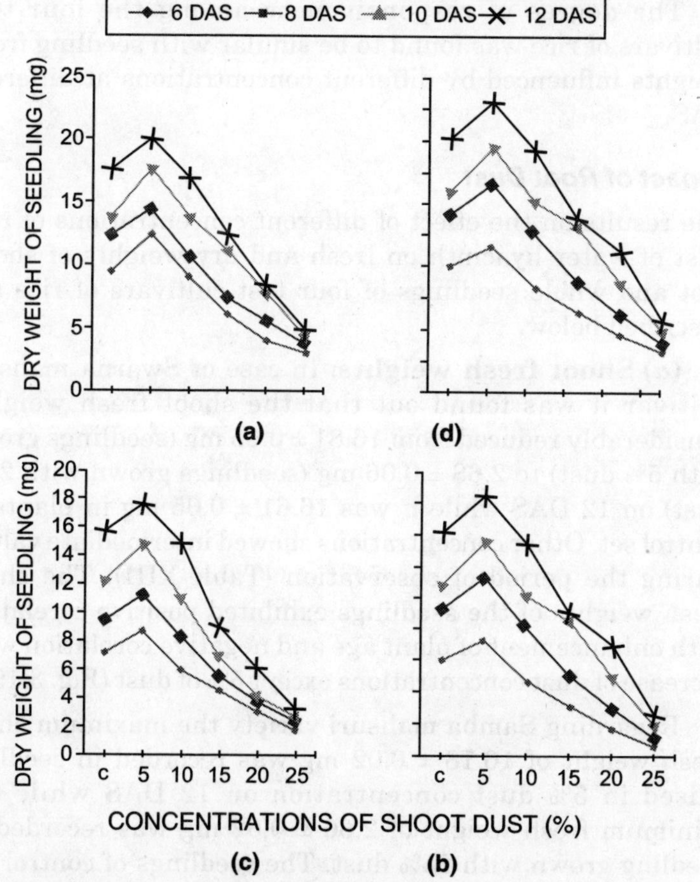

3.18: Impact of different concentrations of shoot dust of water hyacinth *(E. crassipes)* on seedling dry weight of 4 test rice cultivars (a) Swarna mahsuri, (b) Samba mahsuri, (c) Pratikshya, (d) Vijetha

concentrations of shoot dust exhibited positive corelation with advancement of seedling age and negative corelation with increase of dust concentrations except 5% as evidenced from Fig. 3.18 a, b, c and d for Swarna mahsuri, Samba mahsuri, Pratikshya and Vijetha respectively. The data recorded on whole seedlings dry weights influenced by different concentrations of shoot dust at different DAS are presented in Tables-IX, X, XI and XII for Swarna mahsuri, Samba mahsuri, Pratikshya and Vijetha respectively.

The degree of responsiveness among the four test cultivars of rice was found to be similar with seedling fresh weights influenced by different concentrations at different DAS.

Impact of Root Dust

The results on the effect of different concentrations of root dust of water hyacinth on fresh and dry weights of shoot, root and whole seedlings of four test cultivars of rice are described below.

(*a*) Shoot fresh weights: In case of Swarna mahsuri cultivar it was found out that the shoot fresh weights considerably reduced from 16.81 ± 0.05 mg (seedlings grown with 5% dust) to 2.68 ± 0.06 mg (seedlings grown with 25% dust) on 12 DAS while it was 16.61 ± 0.05 mg in plants of control set. Other concentrations showed intermediate values during the period of observation (Table-XIII). The shoot fresh weights of the seedlings exhibited positive corelation with enhancement of plant age and negative corelation with increase of dust concentrations except 5% of dust (Fig. 3.19a).

Regarding Samba mahsuri variety the maximum shoot fresh weight of 16.18 ± 0.02 mg was recorded in seedling raised in 5% dust concentration on 12 DAS while the minimum fresh weight of 2.66 ± 0.02 mg was recorded in seedling grown with 25% dust. The seedlings of control set exhibited 16.08 ± 0.05 mg of fresh weight during the same period of growth. Data of intermediate values were recorded in other seedlings influenced by different concentrations of root dust at varing period of growth (Table-XIV). Like Swarna mahsuri cultivar, this cultivar also exhibited similar trends for shoot fresh weight with growth period and dust concentration (Fig. 3.19b).

Pratikshya cultivar also exhibited more or less same value and similar trends in regards to fresh shoot weight with seedlings age and dust concentrations as was noticed in case of other two cultivars (Table-XV and Fig. 3.19c).

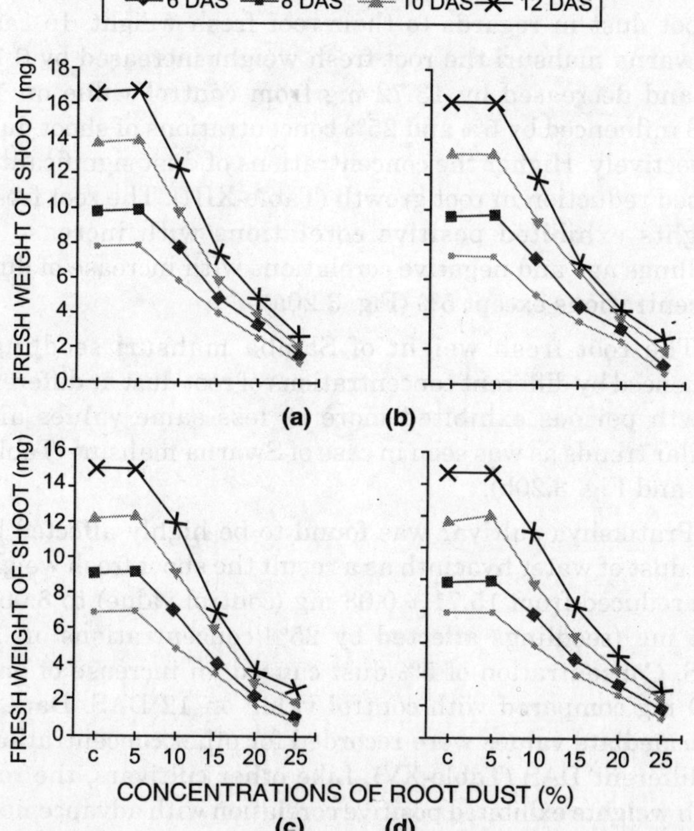

Fig. 3.19: Impact of different concentrations of root dust of water hyacinth *(E. crassipes)* on shoot fresh weight of 4 test rice cultivars (a) Swarna mahsuri, (b) Samba mahsuri, (c) Pratikshya, (d) Vijetha

Table-XVI and Fig. 3.19d indicate the values and trends of shoot fresh weight respectively with influence of dust concentrations and advancement of seedlings age of Vijetha cultivar. The values and trends are more or less same and similar with other cultivars.

Among the four test cultivars, the trends in increase of percentage of seedlings fresh weight was as follows:

Vijetha > Pratikshya > Swarna mahsuri > Samba mahsuri

(*b*) Root fresh weights: All the four test cultivars of rice were significantly affected by different concentrations of root dust in regards to their root fresh weight. In case of Swarna mahsuri the root fresh weight increased by 0.16 mg and decreased by 13.72 mg from control value on 12 DAS influenced by 5% and 25% concentrations of shoot dust respectively. Higher the concentrations of dust significantly caused reduction in root growth (Table-XIII). The root fresh weights exhibited positive corelations with increase of seedlings age and negative corelations with increase of dust concentrations except 5% (Fig. 3.20a).

The root fresh weight of Samba mahsuri seedlings influenced by different concentrations of root dust at different growth periods exhibited more or less same values and similar trends as was seen in case of Swarna mahsuri (Table-XIV and Fig. 3.20b).

Pratikshya cultivar was found to be highly affected by root dust of water hyacinth as a result the shoot fresh weight was reduced from 15.71 ± 0.08 mg (control value) to 3.00 ± 0.05 mg (seedlings affected by 25% concentrations on 12 DAS. Concentration of 5% dust caused an increase of only 0.10 mg compared with control value on 12 DAS. Data of intermediate values were recorded for other concentrations at different DAS (Table-XV). Like other cultivars, the root fresh weights exhibited positive corelation with advancement of seedling age and negative corelation with increase of root dust concentrations in the soil of the trays (Fig. 3.20c).

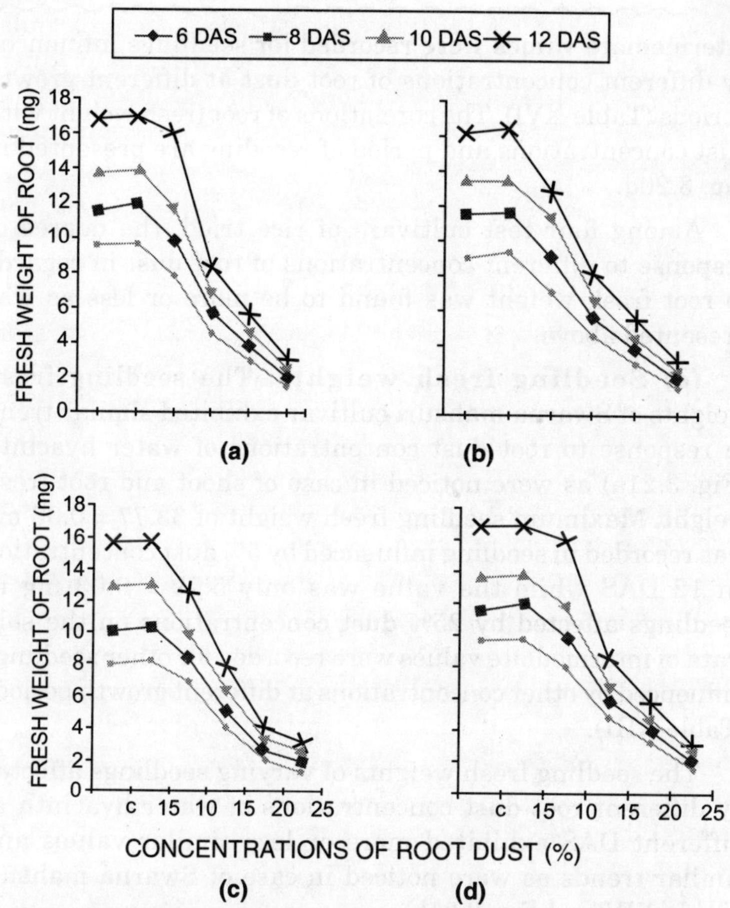

Fig. 3.20: Impact of different concentrations of root dust of water hyacinth *(E. crassipes)* on root fresh weight of 4 test rice cultivars (a) Swarna mahsuri, (b) Samba mahsuri, (c) Pratikshya, (d) Vijetha

The seedlings of Vijetha cultivar also exhibited more or less similarly affected by different concentrations of root dust as a result the shoot fresh weight reduced from 16.89 ± 0.02 mg (Control value) to 3.21 ± 0.06 mg (seedlings affected by 25% dust) on 12 DAS. An increase of 0.10 mg of root fresh weight was recorded for seedlings influence by 5% root dust on 12 DAS compared with respective control values. Data of intermediate values were recorded for seedlings influenced by different concentrations of root dust at different growth periods (Table-XVI). The corelations of root fresh weight with dust concentrations and period of recoding are presented in Fig. 3.20d.

Among four test cultivars of rice tried, the degree of response to different concentrations of root dust in regards to root fresh weight was found to be more or less as was presented above.

(c) Seedling fresh weights: The seedling fresh weights of Swarna mahsuri cultivar exhibited similar trend in response to root dust concentrations of water hyacinth (Fig. 3.21a) as were noticed in case of shoot and root fresh weight. Maximum seedling fresh weight of 33.77 ± 0.03 mg was recorded in seedling influenced by 5% dust concentration on 12 DAS while the value was only 5.79 ± 0.03 mg in seedlings affected by 25% dust concentrations on the soil. Data of intermediate values were recorded for other seedlings influenced by other concentrations at different growth periods (Table-XIII).

The seedling fresh weights of varying seedlings affected by different root dust concentrations of water hyacinth at different DAS exhibited more or less similar values and similar trends as were noticed in case of Swarna mahsuri (Table-XIV and Fig. 3.21b).

Table-XV depicts the seedlings growth response in term of their fresh weight of Pratikshya cultivar to different concentrations of root dust at different DAS. Maximum seedling fresh weight of 30.83 ± 0.06 mg was recorded for seedlings influenced by 5% dust on 12 DAS while minimum weight of 5.60 ± 0.02mg was recorded in seedlings influenced by 25% dust concentration. Data of intermediate values were noticed in other seedlings at different DAS. The seedlings fresh weights of this cultivar exhibited positive corelation with advancement of seedlings age and negative corelation with increase of dust concentrations except 5% at which the seedlings fresh weight were found to be maximum at all stages (Fig. 3.21c).

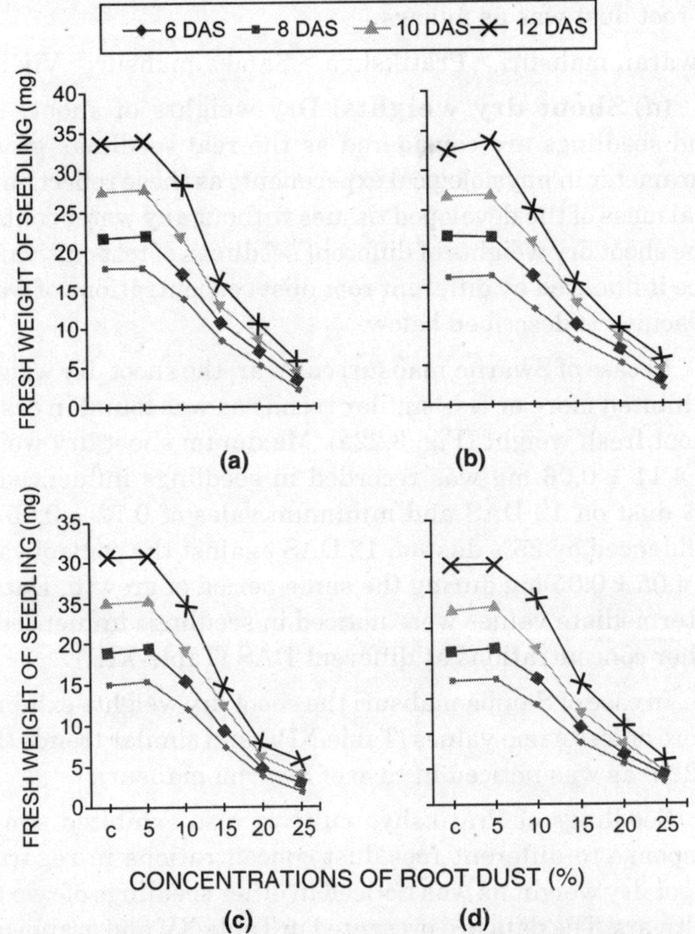

Fig. 3.21: Impact of different concentrations of root dust of water hyacinth *(E. crassipes)* on seedling fresh weight of 4 test rice cultivars (a) Swarna mahsuri, (b) Samba mahsuri, (c) Pratikshya, (d) Vijetha

In case of Vijetha cultivar, the seedlings fresh weights exhibited more or less same values (Table-XVI) and similar trend (Fig. 3.21d) with influence of different concentrations of dust as was noticed in other three test cultivars.

Among the four test cultivars, the degree of reduction in seedling fresh weight influenced by different concentrations of root dust was as follows.

Swaran mahsuri > Pratikshya > Samba mahsuri> Vijetha.

(*d*) Shoot dry weights: Dry weights of shoot, root and seedlings are considered as the real seedlings growth parameter in physiological experiments as these reflect on the real mass of the developed tissues without any water content. The shoot dry weights of different seedlings of test cultivars of rice influenced by different root dust concentrations of water hyacinth is described below:

In case of Swarna mahsuri cultivar, the shoot dry weights exhibited more or less similar trends as was found in case of shoot fresh weight (Fig. 3.22a). Maximum shoot dry weight of 4.11 ± 0.06 mg was recorded in seedlings influenced by 5% dust on 12 DAS and minimum vales of 0.72 ± 0.05 mg influenced by 25% dust on 12 DAS against the control value of 4.05 ± 0.05 mg during the same period of growth. Data of intermediate values were noticed in seedlings influenced by other concentrations at different DAS (Table-XIII).

In case of Samba mahsuri the shoot dry weights exhibited more or less same values (Table-XIV) and similar trends (Fig. 3.22b) as was noticed in case of Swarna mahsuri.

Seedlings of Pratikshya cultivar also exhibited similar response to different root dust concentrations in regard to shoot dry weight as was noticed in other seedlings of two test cultivars. The data are presented in Table-XV and graphically expressed in Fig. 3.22c.

Shoot dry weights of the Vijetha cultivar also significantly reduced by the influence of different concentrations of root dust of water hyacinth at different DAS (Table-XVI). The shoot dry weights exhibited positive corelation with advancement of growth period and negative correlation with increase of dust concentration except 5% (Fig. 3.22d).

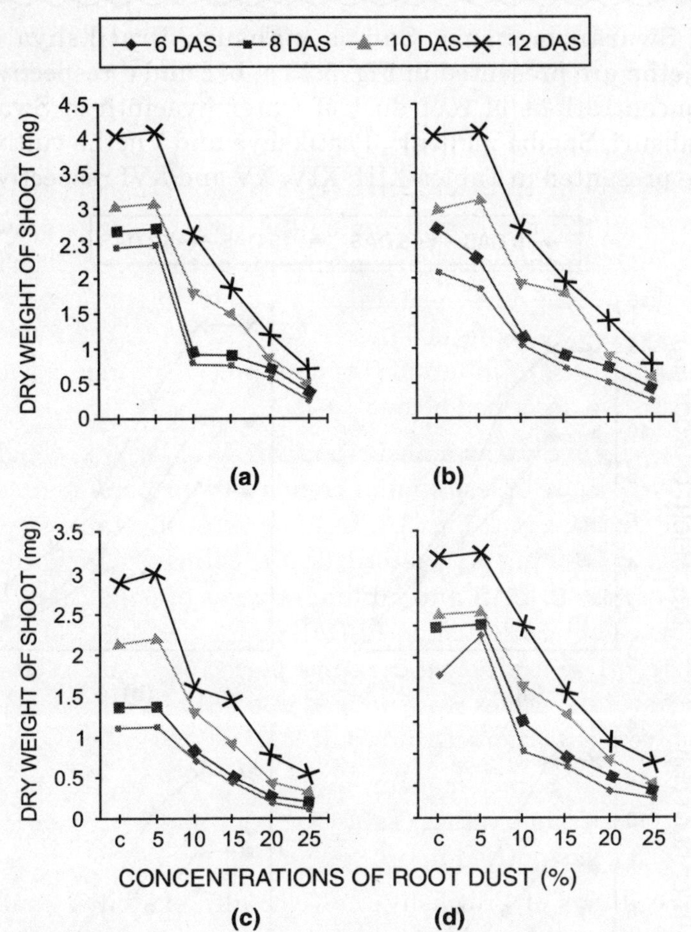

Fig. 3.22: Impact of different concentrations of root dust of water hyacinth *(E. crassipes)* on shoot dry weight of 4 test rice cultivars (a) Swarna mahsuri, (b) Samba mahsuri, (c) Pratikshya, (d) Vijetha

Like shoot fresh weight of seedlings, the responsiveness of shoot dry weights exhibited same trend among the test cultivars to different concentrations of root dust of water hyacinth.

(*e*) Root dry weights: The trends of root dry weights influenced by different concentrations of root dust at different DAS in all seedlings of four test cultivars such as Swaran mahsuri, Samba mahsuri, Pratikshya and Vijetha are presented in Fig. 3.23 a, b, c and d respectively. Concentrations of root dust of water hyacinth of Swarna mahsuri, Samba mahsuri, Pratikshya and Vijetha cultivars are presented in Tables-XIII, XIV, XV and XVI respectively.

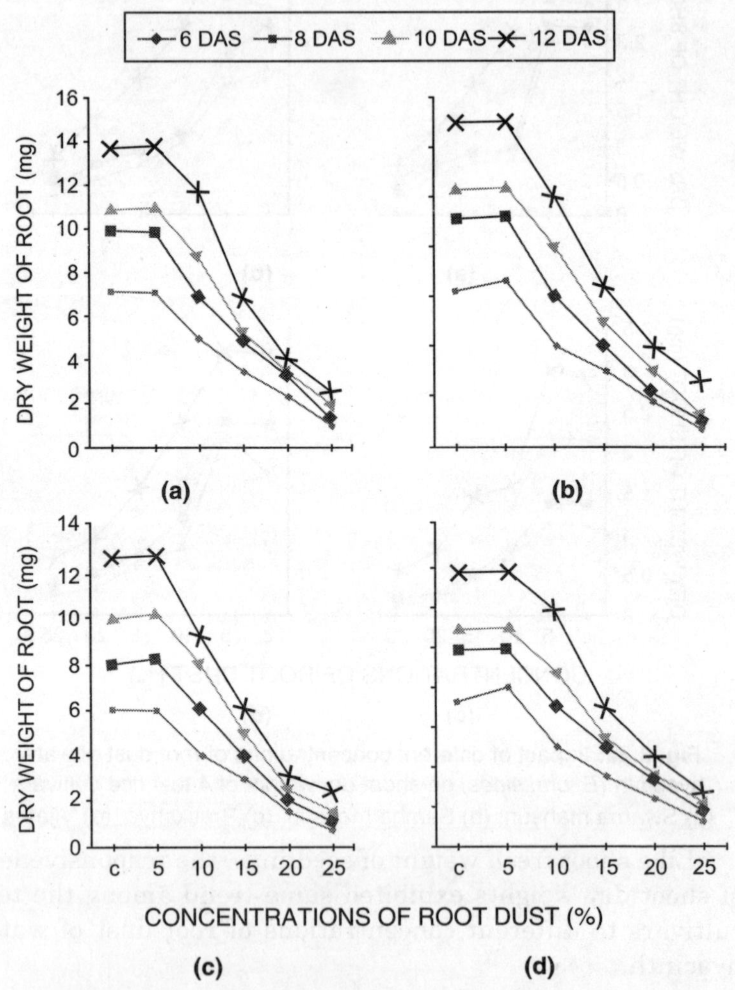

Fig. 3.23: Impact of different concentrations of root dust of water hyacinth *(E. crassipes)* on root dry weight of 4 test rice cultivars (a) Swarna mahsuri, (b) Samba mahsuri, (c) Pratikshya, (d) Vijetha

The degree of responsiveness to different dust concentrations in relation to deduction in root dry weight was found to be similar as was noticed incase of root fresh weight.

(f) Seedlings dry weights: The seedling dry weights of four test cultivars of rice influenced by different concen-

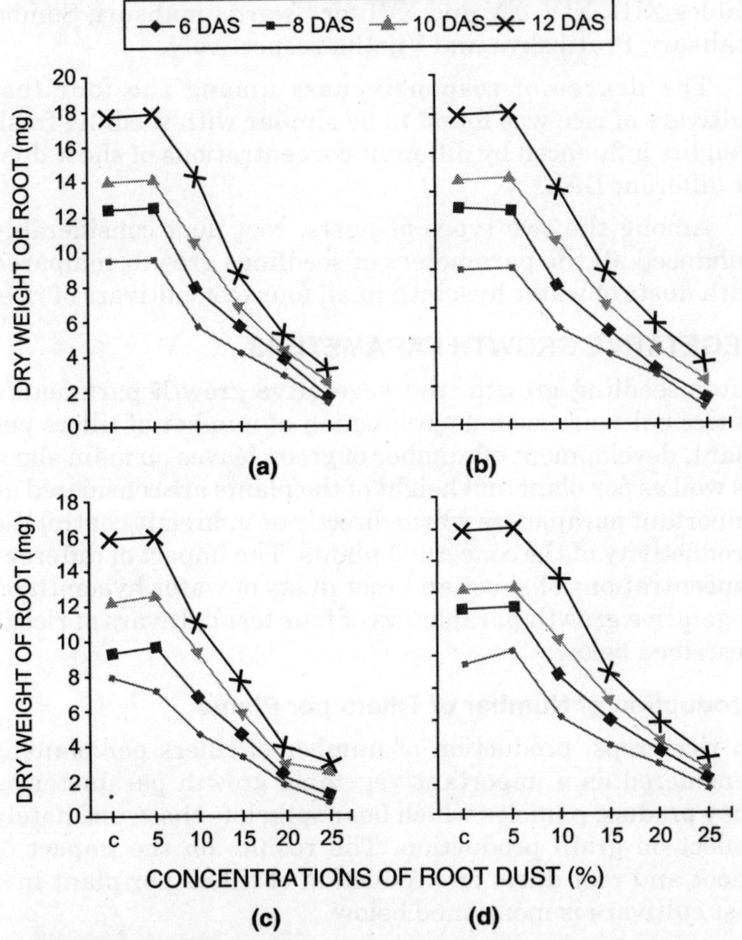

Fig. 3.24: Impact of different concentrations of root dust of water hyacinth *(E. crassipes)* on root dry weight of 4 test rice cultivars (a) Swarna mahsuri, (b) Samba mahsuri, (c) Pratikshya, (d) Vijetha

trations of root dust exhibited positive corelation with advancement of seedling age and negative corelation with increase of dust concentrations except 5% as evidenced from Fig. 3.24 a, b, c and d for Swarna mahsuri, Samba mahsuri, Pratikshya and Vijetha respectively. The data recorded on whole seedlings dry weights influenced by different concentrations of root dust at different DAS are presented in Tables-XIII, XIV, XV and XVI for Swarna mahsuri, Samba mahsuri, Pratikshya and Vijetha respectively.

The degree of responsiveness among the four test cultivars of rice was found to be similar with seedling fresh weights influenced by different concentrations of shoot dust at different DAS.

Among the two types of dusts, root dust considerably enhanced all the parameters of seedlings growth compared with dusts of water hyacinth in all four test cultivars of rice.

VEGETATIVE GROWTH PARAMETERS

After seedling growth, the vegetative growth parameters of rice cultivars such as production of number of tillers per plant, development of number of green leaves on main shoot as well as per plant and height of the plants are considered as important parameters which directly or indirectly control the productivity of the concerned plants. The impact of different concentrations of shoot and root dusts of water hyacinth on vegetative growth parameters of four test cultivars of rice is described below.

Production of Number of Tillers per Plants

In rice crops, production of number of tillers per plant is considered as a important vegetable growth parameter as they produce panicles which bear spikelets those ultimately reflect on grain production. The results on the impact of shoot and root dusts on production of tillers per plant in 4 test cultivars is mentioned below.

Impact of Shoot Dust

(*a*) Swarna mahsuri: In case of Swarna mahsuri cultivars of rice, 5% dust concentrations considerably enhanced the production of number of tillers per plant as results 6.04 ± 0.04 number of tillers were found at flowing stage whereas 25% dust concentration caused production of only 2.28 ± 0.07 number of tillers per plant during the same period of growth. Data of intermediate numbers were recorded in plants affected by different concentrations of dust at varying period of growth (Table-XVII). The production of number of tillers per plant exhibited positive corelation with advancement of plant age and negative corelation with increase of concentrations of shoot dust except 5% (Fig. 3.25 a).

(*b*) Samba mahsuri: The production of number of tillers per plant was found to be maximum (6.93 ± 0.07) in plants influenced by 5% dust at flowering stage. During same period of growth the tiller numbers of 6.0.9 ± 0.05, 5.74 ± 0.06, 52.8 ± 0.05, 3.29 ± 0.04 and 2.22 ± 0.05 were recorded in plants of control set and plants influenced by 10, 15, 20 and 25% shoot dust concentrations. Data of intermediate values were recorded in other plants at different DAS influenced by above concentrations of dust (Table-XVIII). Like Swarna mahsuri, Samba mahsuri also exhibited similar corelation between tillering and plant age as well as dust concentrations as was noticed of Swarna mahsuri (Fig. 3.25b).

(*c*) Pratikshya: In case of pratikshya cultivar, the production of tillers was gradually decreased from 6.04 ± 0.02 (plants influenced by 5% dust) to 5.96, 5.08, 3.0 and 2.01 numbers in plants of control set and plants influenced by 10, 15, 20 and 25% respectively. Data of intermediate values were noticed in plants at different age influenced by varying concentrations of shoot dust in the culture pot (Table-XIX). The development of number of tillers per plants exhibited positive corelation with advancement of plant age and negative corelation with increase of shoot dust concentration in culture pots except 5% (Fig. 3.25c).

(*d*) Vijetha: In this cultivar the production of number of tillers per plant showed more or less same values and

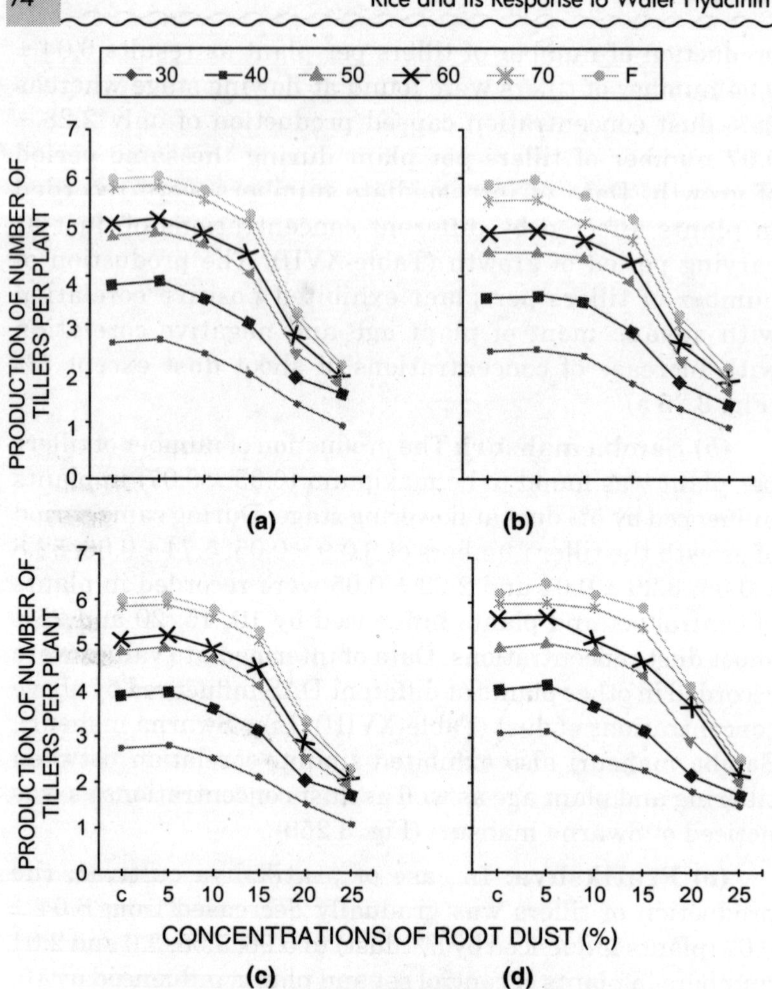

Fig. 3.25: Impact of different concentrations of shoot dust of water hyacinth *(E. crassipes)* on development of number of tillers per plant of 4 test rice cultivars (a) Swarna mahsuri, (b) Samba mahsuri, (c) Pratikshya, (d) Vijetha

similar paterns as were notice in other three test cultivars of rice. The data ranged from 1.51 ± 0.07 (plants influenced by 25% dust at the age of (30 days) to 6.41 ± 0.03 (plants affected by 5% dust at flowering stage) numbers. Other plants exhibited intermediate values in between the above two data at different ages and influenced by different shoot dust concentrations of water hyacinth (Table-XX). The tillering pattern per plant exhibited more or less similar trends as were noticed in other three test cultivars (Fig. 3.25d).

Among the four test cultivars, no significant differences were noticed in relation to production of number of tillers per plant influenced by different concentrations of shoot dust at flowering stage.

Impact of Root Dust

(*a*) Swarna mahsuri: Regarding impact of different concentrations of root dust of water hyacinth on production of number of tillers per plant of this cultivar, the data exhibited more or less same values and similar trends as were noticed in plants influenced by shoot dust (Table-XXI and Fig. 3.26a).

(*b*) Samba mahsuri: This cultivar also exhibited more or less same values and similar trends on tillering response at different ages influenced by varying concentrations of root dust as were observed in plants influenced by different shoot dust concentrations at different ages. (Table-XXII and Fig. 3.26b).

(*c*) Pratikshya: Table-XXIII depicts that maximum number of 5.99 ± 0.02 number of tillers developed per plant influenced by 5% root dust at flowering stage whereas during the same stage plants influenced by 25% dust produced only 2.17 ± 0.06 number of tiller per plant. The data varied from 1.00 ± 0.05 to 5.99 ± 0.02 at different ages influenced by other concentrations of root dust in culture pots. The tillering pattern per plants exhibited positive corelation with increase of plants age and negative corelation with increase of dust concentration in the culture pots (Fig. 3.26c).

(*d*) Vijetha: The plants of this cultivar also produced more or less same number of tillers per plants at different ages influenced by different root dust concentrations of water hyacinth in culture pots as were noticed in other cultivars too (Table-XXIV). Fig. 3.26d indicates the positive corelations between development of number of tillers per plant and advancement of plant age and negative corelations between tillering patterns and increase of root dust concentrations of water hyacinth.

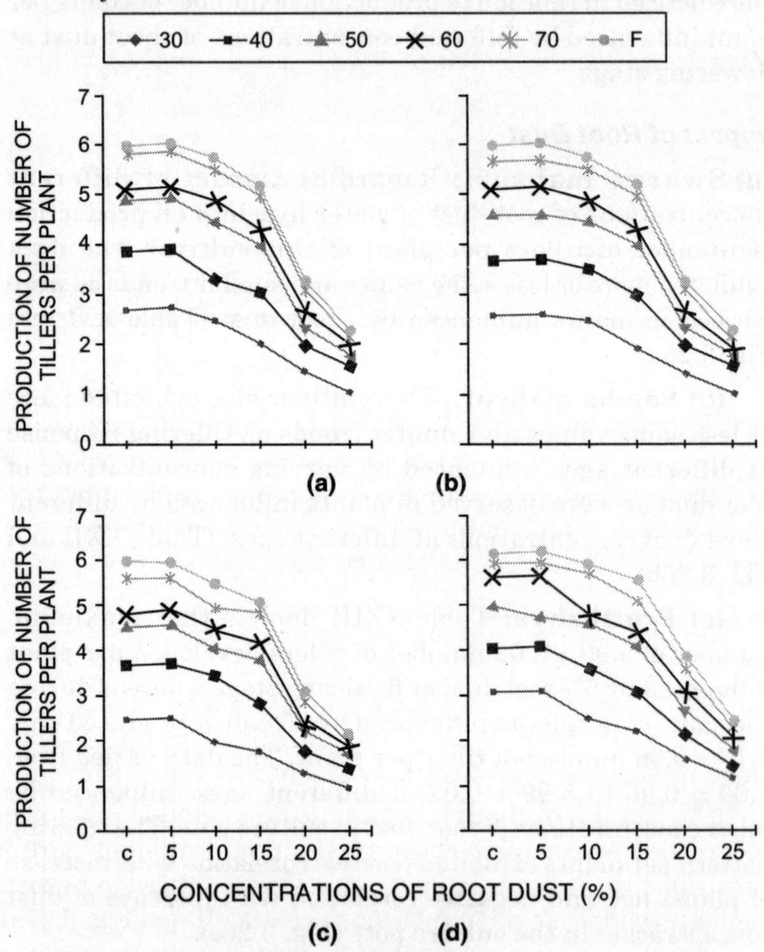

Fig. 3.26: Impact of different concentrations of root dust of water hyacinth *(E. crassipes)* on development of number of tillers per plant of 4 test rice cultivars (a) Swarna mahsuri, (b) Samba mahsuri, (c) Pratikshya, (d) Vijetha

Among the four test cultivars of rice, no significant differences were noticed regarding tillering pattern influenced by root dust of water hyacinth.

Among the two types of dusts (Shoot and root) 5% shoot dust considerably enhanced the tillering compared with root dust in all test cultivars at different ages.

Development of Number of Green Leaves on Main Shoot

The development of number of green leaves on main shoot of rice plants is considered as one of the important vegetative growth parameters as it directly or indirectly controls the growth and productivity of concerned plants. The impact of different concentrations of both shoot and root dusts on production of number of green leaves on main shoot is described below.

Impact of Shoot Dust

(*a*) Swarna mahsuri: The average number of green leaves developed on main shoot of this cultivars varied from 3.43 ± 0.02 (Plants influenced 25% dust at the age of 70 days) to 5.96 ± 0.02 (Plants influenced by 5% dust at the age of 70 days). Intermediate number of green leaves developed on main shoot was recorded in other plants at different ages influenced varying concentrations of shoot dust on culture pots (Table-XVII). The production of number of green leaves on main shoot exhibited positive corelation with advancement of plant age upto 70 days and negative corelations with increase of dust concentrations except 5% (Fig. 3.27a).

(*b*) Samba mahsuri: Regarding development of number of green leaves on main shoot, this cultivar exhibited more or less same values and similar trends as was noticed in Swarna mahsuri cultivar evidenced from (Table-XVII and Fig. 3.27b).

(*c*) Pratikshya: Table-XIX and Fig. 3.27c depict that the development of number of green leaves on main shoot considerably checked by different concentrations of shoot dust of water hyacinth in culture pots. Maximum number of

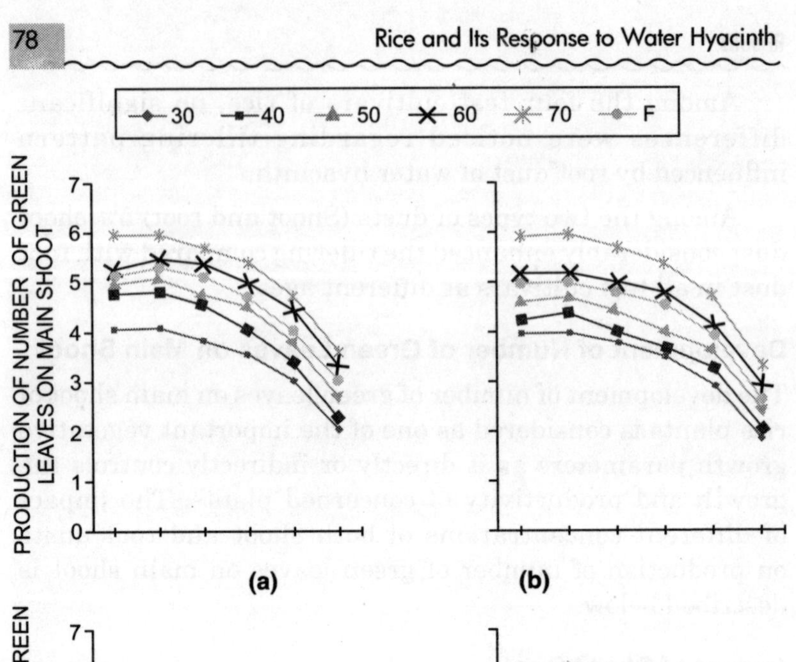

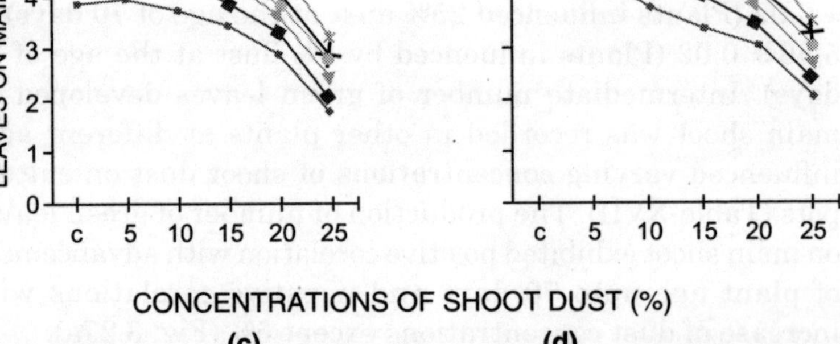

Fig. 3.27: Impact of different concentrations of shoot dust of water hyacinth *(E. crassipes)* on production of number of green leaves on main shoot of 4 test rice cultivars (a) Swarna mahsuri, (b) Samba mahsuri, (c) Pratikshya, (d) Vijetha

green leaves developed on main shoot on 70-day-old plants of these cultivars was 5.92 ± 0.09 influenced by 5% concentration while during the same period of growth 3.23 ± 0.02 number of green leaves recorded in plants influenced by 25% shoot dust. Intermediate number leaves were recorded in plants at different ages influenced by varying concentrations of shoot dust.

(*d*) Vijeth: Plants of this cultivar also produced more or less same number of green leaves on main shoot at different ages influenced by different dust concentrations (Table XX) and similar trends with influence of different dust concentrations at varying developmental stages (Fig. 3.27d) as was noticed in other cultivars.

Among the four test cultivars, no significant differences were noticed regarding development of number of green leaves on main shoot influenced by different shoot dust concentrations of water hyacinth in culture pots.

Impact of root dust

(*a*) Swarna mahsuri: The average number of green leaves developed on main shoot of the cultivars varied from 3.25 ± 0.03 (Plants influenced 25% dust at the age of 70 days) to 5.94 ± 0.02 (Plants influenced by 5% dust at the age of 70 days). Intermediate number of green leaves on main shoot was recorded in other plants at different ages influenced varying concentrations of shoot dust on culture pots (Table-XXI). The production of number of green leaves on main shoot exhibited positive corelation with advancement of plant age upto 70 days and negative corelations with increase of dust concentrations except 5% (Fig. 3.28a).

(*b*) Samba mahsuri: Regarding development of number of green leaves on main shoot, this cultivar exhibited more or less same values and similar trends as was noticed in Swarna mahsuri cultivar evidenced from (Table-XXI and Fig. 3.28b).

(c) Pratikshya: Table-XXII and Fig. 3.28c depict that the development of number of green leaves or main shoot considerably reduced by different concentrations of root dust of water hyacinth in culture pots. Maximum number of green leaves developed on main shoot of 70-day-old plants of these cultivars was 5.86 ± 0.01 influenced by 5% concentration while during the same period of growth 2.90 ± 0.08 number of green leaves recorded in plants influenced by 25% root dust. Intermediate number leaves were recorded in plants at different ages influenced by varying concentrations of root dust.

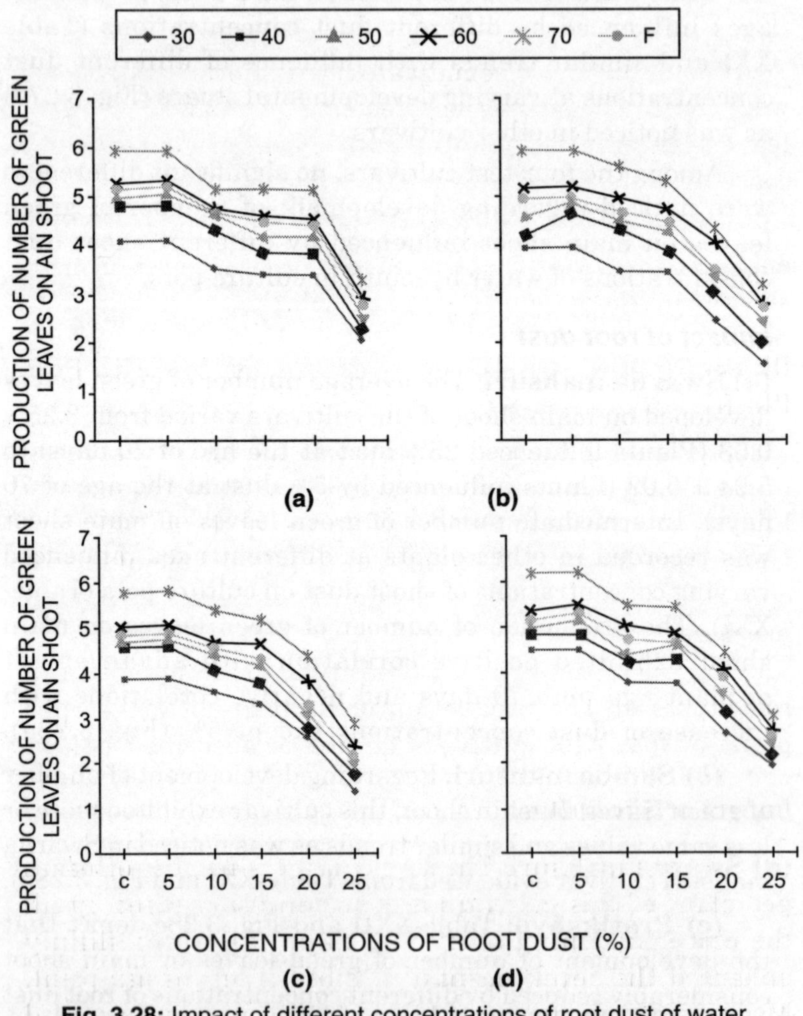

Fig. 3.28: Impact of different concentrations of root dust of water hyacinth *(E. crassipes)* on production of number of green leaves on main shoot of 4 test rice cultivars (a) Swarna mahsuri, (b) Samba mahsuri, (c) Pratikshya, (d) Vijetha

(*d*) **Vijetha:** Plants of this cultivar also produced more or less same number of green leaves on main shoot at different ages influenced by different dust concentrations (Table-XXIV) and similar trends with influence of different dust concentrations and at varying developmental stages (Fig. 3.28d) as was noticed in other cultivars.

Among the four test cultivars, no significant differences were noticed regarding development of number of green leaves on main shoot influenced by different root dust concentrations of water hyacinth in culture pots.

Among the two types of dusts, shoot dust slightly enhanced the development of number of green leaves on main shoot in all the test cultivars of rice plants.

DEVELOPMENT OF TOTAL NUMBER OF LEAVES PER PLANT

The productivity of any crop plant depends on the leaf areas of that plant through photosynthetic activities. Generally higher the photosynthetic area more is the production. Hence, development of total green leaves per plant of rice crop is considered as one of the important vegetable growth parameters which has direct bearing on its productivity. The impact of different concentrations of both shoot and root dusts on the production of total green leaves per plant of four test cultivars of rice is described below.

Impact of Shoot Dust

(*a*) **Swarna mahsuri:** The development of number of leaves per plant of this cultivars is considerably checked by all the concentrations of shoot dust except 5% which slightly enhanced the development of number of leaves per plant. Mean maximum number of 18.95 ± 0.06 leaves were recorded in plants at flowering stage influenced by 5% dust while only 6.10 ± 0.09 number of leaves per plant was recorded in plants influenced by 25% shoot dust. Data of intermediate values were recorded in other plants at different ages influenced by other dust concentrations (Table-XVII). A sharp decline in development of number of leaves per plant was noticed in plants influenced by shoot dust concentrations more than 5%. The leaves developed per plants exhibited positive corelation with increase of plant age and negative corelation with increase of shoot dust concentration in culture pots (Fig. 3.29a).

(*b*) Samba mahsuri: This cultivar also exhibited more or less same values and similar trends in development of number of leaves per plant influenced by different concentrations of dust at varying ages of the plants (Table-XVIII and Fig. 3.29b) as was noticed in case of Swarna mahsuri.

(*c*) Pratikhsya: The development of number of leaves per plant was considerably reduced by the influenced of all concentrations of dust tried except 5% which exhibited slightly higher number of leaves per plant than control plants at different ages. The number of leaves developed per plant ranged from 6.06 ± 0.09 (plant influenced by 25% dust) to 18.69 ± 0.06 (plants influenced by 5% dust) at flowering stage. Data of intermediate values were recorded in plants at different ages influenced by different dust concentrations (Table-XIX). The development of number of leaves per plant exhibited positive corelation with advancement of plant age and negative corelation with increase of dust concentrations (Fig. 3.29c).

(*d*) Vijetha: Like other three cultivars, this cultivar also exhibited more or less same values and similar trends on development of number of leaves per plant at different ages influenced varying concentrations of dust in culture pots (Table-XX and Fig. 3.29d).

Among four test cultivars of rice no significant differences were noticed regarding production of total number of leaves per plant.

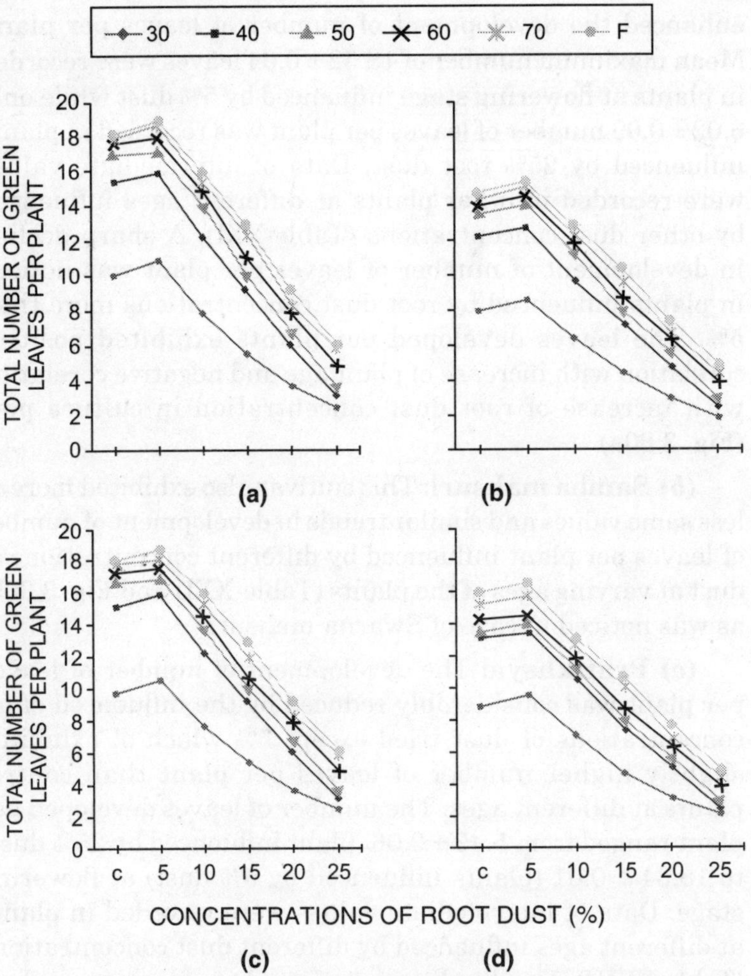

Fig. 3.29: Impact of different concentrations of shoot dust of water hyacinth *(E. crassipes)* on development of number of green leaves per plant of 4 test rice cultivars (a) Swarna mahsuri, (b) Samba mahsuri, (c) Pratikshya, (d) Vijetha

Impact of root dust

(*a*) Swarna mahsuri: The development of number of leaves per plant of this cultivars is considerably checked by all the concentrations of root dust except 5% which slightly enhanced the development of number of leaves per plant. Mean maximum number of 18.52 ± 0.04 leaves were recorded in plants at flowering stage influenced by 5% dust while only 6.02 ± 0.09 number of leaves per plant was recorded in plants influenced by 25% root dust. Data of intermediate values were recorded in other plants at different ages influenced by other dust concentrations (Table-XXI). A sharp decline in development of number of leaves per plant was noticed in plants influenced by root dust concentrations more than 5%. The leaves developed per plants exhibited positive corelation with increase of plant age and negative corelation with increase of root dust concentration in culture pots (Fig. 3.30a).

(*b*) Samba mahsuri: This cultivar also exhibited more or less same values and similar trends in development of number of leaves per plant influenced by different concentrations of dust at varying ages of the plants (Table-XXII and Fig. 3.30b) as was noticed in case of Swarna mahsuri.

(*c*) Pratikhsya: The development of number of leaves per plant was considerably reduced by the influenced of all concentrations of dust tried except 5% which of exhibited slightly higher number of leaves per plant than control plants at different ages. The number of leaves developed per plant ranged from 5.49 ± 0.06 (plant influenced by 25% dust) to 18.34 ± 0.01 (plants influenced by 5% dust) at flowering stage. Data of intermediate values were recorded in plants at different ages influenced by different dust concentrations (Table-XXIII). The development of number of leaves per plant exhibited positive corelation with advancement of plant age and negative corelation with increase of dust concentrations (Fig.-30 c).

(*d*) Vijetha: Like other three cultivars, this cultivar also exhibited more or less same values and similar trends on development of number of leaves per plant at different ages influenced by varying concentrations of dust in culture pots (Table-XXIV and Fig. 3.30d).

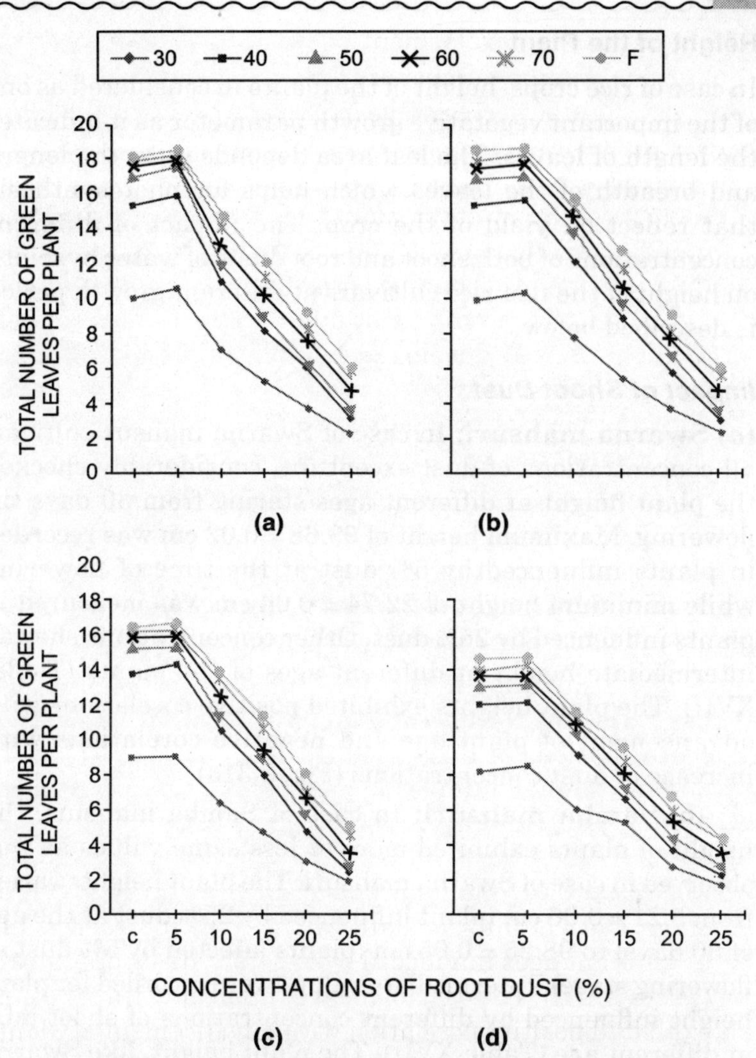

Fig. 3.30: Impact of different concentrations of root dust of water hyacinth *(E. crassipes)* on development of number of green leaves per plant of 4 test rice cultivars (a) Swarna mahsuri, (b) Samba mahsuri, (c) Pratikshya, (d) Vijetha

Among the two types of dust, shoot dust was found to bc slightly effective on development of total number of leaves per plant than the root dust of waters hyacinth.

Height of the Plant

In case of rice crops, height of the plants in considered as one of the important vegetative growth parameter as it indicates the length of leaves. The leaf area depends upon the length and breadth of the leaves which helps for photosynthesis that reflect on yield of the crop. The impact of different concentrations of both shoot and root dusts of water hyacinth on height of the test rice cultivars at different growth period is described below.

Impact of Shoot Dust

(*a*) Swarna mahsuri: In case of Swarna mahsur cultivar, all concentrations of dust except 5%, considerably checked the plant height at different ages staring from 30 days till flowering. Maximum height of 99.68 ± 0.02 cm was recorded in plants influenced by 5% dust at the time of flowering while minimum height of 22.74 ± 0.04 cm was measured in plants influenced by 25% dust. Other concentrations showed intermediate height at different ages of the plants (Table-XVII). The plant heights exhibited positive corelations with advancement of plant age and negative corelations with increase of dust concentrations (Fig. 3.31a).

(*b*) Samba mahsuri: In case of Samba mahsuri, the height of plants exhibited more or less same values as was observed in case of Swarna mahsuri. The plant heights varied from 5.21 ± 0.06 cm (plant influenced by 25% dust at the age of 30 days) to 98.25 ± 0.05 cm (plants affected by 5% dust at flowering stage). Intermediate values were recorded for plant height influenced by different concentrations of shoot dust at different age (Table-XVII). The plant height, like Swarna mahsuri, exhibited positive corelation with increase of dust concentrations except 5% (Fig. 3.31b).

(c) Pratikshya: Like other two test cultivars, this cultivar of rice also exhibited more or less same values (Table-XIX) and similar trends (Fig. 3.31c) in regard to plant heights at different ages influenced by different concentrations of shoot dust of water hyacinth in culture pots.

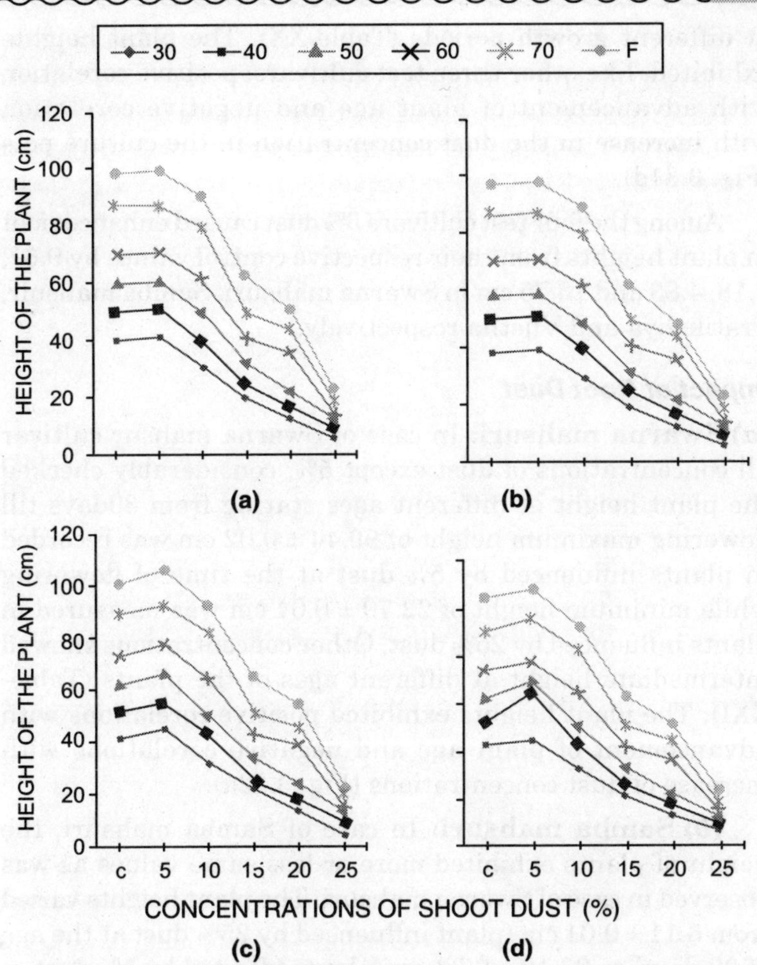

Fig. 3.31: Impact of different concentrations of shoot dust of water hyacinth *(E. crassipes)* on height of the plants of 4 test rice cultivars (a) Swarna mahsuri, (b) Samba mahsuri, (c) Pratikshya, (d) Vijetha

***(d)* Vijetha:** The maximum plant height of 118.77 ± 0.06 cm was recorded in plants affected by 5% shoot dust at the time of flowering whereas during the same stage of growth plant height of only 23.98 ± 0.04 cm was recorded in plants influenced by 25% dust. Data of intermediate values were recorded for other plant affected by different concentrations at different growth periods (Table-XX). The plant heights exhibited, like other three test cultivars, positive corelation with advancement of plant age and negative corelation with increase in the dust concentration in the culture pots (Fig. 3.31d).

Among the four test cultivars 5% dust caused enhancement in plant heights from their respective control values by 9.67, 6.18, 4.83 and 13.75 cm in Swarna mahsuri, Samba mahsuir, Pratikshya and Vijetha respectively.

Impact of Root Dust

(*a*) Swarna mahsuri: In case of Swarna mahsur cultivar all concentrations of dust except 5%, considerably checked the plant height at different ages staring from 30days till flowering maximum height of 99.44 ± 0.02 cm was recorded in plants influenced by 5% dust at the time of flowering while minimum height of 22.70 ± 0.04 cm was measured in plants influenced by 25% dust. Other concentrations showed intermediate height at different ages of the plants (Table-XXI). The plant heights exhibited positive corelations with advancement of plant age and negative corelations with increase of dust concentrations (Fig. 3.32a).

(*b*) Samba mahsuri: In case of Samba mahsuri, the height of plants exhibited more or less same values as was observed in case of Swarna mahsuri. The plant heights varied from 5.11 ± 0.01 cm (plant influenced by 25% dust at the age of 30 days) to 97.12 ± 0.03 cm (plants affected by 5% dust at flowering stage). Data of intermediate values were recorded for plant height influenced by different concentrations of root dust at different age (Table-XXII). The plant height, like Swarna mahsuri, exhibited positive corelation with increase of dust concentrations except 5% (Fig. 3.32b).

(*c*) Pratikshya: Like other two test cultivars, this cultivar of rice also exhibited more or less same values (Table-XXIII) and similar trends (Fig. 3.32c) in regard to plant heights at different ages influenced by different concentrations of root dust of water hyacinth in culture pots.

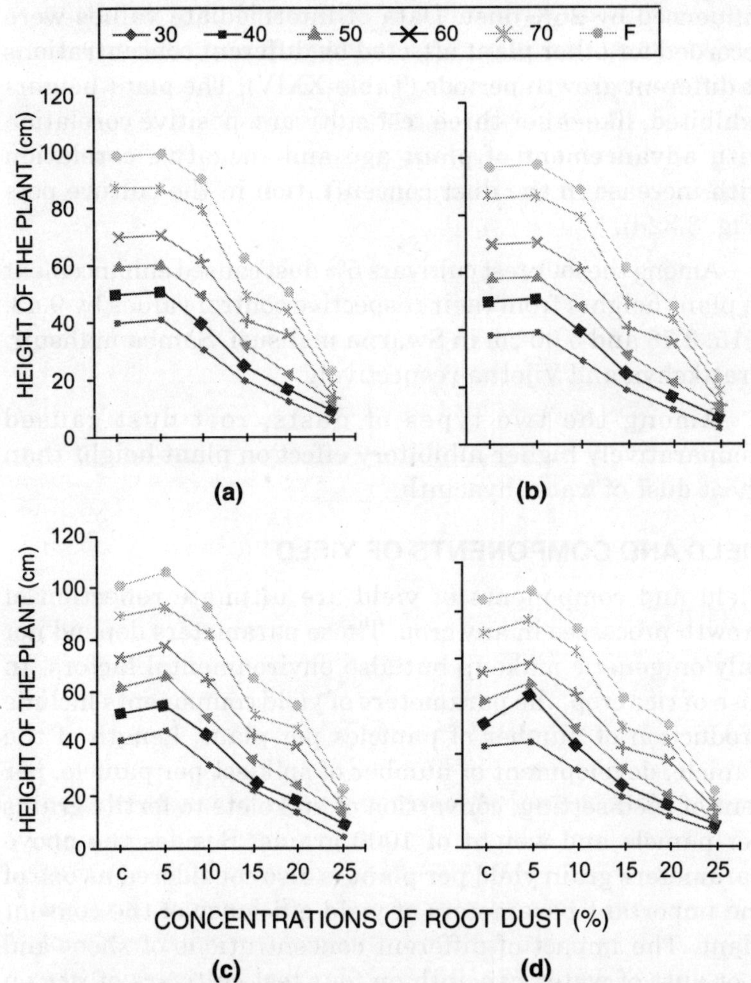

Fig. 3.32: Impact of different concentrations of root dust of water hyacinth *(E. crassipes)* on height of the plants of 4 test rice cultivars (a) Swarna mahsuri, (b) Samba mahsuri, (c) Pratikshya, (d) Vijetha

***(d)* Vijetha:** The maximum plant height of 105.99 ± 0.06 cm was recorded in plants affected by 5% root dust at the time of flowering whereas during the same stage of growth plant height of only 23.00 ± 0.04 cm was recorded in plants influenced by 25% dust. Data of intermediate values were recorded for other plant affected by different concentrations at different growth periods (Table-XXIV). The plant heights exhibited, like other three test cultivars, positive corelation with advancement of plant age and negative corelation with increase in the dust concentration in the culture pots (Fig. 3.32d).

Among the four test cultivars 5% dust caused enhancement in plant heights from their respective control values by 9.43, 0.15, 3.78 and 5.00 cm in Swarna mahsuri, Samba mahsuir, Pratikshya and Vijetha respectively.

Among the two types of dusts, root dust caused comparatively higher inhibitory effect on plant height than shoot dust of water hyacinth.

YIELD AND COMPONENTS OF YIELD

Yield and components of yield are ultimate reflection of growth processes in any crop. These parameters depend not only on genetic makeup but also environmental factors. In case of rice crop, the parameters of yield components include production of number of panicles per plant, Length of the Panicle, development of number of spikiest per panicle, per cent of seed setting, convertion of spikelets to fertile grains per panicle and weight of 1000 grains. Besides the above parameters grain yield per plant is also considered as one of the important parameters of yield efficiency of the consent plant. The impact of different concentrations of shoot and root dust of water hyacinth on four test cultivars of rice on different yield parameters and yield efficiency is mentioned below.

Development of Number of Panicles per Plant

Generally in rice plants a number of tillers develop per plants during their vegetative growth but some of them become fertile by bearing panicles and others remain vegetative only. The fertile tillers are responsible for yield efficiency of the concerned crop. The impact of different concentrations of shoot and root dusts of water hyacinth on development of number of panicles per plant of four test cultivars is described below.

Impact of Shoot Dust

(*a*) Swarna mahsuri: All concentrations of shoot dust of water hyacinth considerably checked the development of panicle per plant as a result an average of only 1.25 ± 0.09 number of panicles were developed per plant influenced by 25% dust concentration whereas plants influenced by 5% dust produced an average of 5.85 ± 0.09 number of panicles per plant. This value was slightly higher than control vale (5.32 ± 0.02). Intermediate number of panicles was noticed in other plants influenced by other concentrations (Table–XXVa). The production of panicles per plant exhibited negative corelation with increase of dust concentrations (Fig. 3.33a).

(*b*) Samba mahsuri:

(*c*) In this test cultivars, an average number of 1.08 ± 0.07 panicles per plant was recorded in plants affected by 25% dust concentration wheresas 5.18 ± 0.04, 5.22 ± 0.05, 3.54 ± 0.04, 2.35 ± 0.01 and 1.65 ± 0.05 numbers of panicles per plants were recorded in plants of control set and plants influenced by 5, 10, 15 and 20% dust respectively (Table XXVIa). Like Swarna mahsuri, this cultivar also exhibited negative corelations between production of panicles per plant and increase of dust concentration (Fig. 3.33a).

(*d*) Pratikshya: The development of number of panicles per plant was considerably reduced by higher concentrations of shoot dust (>5%) as a results average number of 3.02, 2.11, 1.32 and 1.08 panicles were recorded in plants affected by 10, 15, 20 and 25% dust respectively. Plants of control set produced 5.02 ± 0.06 number of panicles per plant whereas the value was 5.05 ± 0.05 for plants influenced by 5% dust (Table-XXVII a). The production of number of tillers showered negative corelation with increase of dust concentrations (Fig. 3.33a).

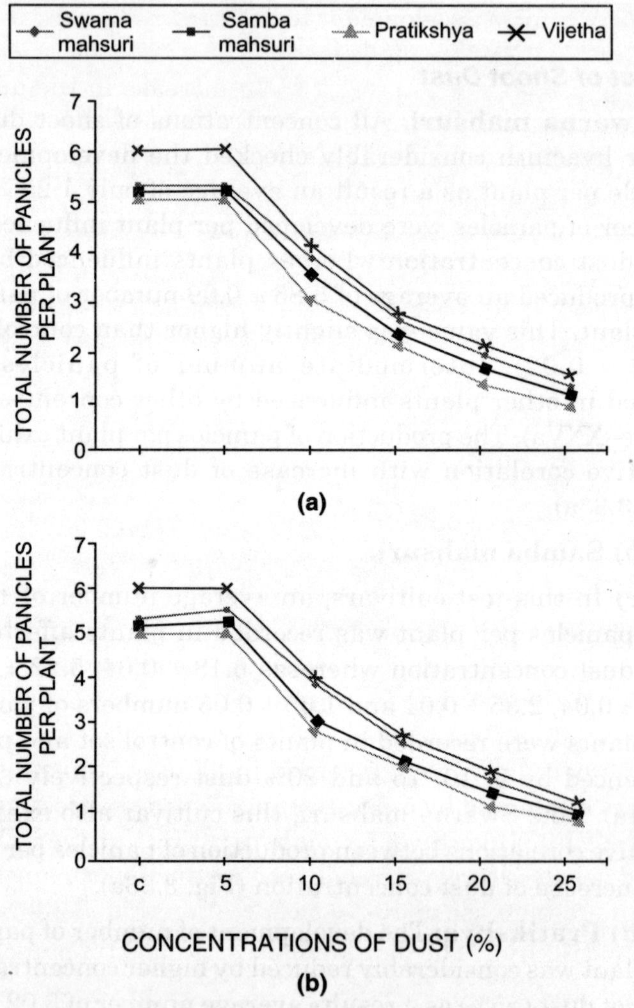

Fig. 3.33: Impact of different concentrations of shoot (a) and root (b) dust of water hyacinth *(E. crassipes)* on development of number of panicles per plant of 4 test rice cultivars

(e) Vijetha: Like other three cultivars, this cultivar also exhibited more or less same vales (Table–XVIII a) and similar corelation between production of number of panicle per plant and duct concentrations in culture pots (Fig. 3.33a).

Among the four test cultivars of rice, the degree of response on panicle development to different concentrations of shoot dust tried was as follows:

Vijetha > Swarna mahsuri > Samba mahsuri > Pratikshya.

Impact of root dust

(a) Swarna mahsuri: All the concentrations of root dust of water hyacinth considerably checked the development of panicles per plant as a result an average of only 1.02 ± 0.01 number of panicles were noticed per plant influenced by 25% dust concentration, whereas plants influenced by 5% dust produced an average of 5.54 ± 0.05 number of panicles per plant. This value was slightly higher than control value (5.32 ± 0.02). Intermediate number of panicles were noticed in other plants influenced by diferent concentrations of root dust (Table–XXV b). The production of panicles per plant exhibited negative corelation with increase of dust concentrations (Fig. 3.33b).

(b) Samba mahsuri: In this test cultivars, an average of 0.91 ± 0.03 number of panicles per plant was recorded in plants affected by 25% dust concentration whereas 5.18 ± 0.04, 5.20 ± 0.07, 3.06 ± 0.04, 2.13 ± 0.01 and 1.41 ± 0.05 numbers of panicles per plants were recorded in plants of control set and plants influenced by 5, 10, 15 and 20% dust respectively (Table–XXVIb). Like Swarna mahsuri, this cultivar also exhibited negative corelations between production of panicles per plant and increase of dust concentration (Fig. 3.33b).

(c) Pratikshya: The development of number of panicles per plant considerably reduced by higher concentrations of root dust (>5%) as a results average numbers of 2.82, 2.01, 1.13 and 1.00 panicles were recorded in plants affected by 10, 15, 20 and 25% dust respectively. Plants of control set produced 5.02 ± 0.06 number of panicles per plant whereas the value was 5.03 ± 0.08 for plant influenced by 5% dust (Table–XXVIIb). The production of number of tillers showered negative corelation with increase of dust concentrations (Fig. 3.33b).

***(d)* Vijetha:** Like other three cultivars, this cultivar also exhibited more or less same vales (Table-XVIIIb) and similar corelation between production of panicle per plant and development of number of panicles per plant (Fig. 3.33b).

Among four test cultivars of rice, the degree of response on panicle development to different concentrations of root dust was as follows:-
Vijetha > Swarna mahsuri > Samba mahsuri > Pratikshya.

Among the two types of dust, all concentrations of shoot dust exhibited slightly higher value than the root dust.

Length of the Panicle

The development of number of grains per panicle depends on the length of the panicle which play a vital role on productivity in cereals in general and rice in particular. In the present investigation, the lengths of panicles influenced by different concentrations of both shoot and root dusts in four test cultivars of rice are mentioned below.

Impact of shoot dust

***(a)* Swarna mahsuri:** All the concentrations of dust considerably reduced the panicle length (except 5%) as a result a mean length of 8.62 ± 0.06 cm of panicle was recorded in plants influenced by 25% dust whereas the values were 20.82, 25.85, 18.44, 13.01 and 11.11 cm in plants of control set and affected by 5, 10, 15 and 20% concentrations of shoot dust respectively (Table–XXVa). The panicle lengths showed negative corelation with increase of shoot dust in culture pot except 5% (Fig. 3.34a).

(*b*) Samba mahsuri: This cultivar also exhibited more or less same values (Table –XXVIa) and similar corelations between panicle length and shoot dust concentrations (Fig. 3.34a).

(*c*) Pratiksya: In this cultivar also higher concentration of dust (>5%) significantly caused reduction in panicle length as a result a mean length of 6.01 ± 0.08 cm panicle was noticed in plants influenced by 25% dust whereas the values were 20.00, 23.11, 16.01, 11.05 and 8.25 cm for plants of control set and plants affected by 5, 10, 15 and 20% of dust respectively (Table–XXVII a). Like other two cultivars, negative corelations between panicle length and increase of dust concentrations in culture pots were noticed in this cultivar also (Fig. 3.34a).

(*d*) Vijetha: The different concentrations of shoot dust affected on the development of panicles. More or less similar lengths of panicles developed in plant and similar corelations with panicle length with dust concetration was noticed as was noticed in other three test cultivars of rice (Table–XXVIII a and Fig. 3.34a).

Among the four tests cultivar of rice, the trend of panicle lengths to different concentrations of dust was as follows:-

Vijetha > Swarna mahsuri < Samba mahsuri > Pratikshya.

Impact of root dust

(*a*) Swarna mahsuri: All the concentrations of dust considerably reduced the panicle length (except 5%) as a result a mean length of 7.42 ± 0.06 cm of panicle was recorded in plants influenced by 25% dust whereas the values were 20.82, 25.83, 18.38, 12.75 and 9.01 cms in plants of control set and affected by 5, 10, 15 and 20% concentrations of root dust respectively (Table–XXV b). The panicle length showed negative corelation with increase of root dust in culture pot except 5% (Fig. 3.34b).

(*b*) Samba mahsuri: This cultivar also exhibited more or less same values (Table–XXVI b) and similar corelation between panicle length and shoot dust concentrations of water hyacinth in the culture pots (Fig.-34 b).

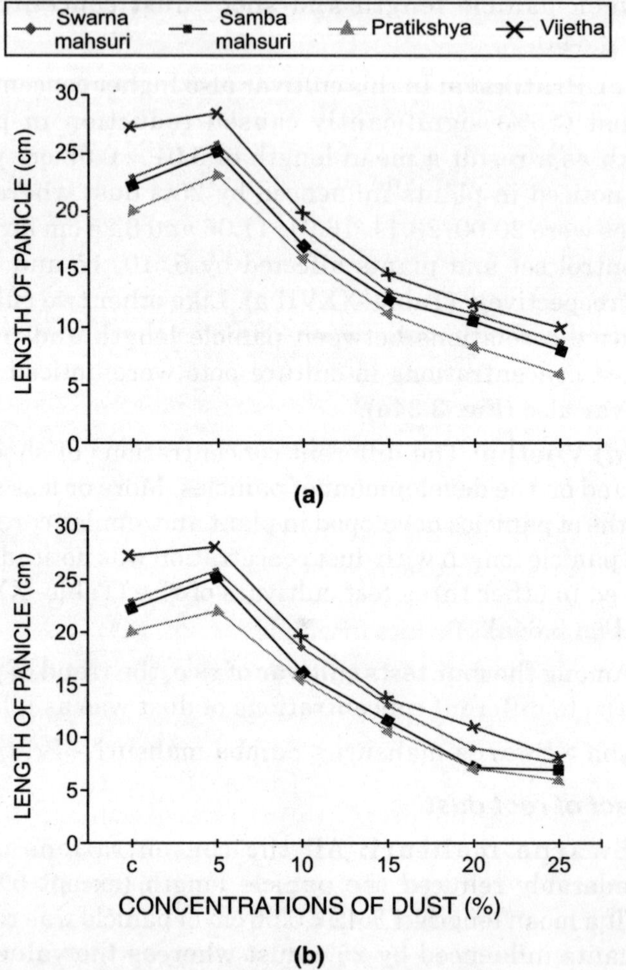

Fig. 3.34: Impact of different concentrations of shoot (a) and root (b) dust of water hyacinth *(E. crassipes)* on length of panicles of 4 test rice cultivars

(c) Pratiksya: In this cultivar also higher concentration of dust (>5%) significantly caused reduction in panicle length as a result a mean length of 5.78 ± 0.01 cm panicle was noticed in plants influenced by 25% dust whereas the values were 20.00, 22.02, 15.46, 10.69 and 7.03 cms in plants of control set and plants affected by 5, 10, 15 and 20% of dust concentrations respectively (Table–XXVII b). Like other two cultivars, negative corelations between panicle length and increase of dust concentrations in culture pots were noticed in this cultivar also (Fig. 3.34b).

(*d*) Vijetha: The different concentration of root dust affected on the panicle development. More or less similar lengths of panicles developed in plant and similar corelations with panicle length with dust concetrations as was noticed in other three test cultivars of rice (Table–XXVIII b and Fig. 3.34b).

Among the four tests cultivar of rice, the trend of panicle length to different concentrations of dust was as follows:

Vijetha > Swarna mahsuri < Samba mahsuri > Pratikshya.

Among the two types of dusts, shoot dusts slightly enhanced the panicle length compared to root dust.

Number of Spikelets / Panicle

The development of number of spikelets per panicle play a vital role in productivity of rice crop as the spikeletes later on convert into grains after proper fertilization and filling. Hence, agronomical point of view this parameter is considered as important parameters of components of yield. The impact of different concentrations of shoot and root dusts of water hyacinth on development of number of spikelets per panicle is described below.

Impact of shoot dust

(*a*) Swarna mahsuri: The development of spikelets on panicle considerably reduced by the influence of different dust concentrations. Maximum number of 169.32 ± 0.04 spikelets per panicle was recorded in plants affected by 5% dust while the value was minimum (28.92 ± 0.01) in plants influenced by 25% consternation. Data of intermediate numbers were observed in other plants influenced by different concentrations of dust (Table–XXV a). The developments of spikelets per panicle exhibited negative corelation with increase of dust consternation in culture pots (Fig. 3.35a).

***(b)* Samba mahsuri:** In this test cultivar, the production of spikelets per panicle significantly reduced from 160.84 ± 0.02 (Plants affected by 5% dust) to 24.56 ± 0.04 (Plants affected by 25% dust). Other concentrations showed intermediate values. No significant differences between plants affected by 5% dust and control plants were noticed as the number of spikerlest per panicle were 160.84 and 160.82 respectively (Table–XXVIa). Like Swaran mahsuri, this cultivar also exhibited negative corelation between production of number of spikelet per panicle and increase of shoot dust concentration in culture pots (Fig. 3.35a).

***(c)* Pratikshya:** The production of number of spikelets per panicle influence by different concentrations of shoot dust is presented in Table–XXVIIa.

The development of spikelets on panicles reduced from 159.92 ± 0.08 (Plant influenced by 5% dust) to 22.11 ± 0.03 (Plants affected by 25% dust). Plants affected by other concentrations of dust showed intermediate values. Like other two cultivars the reduction on production of number of spikelets per plant exhibited positive corelation with increase of dust concentrations in culture pots (Fig. 3.35a).

***(d)* Vijehta:** Table–XXVIII a depicts the development of number of spikelest per panicle in different plants influenced by varying concentrations of shoot dust. All the concentrations significantly reduced the development of number of spikelets per panicle except 5% dust which showed similar value with that of control plants. Fig. 3.35 a indicates the negative corelation between production of number of panicles per plant and increase of dust concentration.

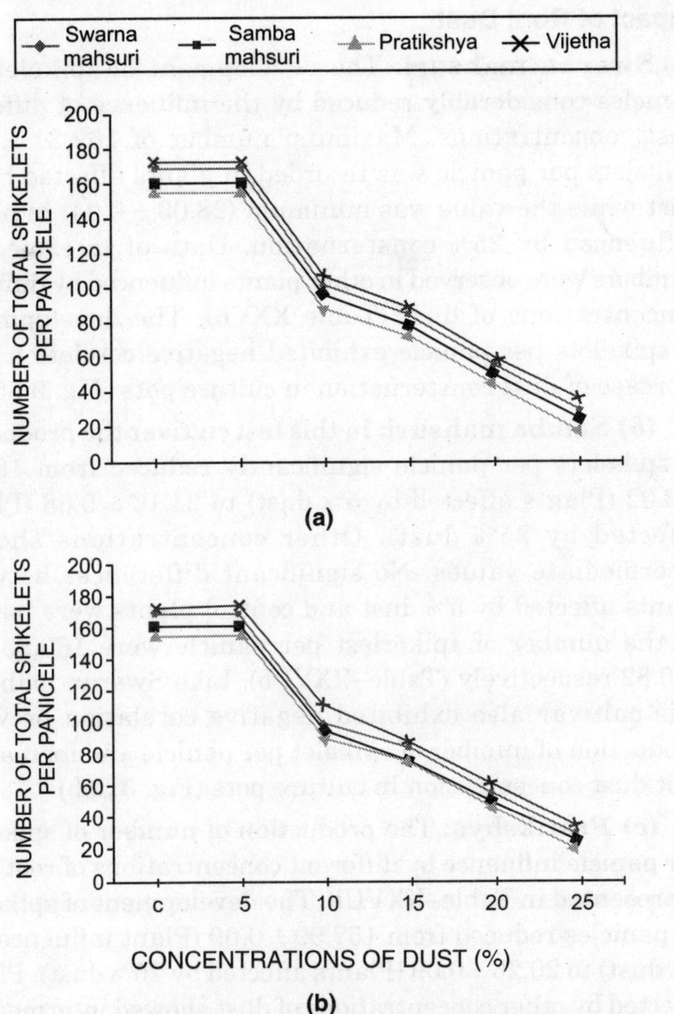

Fig. 3.35: Impact of different concentrations of shoot (a) and root (b) dust of water hyacinth *(E. crassipes)* on production of number of spikelets per panicle of 4 test rice cultivars

Among the four test cultivars, the degree of reduction in development of number of spikelest per panicle in plants influenced by different concentrations of dust was as follows:- Pratikshya > Samba mahsuri > Swarna mahsuri > VIjehta.

Impact of Root Dust

(*a*) Swarna mahsuri: The development of spikelets on panicles considerably reduced by the influence of different dust concentrations. Maximum number of 169.31 ± 0.02 spikelets per panicle was recorded in plants affected by 5% dust while the value was minimum (28.09 ± 0.04) in plants influenced by 25% consternation. Data of intermediate numbers were observed in other plants influenced by different concentrations of dust (Table XXVb). The developments of spikelets per panicle exhibited negative corelation with increase of dust consternation in culture pots (Fig. 3.35b).

(*b*) Samba mahsuri: In this test cultivar the production of spikelets per panicle significantly reduced from 160.83 ± 0.02 (Plants affected by 5% dust) to 24.16 ± 0.08 (Plants affected by 25% dust). Other concentrations showed intermediate values. No significant differences between plants affected by 5% dust and control plants were noticed as the number of spikerlest per panicle were 160.83 and 160.82 respectively (Table–XXVI b). Like Swaran mahsuri, this cultivar also exhibited negative corelation between production of number of spikelet per panicle and increase of root dust concentration in culture pots (Fig. 3.35b).

(*c*) Pratikshya: The production of number of spikelets per panicle influence by different concentrations of root dust is presented in Table–XXVIIb. The development of spikelets on panicles reduced from 157.99 ± 0.09 (Plant influenced by 5% dust) to 20.26 ± 0.09 (Plants affected by 25% dust). Plants affected by other concentrations of dust showed intermediate values. Like other two cultivars the reduction on production of number of spikelets per plant exhibited positive corelation with increase of dust concentrations in culture pots (Fig. 3.35b).

(*d*) Vijehta: Table XXVIIIb depicts the development of number of spikelets per panicle in different plants influenced by varying concentrations of root dust. All the concentrations significantly reduced the development of number of spikelets per panicle except 5% dust which showed similar value with that of control plants. Fig. 3.35b indicates the negative corelation between production of number of panicles per plant and increase of dust concentration.

Among the four test cultivars, the degree of reduction in development of number of spikelets per plant influenced by different concentrations of dust was as follows:

Pratikshya > Samba mahsuri > Swarna mahsuri > VIjehta.

Among the two types of dusts no significant differences were noticed in regards to development of number of spikelets per panicle.

Number of Fertile Grains per Panicle

The development of grains occurs after proper fertilization and nourinshent in spikelest. The farmer again depends upon the viability of pollen and nucleus of megaspore and later upon source and sink relationship. The effects of different concentrations of shoot and root dust of water hyacinth on formation of fully developed grains per panicle of test rice cultivars are described below.

Impact of Shoot Dust

(*a*) Swarna mahsuri: From Table–XXV a it can be noticed that except 5% all concentrations of dust significantly reduced the formation of number of fertile grains per panicle as a result only 3.98 ± 0.01 number of grains were developed per panicles influenced by 25% dust concentration while plants influenced by 5% dust produced 127.41 ± 0.01 number of grains per panicle. Plants of control set produced almost same number of grains per panicle. Other concentrations exhibited intermediate values. Like production of number of spikelets per panicle, formation of grains per panicle exhibited negative corelation with increase of concentrations of the dust (> 5%) as evidenced from Fig. 3.36a.

(*b*) **Samba mahsuri:** This cultivar also produced more or less same number of grains per panicle as was noticed in previous cultivar. Highest number of 114.06 ± 0.09 grains per panicle was recorded in plants influenced by 5% dust while minimum numbers of 2.45 ± 0.08 grains per panicle were recorded in plants influenced by 25% dust. Data of intermediate values were recorded for other plants influenced by different concentrations (Table–XXVIa). The development of grains per panicle exhibited negative corelation with increase of shoot dust concentrations in culture pots except 5% dust (Fig. 3.36a).

(*c*) **Pratikshya:** This cultivar also exhibited more or less same number of grains per panicle (Table–XXVII a) and similar trends (Fig. 3.36a) as was noticed in other two test cultivars.

(*d*) **Vijetha:** In this cultivar, the development of number of fully developed grains per panicle showed slightly higher value than other 3 test cultivars influenced by same concentration of shoot dust. Maximum number of grains developed per panicle (134.78 ± 0.04) was noticed in plants influenced by 5% dust whereas minimum number of 6.18 ± 0.09 grains developed per panicle was recorded in plants affected by 25% dust concentration. Other plants of control and treated sets exhibited intermediate values (Table–XXVIII a). The corelations between development of grains per panicle and different treatments were more or less similar with other three test cultivars of rice (Fig. 3.36a).

Among the four test cultivars the degree of production of number of fully developed or mature grains per panicle was as follows:

Vijetha > Swarna mahsuri > Samba mahsuri > Pratikshya.

Impact of root dust

(*a*) Swarna mahsuri: From Table-XXVb it can be noticed that except 5% all concentrations of dust significantly caused reduction on the formation of number of mature grains per panicle as a result only 3.67 ± 0.04 number of grains were developed per panicles influenced by 25% dust concentration while plants influenced by 5% dust concetration produced 127.28 ± 0.02 number of grains per panicle. Plants of control set produced almost same number of grains per panicle. Other concentrations exhibited intermediate values. Like production of number of spikelets per panicle, formation of grains per panicle exhibited negative corelation with increase in the concentration of dust (> 5%) as evidenced from Fig. 3.36 b.

(*b*) Samba mahsuri: This cultivar also produced more or less same number of grains per panicle as was noticed in previous cultivar. Highest number of 113.86 ± 0.06 grains per panicle was recorded in plants influenced by 5% dust while minimum numbers of 2.31 ± 0.03 grains per panicle were recorded in plants influenced by 25% dust. Data of intermediate values were recorded for other plants influenced by different concentrations (Table–XXVI b). The development of grains per panicle exhibited negative corelation with increase of root dust concentrations in culture pots except 5% dust (Fig. 3.36 b).

(*c*) Pratikshya: This cultivar also exhibited more or less same number of grains per panicle (Table–XXVII b) and similar trends (Fig. 3.36b) as was noticed in other two test cultivars.

(*d*) Vijetha: In this cultivar, the development of number of mature grains per panicle showed slightly higher value than the other 3 test cultivars influenced by same concentration of root dust. Maximum number of grains developed per panicle (135.30 ± 0.07) was noticed in plants influenced by 5% dust whereas minimum number of 5.34

± 0.03 grains developed per panicle was recorded in plants affected by 25% dust concentration. Other plants of control and treated sets exhibited intermediate values (Table–XXVIII b). The corelations between development of mature grains per panicle and different treatments were more or less similar with other three test cultivars of rice (Fig. 3.36b).

Among the four test cultivars, the degree of production of number of mature grains per panicle was as follows:

Vijetha > Swarna mahsuri > Samba mahsuri > Pratikshya.

Among two types of dusts, no significant differences were noticed on production of number of mature grains per panicle between the plants influenced by respective concentration.

Per Cent of Seed Setting

The per cent of seed setting on panicles in rice cultivars play an important of role on productivity of concerned plants. Effects of different concentrations of shoot and root dust of water hyacinth on per cent of seed setting in four test cultivars are described.

Impact of shoot dust

From Fig. 3.37a, it can be noticed that higher the concentration of shoot dust in culture pots lower was the seed setting percentage in all the test cultivars of rice. Shoot dust consternation of 5% exhibited almost similar values on seed setting as was noticed in case of control plants. The data on per cent of seed setting, influenced by different concentrations of shoot dust, in Swarna mahsuri, Samba mahsrui, Pratikshya and Vijetha cultivars are presented in Tables–XXV a, XXVI, XXVII a and XXVIII a respectively.

Among the four test cultivars of rice the degree of per cent of seed setting was as follows:

Vijetha > Swarna mahsuri > Samba mahsuri > Pratikshya.

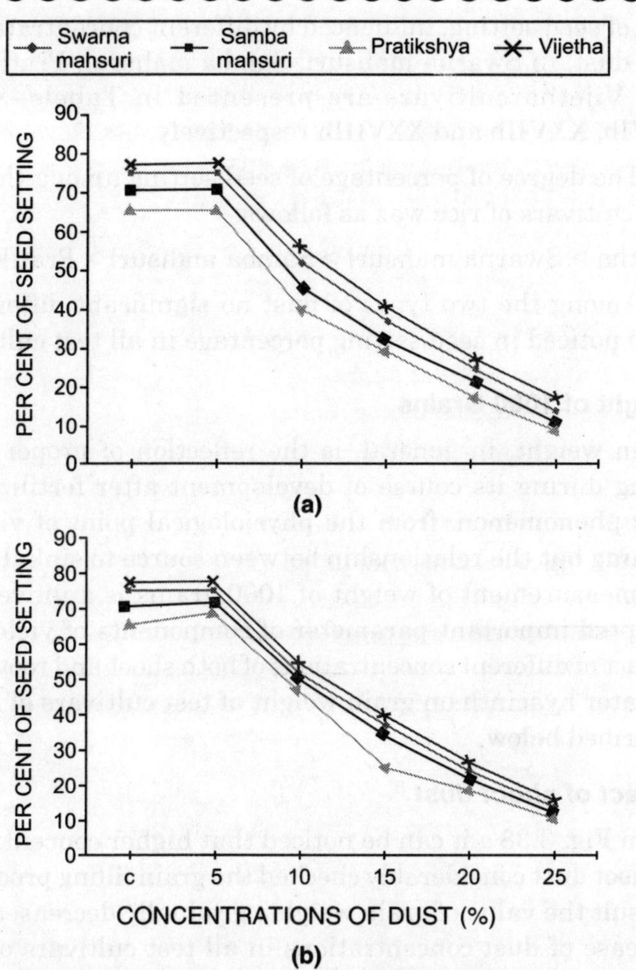

Fig. 3.37: Impact of different concentrations of shoot (a) and root (b) dust of water hyacinth *(E. crassipes)* on % of seed setting of 4 test rice cultivars

Impact of root dust

From Fig. 3.37b, it can be noticed that higher the concentrations of root dust in culture pots lower was the seed setting percentage in all the test cultivars of rice. Shoot dust consternation of 5% exhibited almost similar values on seed setting as was noticed in plants of control set. The data on per cent of seed setting, influenced by different concentrations of root dust, in Swarna mahsuri, Samba mahsrui, Pratikshya and Vijetha cultivars are presented in Tabels–XXVb, XXVIb, XXVIIb and XXVIIIb respectively.

The degree of percentage of seed setting among the four test cultivars of rice was as follows:-

Vijetha > Swarna mahsuri > Samba mahsuri > Pratikshya.

Among the two types of dust no significant differences were noticed in seed setting percentage in all test cultivars.

Weight of 1000 Grains

Grain weight, in general, is the reflection of proper grain filling during its course of development after fertilization. This phenomenon, from the physiological point of view, is nothing but the relationship between source to sink. Hence, the measurement of weight of 1000 grains is a universally accepted important parameter of components of yield. The impact of different concentrations of both shoot and root dusts of water hyacinth on grain weight of test cultivars of rice is described below.

Impact of shoot dust

From Fig. 3.38 a it can be noticed that higher concentration of shoot dust considerably checked the grain filling process as a result the value of grain weights gradually decreased with increase of dust concentrations in all test cultivars of rice. Dust concentration of 5% exhibited no significant differences from respective control values.

Maximum weights of 1000 grains of 18.522, 17.916, 17.166 and 18.951 grams and minimum weights of 3.882, 3.053, 2.511 and 4.912 grains were recorded from plants of Swarna mahsuri (Table–XXV a), Samba mahsuri (Table–XXVI a), Pratikshya (Table–XXVII a) and Vijetha (Table–XXVIII a) influenced by 5% and 25% of dust concentrations respectively.

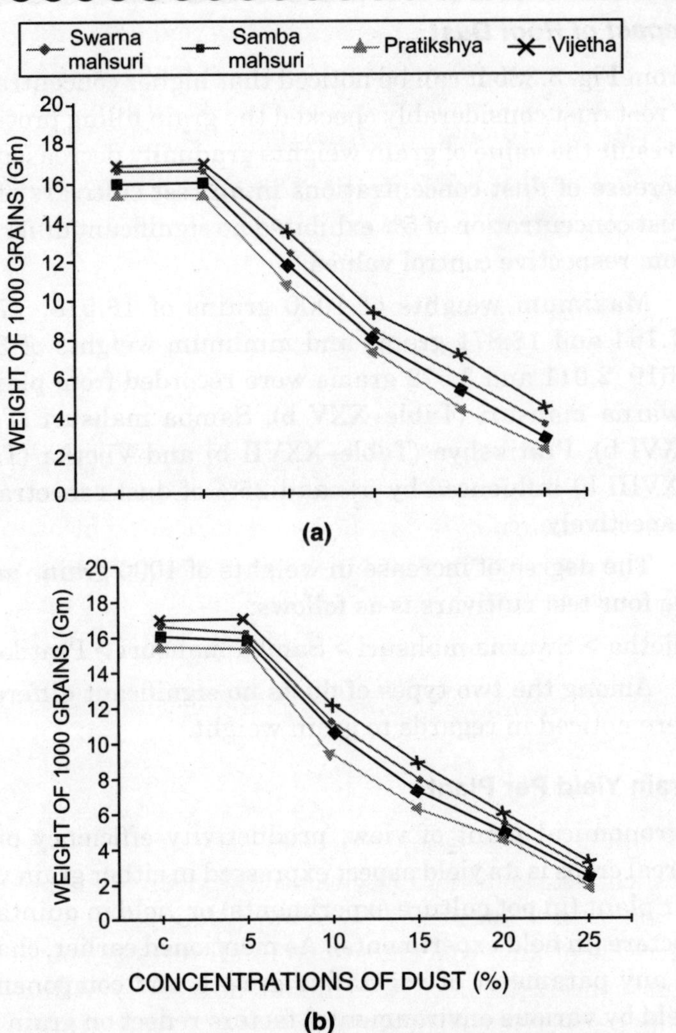

Fig. 3.38: Impact of different concentrations of shoot (a) and root (b) dust of water hyacinth *(E. crassipes)* on weight of 1000 grains of 4 test rice cultivars

Among the four test cultivars, the degree of increase in weights of 1000 grains is as follows:

Vijetha > Swarna mahsuri > Samba mahsuri > Pratikshya.

Impact of Root Dust

From Fig. 3.38b it can be noticed that higher concentrations of root dust considerably checked the grain filling process as a result the value of grain weights gradually decreased with increase of dust concentrations in all test cultivars of rice. Dust concentration of 5% exhibited no significant differences from respective control values.

Maximum weights of 1000 grains of 18.518, 17.830, 17.164 and 18.871 grams and minimum weights of 3.009, 2.519, 2.011 and 3.572 grams were recorded from plants of Swarna mahsuri (Table–XXV b), Samba mahsuri (Table–XXVI b), Pratikshya (Table–XXVII b) and Vijetha (Table–XXVIII b) influenced by 5% and 25% of dust concetrations respectively.

The degree of increase in weights of 1000 grains among the four test cultivars is as follows:

Vijetha > Swarna mahsuri > Samba mahsuri > Pratikshya.

Among the two types of dusts no significant differences were noticed in regards to grain weight.

Grain Yield Per Plant

Agronomical point of view, productivity efficiency of any cereal crops is its yield aspect expressed in either grain yields per plant (in pot culture experiments) or yield in quintal per hectare (in field experiments). As mentioned earlier, changes in any parameter of vegetative growth and components of yield by various environmental factors reflect on grain yield of the concerned crop. The effects of different concentrations of both shoot and root dust of water hyacinth on grain yield per plant of four test cultivars of rice are described below.

Impact of Shoot Dust

(*a*) Swarna mahsuri: From Table–XXV a it can be noticed that all concentrations of dust except 5% significantly reduced the grain yield per plant as a result almost all negligible yield (0.019 ± 0.02 g) per plants was recorded in plants influenced by 25% dust whereas highest yield per plant (13.805 ± 0.09 gm) was recorded in plants affected by 5% dust. The plants of control set yielded 12.531 ± 0.05 gm of seeds per plant. Data of intermediate values were recorded for other plants influenced by 10, 15 and 20% dust. The grain yield per plant exhibited negative corelations with increase of dust consternations (except 5%) in culture pots (Fig. 3.39a).

***(b)* Samba mahsuri:** In this test cultivar, the grain yield per plant exhibited more or less same values (Table–XXVI a) and similar trends (Fig. 3.39a) as was notice in case of Swarna mahsuri.

***(c)* Pratikshya:** In this cultivar, maximum yield per plant (9.633 ± 0.05 g) was noticed in plants affected by 5% dust whereas it was negligible (0.007 ± 0.002 g) in plants affected by 25% dust. Data of intermediate values were recorded in other plants influenced by different concentrations of shoot dust (Table–XXVII a). The corelations between grain yield per plant and different concentrations of shoot dust were found to be almost similar as was noticed in case of other 2 test cultivars (Fig. 3.39 a).

***(d)* Vijetha:** The influence of different concentrations of shoot dust on grain yield per plant is presented in Table–XXVII a. Maximum grain yield per plant (15.453 ± 0.06 g) was recorded in plants influenced by 5% dust whereas the values were 15.27 ± 0.02 and 0.045 ±0.005 g in plants of control set and plants affected by 25% concentration of dust respectively. Data of intermediate values were noticed in plants of other sets.

This cultivar also exhibited similar corelation between grain yield per plant and increase of dust concentrations in culture pots as was noticed in case of other 3 test cultivars (Fig. 3.39a).

Among the four test cultivars of rice, the degree of yield performance per plant in response to shoot dust effects as was follows:

Vijetha > Swarna mahsuri > Smaba mahsuri > Pratikshya.

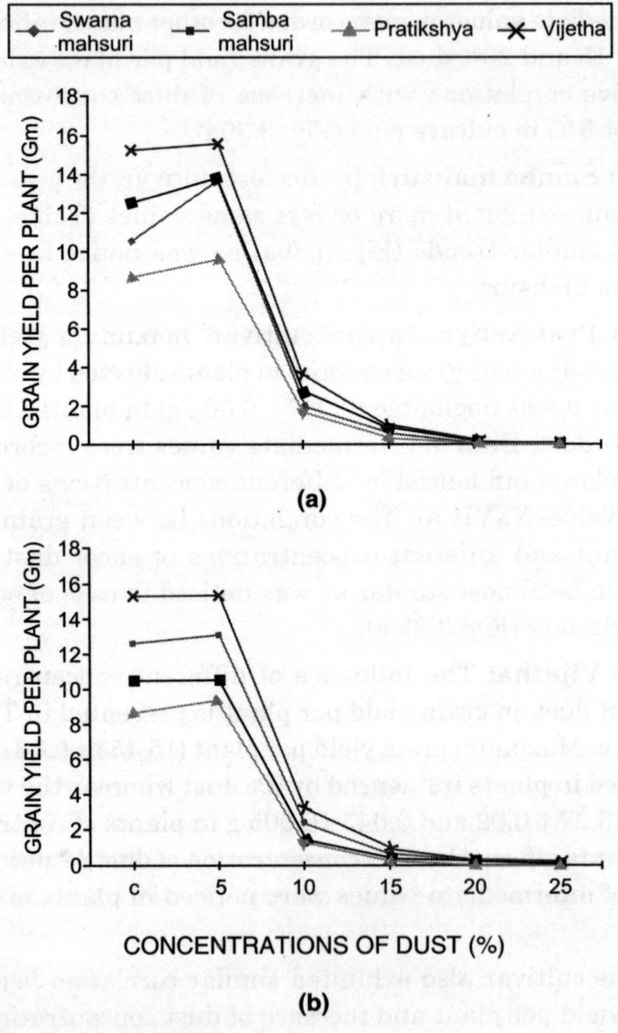

Fig. 3.39: Impact of different concentrations of shoot (a) and root (b) dust of water hyacinth *(E. crassipes) on grain yield per plant of 4 test rice cultivars*

Impact of Root Dust

(*a*) Swarna mahsuri: From Table–XXV b it can be noticed that all concentrations of dust except 5% significantly reduced the grain yield per plant as a result almost negligible yield (0.011 ± 0.05 g) per plants was recorded in plants influenced by 25% dust whereas highest yield per plant (13.058 ± 0.08 gm) was recorded in plants affected by 5% dust. The plants of control set yielded 12.531 ± 0.05 g grains per plant. Data of intermediate values were recorded for other plants influenced by 10, 15 and 20% dusts. The grain yield per plant exhibited negative corelation with increase of dust consternations (except 5%) in culture pots (Fig. 3.39b).

(*b*) Samba mahsuri: In this test cultivar the grain yield per plant exhibited more or less same values (Table–XXVI b) and similar trends (Fig. 3.39b) as was notice in case of Swarna mahsuri.

(*c*) Pratikshya: In this cultivar, maximum yield per plant (9.336 ± 0.09 g) was recorded in plants affected by 5% dust whereas it was almost nil (0.004 ± 0.001 g) in plants affected by 25% dust. Data of intermediate values were recorded in other plants influenced by different concentrations of root dust (Table XXVIIb). The corelations between grain yield per plant and different concentrations of root dust in culture pots were found to be almost similar as was noticed in case of other 2 test cultivars (Fig. 3.39b).

(*d*) Vijetha: The influence of different concentrations of root dust on grain yield per plant is presented in Table–XXVII b. Maximum grain yield per plant (15.397 ± 0.05 g) was recorded in plants influenced by 5% dust whereas the values were 15.27 ± 0.02 and 0.023 ± 0.001 g in plants of control set and plants affected by 25% concentration of dust respectively. Data of intermediate values were noticed in plants of other sets.

This cultivar also exhibited similar corelation between grain yield per plant and increase of dust concentrations in culture pots as was noticed in case of other 3 test cultivars (Fig. 3.39b).

Among the four test cultivars of rice, the degree of yield performance per plant in response to root dust effects as was follows:

Vijetha > Swarna mahsuri > Smaba mahsuri > Pratikshya.

Among the two types of dusts shoot dusts exhibited slightly higher values than the root dusts.

❑❑❑

4 Discussion

It is well-known that every plant produces secondary metabolites or products those include phenolic acids, terpenoids, alkaloids, flavonoids. To maintain the internal level of such secondary metabolites in permissible level, the plant distribute them within the plants and release the same in due course through leachation, volatilization, abscission or exudation (Singh and Bawa, 1982). Leaching and flow from aerial parts occur during rain, dew, fog, mist etc. These substances sometimes affect adversely on many crop plants. Chetty (1988) reported that *Eichharnia crassipes* plants could grow very fast by releasing high amount of vanillic acid, p-hydorxy- benzoic, ferulic and trans-p-coumaric acids and by conserving dihydorxy- phenolic compounds such as protocatechuic, chlorogenic, gentisic, caffeic acids and gibberellin like substances. Sircar and Kundu (1959, 1960) and Sircar and Chakravotry (1961) reported the growth regulation of chemicals present in water hyacinth roots. Sircar (1967) reported that indole acetic acid (IAA), indole acetonitril (IAN), tryptophan, arabinose, auxin-sugar complex and indole positive compounds are present in roots of *E. crassipes*. Further Sircar *et al.* (1993) reported the presence of GA_3 like substances in water hyacinth shoot. The impact of different concentrations of shoot and root dusts of *E. crassipes* on seeds germination, seedling growth, vegetative growth, yield and components of yield of four test cultivars of rice is discussed below.

SEED GERMINATION

The seed is a miniature plant in a latent state encompassing all the characteristics of the types or cultivars to which it belongs. It is the terminal point in the life cycle of the mother plant as well as the starting point in the life cycle of the plant that follows it. The transition of the seed from resting phase to one of activity is known as germination (Gelmond, 1981). Evenari (1961) defined germination as "the sun total of all the physiological processes occurring inside the seed, which start with inhibition of water and ends with protrusion of the embryonic root in dicots and coleorhiza in monocots". Ching (1972) defined germination as a stage in the "developmental process from fertilized egg cell to mature plant which is genetically programmed and environmentally modulated". Each developmental phase exhibits a characteristics pattern of metabolism controlled by enzyme activities that differ in kind, rate and location. The rate of enzyme activities are controlled by the quantity of the active enzyme, substrate(s), cofactor(s), coenzyme(s), presence of inhibitor(s) or stimulator(s). physical and chemical micro-environment including temperature, light, pH, hydration, ionic strength etc.

Generally, during seed germination the following type of metabolic processes are being carried out in seeds:

(*a*) Imbibition of water that leads to hydration of organelles.

(*b*) Sub-cellular organization of the embryo and/or endosperm.

(*c*) Alternation in the activity of phytochrome (if operated).

(*d*) Activity of enzyme.

(*e*) *de-novo* synthesis of the enzymes.

(*f*) Hydrolysis of stored metabolites in seed such as fats, starch, protein etc.

(*g*) Formation of organic molecules and their translocation to the new centers of growth.

(*h*) Synthesis of nucleic acids and proteins which regulate the synthesis of other cell-building materials.

(*i*) Oxygen uptake and respiration.

(*j*) Synthesis of membranes and other cellular constituents.

(*k*) Synthesis and their utilization of phytohormones.

(*l*) Enlargement of the membrane of the cell and repetition of cell divisions.

(*m*) Variation in CO_2 and O_2 levels.

(*n*) The schematic representation of mobilization of different metabolites during germination process in seeds is shown below.

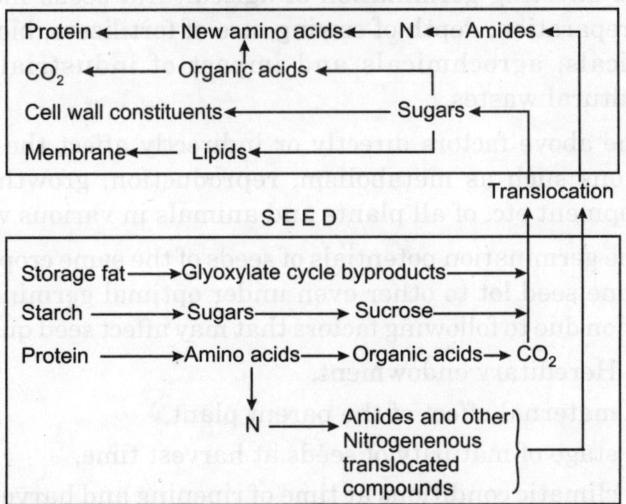

Schematic representation of mobilization of different metabolites in germinating seeds (adapted from Mali, 1981)

Factors Controlling Germination

In nature every organism has its own environment. The term 'environment' ethnologically means the surroundings. So, environment is a complex of so many parameters such as light, temperature, soil, water etc. Any external forces, substances or conditions, which surround and affect the life style of an organism, in any way, become a factor of its environment. These are called as environmental or ecological factors. The ecological factors of the environment are mainly of two types such as (1) biotic factor (living factors) and (2) abiotic factors (non-living factors).

Biotic factors include all kinds of interactions between different forms of life, while abiotic factors are the external factors that affect germination of all sorts of seeds, which include a climatic factor viz. (a) light, temperature, humidity, rain fall etc., (b) tropographic factors viz. physical geography of the earth and (c) adaphic factors viz. physical and chemical properties of the soil. Besides the above, other external factors affecting germination of agricultural seeds include soil preparation, depth of sowing, use of fertilizers, biocidal chemicals, agrochmicals and impact of industrial and agricultural wastes.

The above factors directly or indirectly affect the vital functions such as metabolism, reproduction, growth and development etc. of all plants and animals in various ways.

The germination potentials of seeds of the same crop vary from one seed lot to other even under optimal germination condition due to following factors that may affect seed quality:

(*a*) Hereditary endowment,

(*b*) maternal effect of the parent plant,

(*c*) stage of maturity of seeds at harvest time,

(*d*) climatic conditions at time of ripening and harvesting of the seed,

(*e*) seed size,

(*f*) seed processing,

(*g*) age of seeds,

(*h*) factors affecting viability,

(*i*) seed-borne diseases and

(*j*) seed dormancy.

From the present investigation, it was marked that all concentrations of both shoot and root dusts considerably checked the process of germination which might have caused by various phenolic and phototoxic chemicals present in the dust directly or indirectly by arresting α-amylase activities. The synthesis of gibberellins, a types of phytohormone responsible for germination and protrusion of embryonic axis by the process of elongation, might have affected by the phytotoxic chemicals present in the dust. Del Moral and Muller (1970) and Muller and Choe (1971) reported that during the process of Eucalyptus-litter decomposition, the allelochemicals (phenolic compounds, terpenses, alkaloids, nitrates etc.) form complexes with organic soil constituents which alter the physico-chemical nature of the soil by increasing their effective toxicity. Choe (1972) reported that different endogenous hormones are lost or leached out to the surrounding by exogenous application of growth regulative chemicals present around the germinating seeds. Since the secondary metabolites present in the dust are phyototoxic in nature, they might have inhibited the germination process resulting decreased trend in germination in all the test cultivars of rice. Such type of inhibitory effects on seed germination by different concentrations of *Eichhornia crassipes* shoot and root leachates on rice (*Oryza sativa* L cv 1014), ragi (*Elusine coracana* Gaertn. cv AKP-21), greengram (*Phaseolus aureus* Roxb. cv K-8511), blackgram (*Phaseolus radiatus* L. cv T-2), mustard (*Brassica juncea* (L) Czer. cv M-27) and til (*Sessamum orientale* L. cv Sl-14) was reported by Mohanty (1995). Concentration of 5% dust of both shoot and root slightly stimulated the percentage of seed germination which might be due to presence of lower concentrations of GA-like substances. Further, the germination vigour of any seed is controlled by both internal genetic and external environmental factors (Muralikrishna and Saxena, 1981). The requisite amount of growth regulatoring compounds present in *E. crassipes* might have enhanced the rate of germination as a result of which higher rate of germinations was noticed in seed influenced by 5% concentration. The variation in rate of germination in different test cultivars of rice might be due to the varietal response to test dusts. Saxena and Singh (1987) and Saxena (1988) have reported that osmotic potential helps in making all the essential preparation of germination. The delay or inhibition in the process of germination or inducement of seed dormancy is generally caused by different phenolic compounds present in leachates. Those substances directly check or arrest the amylase and protease activities in the aleurone layer and directly or indirectly inhibit the synthesis of gibberellins which usually induce and activate the synthesis of hydrolysing enzymes responsible for better germination. Sing and Saxena (1991) also have reported that seed germination is controlled by osmotic potential which further regulates the activation of hydrolytic enzymes. The present findings corroborate with reports of Gopal and Goel (1993) who reported that aqueous extracts of various parts of many plants were found to enhance the germination of *Cyperus rotundus* L, *Lycopersicon esculentum* Mill., *Corchorus capsularirs* L. and *Ciser arietinum* L.

So, as a whole, higher amount of allelochmics present in both types of dust of water hyacinth might have checked the germination process by inhibiting partially or fully various metabolic activities through several essential enzyme activities.

SEEDLING GROWTH

Establishment of seedlings followed after germinations is the second important developing stage of any higher plant. Newly developing areas, generally, occur during this process where all necessary constituents of cell, cell wall and cell inclusions are synthesised which ultimately reflect on seedling vigour. These complicated processes are again controlled by various internal characteristics features and/or external environmental factors. Generally seedling growth is measured in term of growth and development of shoot, root and whole seedling. The impact of allelochemicals, released by various plants into the soil or to the atmosphere, on the seedling establishment of any plant cannot be ignored (Kohli and Gaba, 1989). In the present investigation, it was observed that all the concentrations of both shoot and root dusts (except 5%) more or less arrested or inhibited per cent of seed germination which alternatively regulated the seedling growth in all test cultivars. Generally the growth and development of seedlings are controlled by cell differentiation and morphogenesis, which are influenced by endogenous plant growth regulators and translocation of carbohydrates and other metabolites from the site of synthesis/storage to the site of action. Yomo (1960) and Paleg (1960a, 1961) reported that gibberellins and endogenous growth regulator, which synthesis in the embryo region move to the aleurone layer of the seed and this layer is responded by amylase and RNase activities.

In the present investigation, the different phytotoxic chemicals present in dusts of both shoot and root except 5% might have adversely affected the process of gibberellins synthesis, interfered in α-amylase and protease activities and synthesis of various metabolites essential for seedling growth resulting decrease in the seedling vigour such as fresh and dry weights of shoot, root and whole seedlings of test cultivars of rice. Padhy *et al.* (2006a) reported that aqueous leaf/phyllode and bark leachates of *Eucalyptus globules*, *Acacia nilotica* and *Acacia auriculaeformis* were found to be mito-repressive and brought about cytological abnormalities due to the influenced of various allelochemcis present in leachates. The findings of present investigation suggest that higher the concentrations of shoot and root dust (> 5 %) might have containing higher amount of phytotoxic chemicals which checked all the seedling growth parameters. Reports of Singh and Nandal (1983) on wheat, mustard and chick pea seedlings, Kohli *et al.* (1988) on green gram and cow pea, Lisanwork and Michelson (1993) on chick pea, maize and pea, Jayakumar *et al.* (1990) on groundnut, Padhy *et al.* (1992) on ragi and Gantayat (2001) on some gram seeds treated with leaf-litter leachates of *Eucalyptus globulus* corroborate the findings of present study. Narwal (1994 c) suggested that the present knowledge or informations on the role of allelopathic effect on crop growth and production is not sufficient to draw any concrete conclusion. Hence, much more technological researches are needed for better knowledge on the biochemical aspects and physiological process of growth of any crop. Further, the relation of cell multiplication to synthesis of growth regulator influence(s) of the later on cell differentiation and cell morphogenesis, translocation of metabolites from source to sink are needed for batter knowledge on physiological and biochemical changes that occur during seedlings growth. Mukharji and Chakraverty (1977) reported that amylase activities in rice endosperm was significantly depressed in seeds germinated and grown in sodium salt of N-formyl-hydroxy-amino acetic acid (Hadacidin). Chakraverty (1983) reported that Hadacidin acted both by depressing the biosynthesis of cytokines and gibberellins in *Phaseolus mungo* which in turn disrupted normal elongation mechanism. From the above point of view, it is quite logical to interpret that the phytotoxic compounds released into the soil from different concentrations of dust and absorbed by concerned plants might have induced the inhibition in seedling height or might be probably due to decrease of cell division as well as inhibition in cell elongation in test rice cultivar seedlings.

VEGETATIVE GROWTH

It is a well established fact that the plant growth and development are controlled by different factors. Growth analysis is one of the prime importance in the study of photosynthetic efficiency in relation to plant productivity. An increase in agriculture productivity requires enhancement of total photosynthesis per unit land area. Thus, the photosynthetic area depends upon mineral nutrition, plant protection majors and water management (Palit *et al.*, 1976). Vegetative growth of any crops directly or indirectly useful for selection of desirable agronomic characters which are highly corelated with yield. Sinha and Swain (1978) and Patanaik (1998) reported positive correlations between production of number of tillers with crop maturity and plant height in finger millet. Vergara *et al.* (1966) suggested that study on production of leaves per plant and height of the plant, particularly in monocarpic plants, is a prime important as those parameters have direct relationship with yield efficiency of the concerned plants. The effect of different concentrations of both shoot and root dust of water hyacinth on various parameters of vegetative growth are discussed below.

In most of the monocarpic plants, tillering takes place at the earlier part of the plant life and because each has the capacity to become a virtually independent replica of the main shoot. Tillering represents a powerful mechanism for adjustment of plants to the environment. It is quite common that most of the visible tillers die without producing panicles and there may be many buds which never reach the visible stage (Davidson, 1964). The development of number of tillers also depends on variety of the crops, environmental factors such as changes in temperature, humidity, photoperiod and application of different agro-chemicals (Langer, 1963; Barley and Naidu, 1964; Bremner. 1969 a and Carnel, 1969 a) and longer vegetative growth periods in rice (Khan *et al.,* 1987), barley (Aspinall, 1961) and wheat (Bremner, 1969b). The reduction in production of tiller per plant in all test cultivars of rice by the influence of different kinds of dust might be due to release and subsequent accumulation of stimulatory or inhibitory water-soluble phytochemical substance from dusts that affected the physico-chemical properties of soil. Similar allelopathic observation are reported by various workers for different crops (Partick and Koch, 1958; Muller, 1970; Lodhi, 1978; Hussain *et al.,* 1984; Ayaz *et al.,* 1989 and Shivanna *et al.,* 1992).

The production of green leaves on main shoot as well as on whole plant is a type of architecture of the plant which directly or indirectly has bearing on the yield. The production of yield depends on increase of leaf surface area (source) that has direct relationship with sink (site of action). Any alteration in production of leaves and plant height by different internal and external factors cause imbalance between source and sink relationship. The application of various concentrations of both shoot and root dust (except 5%) directly or indirectly caused imbalance in the metabolic status. The reduction on development of number of leaves on main shoot as well as on whole plant might have influenced due to translocation of phototoxic-active ingredients present in dusts from leaves to shoot apex and the apical buds might have been affected by such allelochemics which alternatively have interfered in different metabolic processes during ontogenesis.

Plant height, generally, increased in rice plants due to longitudinal growth of leaf sheath and blade by cell elongation which is regulated by endogenous plants growth substances such as gibberellins and auxins. Cleland (1964) suggested that gibberellins play an important role on the growth of grass leaves. Phillips and Jones (1964) suggested that higher level of gibberellins occur in apices of stem and root, young leaves and embryo as well as endosperm of developing seeds. The movement of gibberellins is generally carried out from site of synthesis to the site of action along with the metabolites where they accumulate and act accordingly to the need of the plant. Any alteration in process of trans accumulation and action results or reflects on growth and development of concerned plant. In the present investigation higher concentrations (> 5%) of both shoot and root dusts might have prevented the synthesis, translocation, accumulation and / or action of gibberellins there by the heights of the test rice plants were significantly decreased. Similar findings were reported by other workers in variety of plants affected by allelopathic affect of different weeds and crops (Tripathy, 2000; Patanik, 1998; Sabata, 2008 and Gantayat, 2001).

The enhancement in different vegetative growth para-meters studied in test cultivars of rice compare to their respective control plants by the influence of 5% concentrations of both the types of dust indicates that presence of requisite amount of growth promoting substance leached by 5% dust might have accelerated the growth and development parameters. It has already been mentioned that some growth regulating allelochemicals might be present at lower concentration due to translocation of the same from root to shoot of *E. crassipes*. Therefore, the shoot might have contained higher level of allelochemicals as results of which shoot dusts stimulated the shoot growth than the root growth during seedling stage. Further the GA-Like substance present in shoot dust might have accelerated the plant growth by means of quick and higher rate of cell elongation. Better plant growth was found due to influence of shoot dust in comparison to root dust which might be due to the lethal dose of some allelochemics present at higher concentrations. Since no detailed work in this respect has done yet, it needs further in detailed studies to draw any concrete conclusions.

YIELD AND YIELD COMPONENTS

Productivity of any cereal crops depends on their vegetative growth and components of yield parameters such as production of number fertile tillers per plant, length of the panicle, per cent of seed setting and grain weight. These parameters depend not only on genetic makeup of the plants and environmental factors but also to some extent cultural practices. It has been reported that grain yield in wheat (Pearman *et al.* 1978; Abbas *et al.,* 1983 and Jain and Khanna, 1978); rice (Vergara *et el.,* 1964; Yoshida, 1972; Murty and Sahu, 1977; Palit *et al.* 1978; Sahu and Murty, 1978; Padhy, 1980; Das, 1999 and Tripathy, 2000); oat (Mathur *et al.,* 1980); barely (Quaseem *et al.*, 1978); finger-millet (Das and Sinha, 1986; Acharya, 1984 and Pataniak, 1998) and other cereals is determined by the growth characters like production of leaves per plant, plant height, number of fertile tillers per plants etc. which in turn are influenced by changes in internal genetic characters of the plant and external environmental factors. When any change occurs in vegetative growth characters due to cultural and / or environmental factors that reflects on the productivity of the concerned crops.

The plants of test cultivars of rice influenced by different concentrations (except 5%) of both types of dusts exhibited lesser number of fertile tillers per plant, length of the panicle, lesser seed setting and grain weights compared with their respective control plants. These inhibitory effects might be due to presence of phototoxic allelohemics of water hyacinth plant after releasing from dusts into the soil resulting lower yield rate per plant. Further phytochmicals released from higher concentrations of both shoot and root dusts might have acted as anti-auxin inhibitor reusing poor vegetative growth. Lower concentrations of dust (5%) might have favoured for translocation of growth regulating substances responsible for flaral induction at the shoot apex resulting production of more number of fertile tillers per plant. Further higher the quantity of anti-auxin or inhibitors released from dusts lower was the vegetative growth and yield. The death of unproductive tillers is another cause of lowering the formation of number of fertile tiller per plant. The tiller death is also a response to internal and external competitive stresses and any one or all of the components of the environment may be involved on production of less number of fertile tillers per plant in cereats. (Asana *et al*, 1966 and Rawson, 1967) Further, Bremner (1969b), Chaturvedy and Zabka (1969) and Shinoty and Waver (1970) reported that chemicals of anti-auxin nature retard tillering or branching, fructification or grain setting, translational and accumulation of metabolites from source to sink. Since, allelochemics include number of phenolic acids, terpenoids, organic cyanides, organic acids and other phytotoxic substances which might have interfered in the oxido-reduction reaction, nucleotides and giberellin biosyntheses and / or preventing synthesis, translocation and accumulation of metabolites resulting in poor production of dry matter and grains (Basu *et al*, 1987).

Production of number of spikerlet initials on panicle depends on the vegetative growth, translocation and accumulation of growth substance essential for spikelet initiation on panicles (Evanas, 1960; Williams, 1966 and Rawson, 1970). The determination of development of spikelet number on panicle is generally under genetic control but Cooper (1956) and Fisher (1973) reported that development of spikelet initials on panicle is controlled by cumultative low temperature and day length depending upon the nature of the cultivar and place of cultivation. In the present investigation, reduction in development of spikelets per panicle might be due to the phytochemicals released from the dust into the soil and absorption of same by plants might have checked or arrested on spikelet initiation and development on panicles.

Grain setting is another important event in the series of reproduction parameters which determines production of number of mature grain per unit leaf area. The grain numbers per panicle largely depend on the photosynthetic efficiency of the crop during grain filing which may be transformed into overall growth and economics of the yield (Dabadghao *et al.*, 1973; Gerakis, *et al.*, 1975; De Puit and Caldwell, 1975 and Rawson and Bremnber, 1981). Reports are available on source and sink relationship in rice (Yoshida *et al.* 1972; Horiuchi, 1977 and Rao and Murty, 1993).

The decrease in yield and components of yield affected by both types of dusts of *E. crassipes* in the present investigation probably due to denature of photosynthetic pigments and other macromolecules. The activity of enzymes like catalase peroxidase, DNase, RNase and ATPase were considerably altered in the ragi leaves affected by aqueous leachates of *Eucalyptus globulus* resulting imbalance in metabolic status which influenced yield efficiency of that crop (Patanaik, 1998). Similarly Das (1999) and Tripathy (2000) reported role of such enzymes in the rice leaves on grain yield per plant influenced by different industrial effluents and aqueous lactates of *Acacia auriculaleformis* and *Acacia nilotica* respectively. Hence, it may be concluded that the phytochemcials released by both types of dusts of water hyacinth directly or indirectly altered the physico-chemical properties of the soil which directly or indirectly controlled the vegetative growth which ultimately reflected on the yield efficiency in four test cultivars of rice.

The enhancement of grain yield per plant influenced by 5% dust might be due to positive influence on vegetative growth and components of yield parameters which directly reflected on yield.

Among the four test cultivars of the rice, Pratikshya was found to be more susceptible followed by Samba mahsuri, Swarna mahsuri and Vijetha to different concentrations of both shoot and root dusts of water hyacinth.

Hence, in a nut-shell, it is concluded that water hyacinth plants can be utilized at lower amount in rice filed for better growth and yield of rice crops. Precautions to be taken for irradication of dense growth of water hyacinth found in rice field during and after the crop growth. So, water hyacinth can be used a good or bad material for rice crop depending upon their control by cultivators. Further awareness be created among farmers by involving the Non-Government Organisations (NGOs) regarding the usefulness and harmfulness of the water hyacinth.

❑❑❑

5

Summary

Both laboratory and field experiments were performed to find out the allelopathic effects of different concentrations of both shoot and root dust of water hyacinth *(Eichhornia crassipes)* on seed germination, seedling growth, vegetative growth, yield performance and components of yield of four rice (*Oryza sativa* L.) cultivars viz. Swarna mahsuri (MTU-7029), Samba mahsuri (BPT-5204), Pratikshya (ORS-2015) and Vijetha (MTU-1001) widely cultivated by farmers of India in general and Odisha in particular for their better yield performance and nutritive value. The followings are the salient observations of the present study.

1. Seed germinations were greatly affected by all concentrations of both shoot and root dusts (except 5%) in all test cultivars of rice.
2. Among two types of dust, root dusts were found to be more adversely affective on the process of germination in all cultivars.
3. Among the four test cultivars, the degree of response to both type of dusts was as follows :-
   Vijetha > Swarna mahsasuri > Samba mahsauri > Pratikshya.
4. The seedling growth and their fresh and dry weights exhibited positive corelations with enhancement of plant age and negative coreralation with increase of dust concentration (except 5%) in all test cultivars of rice.

5. Vegetative growth parameters such as development of number of tillers per plant, number of green leaves on main shoot as well as whole plant and height of the plants recorded from plants, raised in pot culture method, were considerably reduced by the influence of all concentrations (except 5%) of both shoot and root dusts of water hyacinth.
6. The yield parameters such as development of number of panicles per plants, length of panicles, number of spikelets per panicle, total number of spikelets per panicle, seed setting percentage, weight of 1000 grains and yield per plant were considerably reduced by the influence of all concentrations (except 5%) of both types of dusts.
7. Among the four test cultivars of rice, the degree of yield performance per plant in response to both types of dusts was as follows :

   Vijehta >Swarna mahsuri > Samba mahsuri>Pratikshya.
8. The enhancement of grain weight and yield per plant influenced by dust concentration of 5% was due to positive influence on parameters of vegetative growth and components of yield which directly reflected on yield.
9. Among the both type of dusts, shoot dust exhibited higher values in all parameters studied than root dusts.
10. The impact of allelochemicals released from water hyacinth plants on crop plants needs indepth research at molecular and sub-molecular levels to draw any concrete conclusions.

Hence, in a nut-shell, it is concluded that water hyacinth plants can be utilized at lower amount in rice fields for better growth and yield of rice crops. Precautions to be taken for eradication of dense growth of water hyacinth found in rice fields during and after the crop growth. This weed can be utilized as good material for rice crop with adopting proper precaution measures. Further awareness be created among farmers by involving the Non-Government Organisation (NGOs) regarding the beneficial and harmful effects of this aquatic weed (water hyacinth).

❑❑❑

Tables

Table-I: *Effect of different concentrations of shoot (a) and root (b) dust of water hyacinth (E. crassipes) on seed germination of Swarna mahsuri cultivar of rice*

(Each value is mean of 5 replicates ± SE)

Dust conc. (%)	% of germination at different days after sowing (DAS)			
	3	4	5	6
(a) Shoot dust				
C	64.40 ± 0.34	86.20 ± 0.99	91.80 ± 0.97	100.00 ± 0.85
05	72.00 ± 0.81	95.20 ± 0.70	98.00 ± 0.55	99.00 ± 0.44
10	60.60 ± 0.77	65.40 ± 0.48	70.40 ± 0.51	76.00 ± 0.55
15	35.00 ± 0.91	39.00 ± 0.88	41.60 ± 0.71	50.20 ± 0.46
20	24.00 ± 0.71	26.20 ± 0.66	31.00 ± 0.82	35.00 ± 0.55
25	10.80 ± 0.46	14.00 ± 0.71	16.80 ± 0.55	20.00 ± 0.52
(b) Root dust				
C	64.40 ± 0.34	86.20 ± 0.99	91.80 ± 0.97	100.00 ± 0.85
05	66.20 ± 0.44	89.00 ± 0.88	94.60 ± 0.49	98.00 ± 0.82
10	52.00 ± 0.44	54.40 ± 0.61	61.00 ± 0.59	70.80 ± 0.73
15	34.00 ± 0.78	38.00 ± 0.39	40.80 ± 0.80	48.00 ± 0.70
20	23.20 ± 0.32	25.60 ± 0.84	30.60 ± 0.64	34.00 ± 0.77
25	9.00 ± 0.70	13.00 ± 0.55	15.00 ± 0.79	18.20 ± 0.91

Table-II: *Effect of different concentrations of shoot (a) and root (b) dust of water hyacinth (E. crassipes) on seed germination of Samba mahsuri cultivar of rice*

(Each value is mean of 5 replicates ± SE)

Dust conc. (%)	% of germination at different days after sowing (DAS)			
	3	4	5	6
(a) Shoot dust				
C	63.20 ±0.62	80.40 ±0.95	92.80 ±0.94	100.00 ±0.86
05	70.00 ±0.88	90.40 ±0.48	97.00 ±0.60	98.80 ±0.48
10	58.20 ±0.82	64.40 ±0.72	69.00 ±0.53	75.80 ±0.55
15	34.00 ±0.59	38.00 ±0.38	40.40 ±0.61	49.00 ±0.71
20	23.20 ±0.79	25.00 ±0.66	29.00 ±0.41	33.60 ±0.49
25	8.00 ±0.62	13.00 ±0.95	15.00 ±0.94	18.60 ±0.86
(b) Root dust				
C	63.20 ±0.82	80.40 ±0.95	92.80 ±0.94	100.00 ±0.86
05	65.60 ±0.39	87.00 ±0.88	93.00 ±0.90	95.40 ±0.79
10	45.00 ±0.41	55.80 ±0.82	60.40 ±0.72	69.00 ±0.88
15	33.20 ±0.77	36.00 ±0.62	39.00 ±0.55	47.80 ±0.60
20	22.00 ±0.58	24.60 ±0.76	28.40 ±0.77	32.00 ±0.44
25	7.00 ±0.67	11.00 ±0.82	13.00 ±0.75	16.00 ±0.79

Table-III: *Effect of different concentrations of shoot (a) and root (b) dust of water hyacinth (E. crassipes) on seed germination of Pratikshya cultivar of rice*

(Each value is mean of 5 replicates ± SE)

Dust conc. (%)	% of germination at different days after sowing (DAS)			
	3	4	5	6
(a) Shoot dust				
C	60.00 ±0.36	70.00 ±0.97	88.00 ±0.22	100.00 ±0.87
05	69.00 ±0.49	75.00 ±0.81	90.00 ±0.90	97.80 ±0.77
10	57.40 ±0.83	62.00 ±0.41	68.80 ±0.81	73.00 ±0.52
15	32.00 ±0.44	37.60 ±0.29	38.00 ±0.48	47.20 ±0.72
20	22.20 ±0.71	24.00 ±0.61	27.40 ±0.41	30.00 ±0.81
25	6.00 ±0.88	10.00 ±0.51	14.00 ±0.44	15.20 ±0.56
(b) Root dust				
C	60.00 ±0.36	70.00 ±0.97	88.00 ±0.22	100.00 ±0.87
05	64.00 ±0.44	74.00 ±0.88	85.00 ±0.48	96.00 ±0.77
10	42.40 ±0.45	52.60 ±0.44	59.00 ±0.71	67.00 ±0.77
15	30.00 ±0.44	35.00 ±0.78	37.20 ±0.66	45.80 ±0.91
20	20.60 ±0.47	22.60 ±0.72	25.00 ±0.88	28.20 ±0.89
25	5.00 ±0.90	8.00 ±0.29	12.00 ±0.82	14.00 ±0.84

Table-IV: *Effect of different concentrations of shoot (a) and root (b) dust of water hyacinth (E. crassipes) on seed germination of Vijetha cultivar of rice*

(Each value is mean of 5 replicates ± SE)

Dust conc. (%)	% of germination at different days after sowing (DAS)			
	3	4	5	6
(a) Shoot dust				
C	65.40 ±0.32	88.80 ±0.91	94.00 ±0.92	100.40 ±0.81
05	73.00 ±0.41	96.00 ±0.49	98.00 ±0.30	100.00 ±0.79
10	61.00 ±0.42	67.00 ±0.32	71.00 ±0.44	78.00 ±0.64
15	37.00 ±0.29	41.20 ±0.89	44.60 ±0.76	51.80 ±0.91
20	26.40 ±0.79	30.80 ±0.92	32.00 ±0.48	36.40 ±0.66
25	11.00 ±0.89	15.00 ±0.88	18.00 ±0.88	22.80 ±0.94
(b) Root dust				
C	65.40 ±0.32	88.80 ±0.91	94.00 ±0.92	100.40 ±0.81
05	68.00 ±0.36	91.00 ±0.81	95.00 ±0.97	99.00 ±0.72
10	60.80 ±0.41	65.00 ±0.62	70.60 ±0.91	75.00 ±0.51
15	36.00 ±0.81	40.40 ±0.55	42.40 ±0.88	50.20 ±0.44
20	25.20 ±0.88	28.80 ±0.41	31.60 ±0.86	35.00 ±0.32
25	10.00 ±0.91	14.00 ±0.77	16.00 ±0.51	20.40 ±0.88

Table-V: *Effect of different concentrations of shoot (a) and root (b) dust of water hyacinth (E. crassipes) on seedling growth of Swarna mahsuri cultivar of rice*

(Each value is mean of 10 samples ± SE)

Dust conc. (%)	Reading taken at different days after soaking (DAS)											
	6			8			10			12		
	SL	RL	TL	SL	RL	TL	SL	RL	TL	SL	RL	TL
(a) Shoot dust												
C	6.77 ±0.04	6.90 ±0.05	13.67 ±0.01	6.95 ±0.06	7.70 ±0.08	14.65 ±0.08	7.35 ±0.05	7.91 ±0.04	15.26 ±0.06	8.01 ±0.06	8.32 ±0.04	16.33 ±0.04
05	6.82 ±0.07	6.98 ±0.04	13.80 ±0.02	7.00 ±0.04	7.82 ±0.07	14.82 ±0.02	7.45 ±0.07	7.99 ±0.06	15.44 ±0.01	8.15 ±0.05	8.54 ±0.06	16.69 ±0.05
10	5.68 ±0.06	5.82 ±0.04	11.50 ±0.04	5.92 ±0.04	6.65 ±0.05	12.57 ±0.02	6.31 ±0.07	6.88 ±0.08	13.19 ±0.05	6.39 ±0.06	7.92 ±0.06	14.31 ±0.02
15	3.02 ±0.05	3.05 ±0.08	6.07 ±0.02	3.21 ±0.08	4.01 ±0.07	7.22 ±0.04	3.80 ±0.05	4.05 ±0.04	7.85 ±0.03	4.20 ±0.09	4.80 ±0.07	9.00 ±0.03
20	1.31 ±0.05	1.45 ±0.08	2.76 ±0.05	1.90 ±0.06	1.56 ±0.08	3.46 ±0.08	2.35 ±0.04	2.49 ±0.02	4.84 ±0.05	2.95 ±0.09	2.21 ±0.08	6.16 ±0.07
25	0.80 ±0.04	0.82 ±0.07	1.62 ±0.04	1.02 ±0.02	1.04 ±0.06	2.28 ±0.02	1.72 ±0.06	2.19 ±0.08	2.91 ±0.02	2.01 ±0.04	2.32 ±0.07	4.33 ±0.06
(b) Root dust												
C	6.77 ±0.07	6.90 ±0.05	13.67 ±0.03	6.95 ±0.06	7.70 ±0.08	14.65 ±0.04	7.35 ±0.05	7.91 ±0.04	15.26 ±0.02	8.01 ±0.06	8.32 ±0.04	16.33 ±0.04
05	6.85 ±0.07	6.95 ±0.04	13.80 ±0.05	6.99 ±0.06	7.80 ±0.02	14.79 ±0.08	7.39 ±0.08	7.96 ±0.09	15.35 ±0.02	8.06 ±0.04	8.35 ±0.03	16.41 ±0.08
10	5.65 ±0.05	5.77 ±0.08	11.42 ±0.03	5.85 ±0.07	6.05 ±0.04	11.90 ±0.05	6.25 ±0.08	6.32 ±0.02	12.57 ±0.04	6.31 ±0.06	7.42 ±0.04	13.73 ±0.04
15	3.01 ±0.08	3.25 ±0.02	6.26 ±0.06	3.25 ±0.09	4.01 ±0.04	7.26 ±0.01	3.80 ±0.09	4.21 ±0.07	8.01 ±0.03	4.17 ±0.02	4.62 ±0.09	8.79 ±0.06
20	1.25 ±0.05	1.75 ±0.08	3.00 ±0.02	1.65 ±0.06	2.49 ±0.08	4.14 ±0.07	2.25 ±0.04	2.89 ±0.02	5.14 ±0.06	2.90 ±0.09	3.02 ±0.08	5.92 ±0.06
25	0.72 ±0.06	1.01 ±0.04	1.73 ±0.04	1.00 ±0.01	1.02 ±0.07	2.02 ±0.04	1.62 ±0.04	2.00 ±0.08	3.62 ±0.5	2.00 ±0.03	2.22 ±0.02	4.22 ±0.02

SL = shoot length (cm.) RL = root length (cm.) TL = total length of seedling (cm.)

Table-VI: *Effect of different concentrations of shoot (a) and root (b) dust of water hyacinth (E. crassipes) on seedling growth of Samba mahsuri cultivar of rice*

(Each value is mean of 10 samples ± SE)

Dust conc. (%)	Reading taken at different days after soaking (DAS)											
	6			8			10			12		
	SL	RL	TL	SL	RL	TL	SL	RL	TL	SL	RL	TL
(a) Shoot dust												
C	6.67 ±0.06	6.88 ±0.06	13.55 ±0.05	6.85 ±0.07	7.60 ±0.09	14.45 ±0.08	7.05 ±0.08	7.90 ±0.07	14.95 ±0.07	8.00 ±0.04	8.22 ±0.09	16.22 ±0.05
05	6.69 ±0.07	6.92 ±0.06	13.61 ±0.06	6.95 ±0.02	7.46 ±0.04	14.41 ±0.06	7.04 ±0.06	7.69 ±0.05	14.73 ±0.04	8.09 ±0.07	8.26 ±0.04	16.35 ±0.03
10	5.06 ±0.06	5.46 ±0.08	10.52 ±0.06	5.52 ±0.03	6.14 ±0.04	11.66 ±0.05	6.01 ±0.07	6.41 ±0.06	12.42 ±0.05	6.37 ±0.05	7.01 ±0.04	13.38 ±0.06
15	2.59 ±0.08	3.02 ±0.07	5.61 ±0.07	3.12 ±0.04	3.52 ±0.06	6.64 ±0.05	3.62 ±0.03	4.00 ±0.08	7.62 ±0.04	4.05 ±0.05	4.70 ±0.07	8.75 ±0.05
20	1.22 ±0.04	1.25 ±0.08	2.47 ±0.06	1.51 ±0.06	1.40 ±0.09	2.91 ±0.06	2.01 ±0.07	2.44 ±0.04	4.45 ±0.03	2.61 ±0.07	2.64 ±0.04	5.25 ±0.06
25	0.74 ±0.09	0.62 ±0.07	1.36 ±0.07	1.00 ±0.06	1.00 ±0.04	2.00 ±0.05	1.41 ±0.06	2.06 ±0.07	3.47 ±0.06	1.62 ±0.06	2.26 ±0.07	3.88 ±0.07
(b) Root dust												
C	6.67 ±0.66	6.88 ±0.06	13.55 ±0.05	6.85 ±0.07	7.60 ±0.09	14.45 ±0.08	7.05 ±0.08	7.90 ±0.07	14.95 ±0.06	8.00 ±0.04	8.22 ±0.09	16.22 ±0.06
05	6.69 ±0.07	6.85 ±0.06	13.54 ±0.06	7.01 ±0.02	7.69 ±0.04	14.96 ±0.03	7.91 ±0.06	7.95 ±0.05	15.86 ±0.04	8.08 ±0.07	8.24 ±0.09	16.32 ±0.02
10	5.00 ±0.06	5.26 ±0.08	10.26 ±0.07	5.46 ±0.03	5.62 ±0.04	11.08 ±0.04	5.92 ±0.07	6.05 ±0.06	11.97 ±0.05	6.29 ±0.05	7.00 ±0.04	13.29 ±0.04
15	2.26 ±0.08	2.75 ±0.07	5.01 ±0.08	3.11 ±0.04	3.32 ±0.06	6.43 ±0.05	3.44 ±0.03	3.85 ±0.08	7.29 ±0.04	3.92 ±0.05	4.21 ±0.07	8.13 ±0.06
20	1.20 ±0.04	1.20 ±0.08	2.40 ±0.05	1.42 ±0.06	1.41 ±0.09	2.83 ±0.08	2.00 ±0.07	2.41 ±0.04	4.41 ±0.05	3.12 ±0.07	3.61 ±0.04	6.73 ±0.05
25	0.66 ±0.09	0.61 ±0.07	1.27 ±0.08	0.90 ±0.06	0.90 ±0.04	1.80 ±0.05	1.24 ±0.06	1.92 ±0.07	3.16 ±0.05	1.44 ±0.06	2.12 ±0.07	3.56 ±0.05

SL = shoot length (cm.) RL = root length (cm.) TL = total length of seedling (cm.)

Table-VII: *Effect of different concentrations of shoot (a) and root (b) dust of water hyacinth (E. crassipes) on seedling growth of Pratikshya cultivar of rice*

(Each value is mean of 10 samples ± SE)

Dust conc. (%)	Reading taken at different days after soaking (DAS)											
	6			8			10			12		
	SL	RL	TL	SL	RL	TL	SL	RL	TL	SL	RL	TL
(a) Shoot dust												
C	6.07	6.20	12.27	6.25	7.30	13.55	7.00	7.61	14.61	7.99	8.12	16.11
	±0.09	±0.06	±0.08	±0.09	±0.06	±0.06	±0.03	±0.07	±0.04	±0.08	±0.09	±0.08
05	6.10	6.30	12.40	6.30	7.34	13.64	7.02	7.62	14.64	8.01	8.24	16.25
	±0.05	±0.08	±0.06	±0.06	±0.04	±0.03	±0.03	±0.07	±0.04	±0.09	±0.06	±0.02
10	4.51	5.09	9.60	5.00	6.09	11.09	6.00	6.27	12.27	6.29	7.00	13.29
	±0.08	±0.05	±0.04	±0.07	±0.04	±0.05	±0.06	±0.08	±0.07	±0.09	±0.06	±0.04
15	2.09	3.00	5.09	2.79	3.22	6.01	3.02	3.92	6.94	4.02	4.38	8.40
	±0.04	±0.07	±0.05	±0.05	±0.07	±0.06	±0.06	±0.08	±0.05	±0.05	±0.08	±0.06
20	1.12	1.06	2.18	1.50	1.16	2.66	2.00	2.09	4.09	2.49	2.21	4.70
	±0.08	±0.09	±0.02	±0.06	±0.09	±0.08	±0.06	±0.05	±0.02	±0.06	±0.01	±0.02
25	0.66	0.42	1.08	0.89	0.79	1.68	1.31	2.01	3.32	1.40	2.18	3.58
	±0.06	±0.05	±0.01	±0.08	±0.04	±0.05	±0.07	±0.03	±0.04	±0.07	±0.03	±0.01
(b) Root dust												
C	6.07	6.20	12.27	6.25	7.30	13.55	7.00	7.61	14.61	7.99	8.12	16.11
	±0.09	±0.06	±0.08	±0.09	±0.06	±0.06	±0.03	±0.07	±0.04	±0.08	±0.09	±0.08
05	6.09	6.22	12.31	6.28	7.32	13.60	7.00	7.65	14.65	8.00	8.19	16.19
	±0.05	±0.08	±0.06	±0.06	±0.04	±0.03	±0.03	±0.07	±0.04	±0.09	±0.06	±0.02
10	4.42	5.02	9.44	4.96	5.61	10.57	5.90	6.02	11.92	6.16	6.92	13.08
	±0.08	±0.05	±0.04	±0.07	±0.04	±0.05	±0.06	±0.08	±0.07	±0.09	±0.06	±0.04
15	2.03	2.65	4.68	2.62	3.09	5.71	3.01	3.79	6.80	3.66	4.09	7.69
	±0.04	±0.07	±0.05	±0.05	±0.07	±0.06	±0.06	±0.08	±0.05	±0.05	±0.08	±0.06
20	1.01	1.02	2.03	1.40	1.16	2.56	1.61	2.01	3.62	2.31	2.26	4.57
	±0.08	±0.09	±0.02	±0.06	±0.09	±0.08	±0.06	±0.05	±0.02	±0.06	±0.01	±0.02
25	0.42	0.41	0.83	0.69	0.83	1.52	0.89	1.91	2.80	1.00	2.24	3.24
	±0.06	±0.05	±0.01	±0.08	±0.04	±0.05	±0.07	±0.03	±0.04	±0.07	±0.03	±0.01

SL = shoot length (cm.) RL = root length (cm.) TL = total length of seedling (cm.)

Table-VIII: *Effect of different concentrations of shoot (a) and root (b) dust of water hyacinth (E. crassipes) on seedling growth of Vijetha cultivar of rice*

(Each value is mean of 10 samples ± SE)

Dust conc. (%)	Reading taken at different days after soaking (DAS)											
	6			8			10			12		
	SL	RL	TL	SL	RL	TL	SL	RL	TL	SL	RL	TL
(a) Shoot dust												
C	6.87 ±0.08	6.95 ±0.03	13.82 ±0.04	6.98 ±0.06	7.78 ±0.03	14.76 ±0.05	7.65 ±0.06	7.99 ±0.05	15.64 ±0.05	8.07 ±0.09	8.34 ±0.09	16.41 ±0.08
05	6.88 ±0.04	6.99 ±0.08	13.87 ±0.05	7.06 ±0.07	7.83 ±0.05	14.89 ±0.06	7.69 ±0.02	8.04 ±0.06	15.73 ±0.04	8.16 ±0.07	8.56 ±0.07	16.72 ±0.06
10	5.87 ±0.03	5.84 ±0.07	11.71 ±0.02	5.94 ±0.04	6.72 ±0.05	12.66 ±0.05	6.38 ±0.02	6.97 ±0.04	13.35 ±0.03	6.40 ±0.06	7.95 ±0.05	14.35 ±0.05
15	3.38 ±0.06	3.79 ±0.02	7.17 ±0.01	3.57 ±0.08	4.03 ±0.09	7.60 ±0.08	3.88 ±0.02	4.60 ±0.03	8.48 ±0.02	4.69 ±0.06	4.89 ±0.07	9.58 ±0.04
20	2.12 ±0.04	2.52 ±0.05	4.64 ±0.03	2.41 ±0.07	2.88 ±0.04	5.29 ±0.06	2.70 ±0.06	3.31 ±0.08	6.01 ±0.06	3.59 ±0.07	3.44 ±0.06	7.03 ±0.03
25	0.82 ±0.03	1.21 ±0.06	2.03 ±0.05	1.05 ±0.08	1.51 ±0.07	2.56 ±0.03	1.75 ±0.09	2.22 ±0.07	3.97 ±0.06	2.31 ±0.06	2.42 ±0.04	4.73 ±0.05
(b) Root dust												
C	6.87 ±0.08	6.96 ±0.03	13.83 ±0.05	6.93 ±0.06	7.78 ±0.03	14.71 ±0.05	7.65 ±0.06	7.98 ±0.05	15.63 ±0.04	8.07 ±0.09	8.34 ±0.09	16.41 ±0.06
05	6.86 ±0.08	6.97 ±0.03	13.83 ±0.03	7.00 ±0.06	7.82 ±0.03	14.82 ±0.02	7.62 ±0.08	7.99 ±0.06	15.61 ±0.06	8.10 ±0.07	8.36 ±0.03	16.46 ±0.05
10	5.81 ±0.07	5.82 ±0.04	11.63 ±0.06	5.91 ±0.04	6.65 ±0.03	12.56 ±0.03	6.88 ±0.06	6.82 ±0.08	13.10 ±0.07	6.39 ±0.06	7.62 ±0.08	14.01 ±0.07
15	3.21 ±0.04	3.62 ±0.05	6.83 ±0.4	3.28 ±0.08	4.02 ±0.07	7.30 ±0.06	3.82 ±0.08	4.50 ±0.09	8.32 ±0.08	4.49 ±0.08	4.86 ±0.09	9.35 ±0.08
20	1.65 ±0.08	2.00 ±0.04	3.65 ±0.07	2.00 ±0.08	2.52 ±0.04	4.52 ±0.05	2.31 ±0.06	2.91 ±0.07	5.22 ±0.06	3.20 ±0.05	3.12 ±0.06	6.32 ±0.05
25	0.75 ±0.02	1.06 ±0.08	1.81 ±0.06	1.03 ±0.09	1.32 ±0.07	2.35 ±0.08	1.71 ±0.03	2.01 ±0.05	3.72 ±0.04	2.06 ±0.06	2.25 ±0.09	4.31 ±0.07

SL = shoot length (cm.) RL = root length (cm.) TL = total length of seedling (cm.)

Table-IX: *Effect of different concentrations of shoot dust of water hyacinth (E. crassipes) on fresh and dry weights of seedlings of Swarna mahsuri cultivar of rice*

(Each value is mean of 10 samples ± SE)

Dust conc. (%)	Days after sowing (DAS)	Fresh weight (mg.)			Dry weight (mg.)		
		Shoot	Root	Seedling	Shoot	Root	Seedling
C	6	7.82 ±0.02	9.65 ±0.05	17.47 ±0.02	2.45 ±0.01	7.08 ±0.05	9.53 ±0.03
	8	9.82 ±0.04	11.62 ±0.03	21.44 ±0.03	2.70 ±0.06	9.72 ±0.08	12.42 ±0.05
	10	13.62 ±0.02	13.66 ±0.04	27.28 ±0.02	3.06 ±0.05	10.91 ±0.07	13.97 ±0.04
	12	16.61 ±0.05	16.83 ±0.04	33.44 ±0.02	4.05 ±0.05	13.70 ±0.03	17.75 ±0.04
5	6	9.63 ±0.04	10.92 ±0.05	20.55 ±0.06	3.01 ±0.03	9.41 ±0.02	12.42 ±0.04
	8	11.41 ±0.03	13.22 ±0.06	24.63 ±0.047	3.19 ±0.05	11.25 ±0.06	14.44 ±0.03
	10	15.91 ±0.02	16.83 ±0.05	32.74 ±0.04	3.91 ±0.06	13.62 ±0.05	17.53 ±0.01
	12	18.67 ±0.07	19.63 ±0.02	38.30 ±0.06	4.98 ±0.02	15.93 ±0.05	20.01 ±0.06
10	6	7.33 ±0.02	8.62 ±0.04	15.95 ±0.01	2.11 ±0.06	7.04 ±0.05	9.15 ±0.04
	8	8.79 ±0.05	10.01 ±0.06	18.80 ±0.02	2.68 ±0.05	08.05 ±0.08	10.73 ±0.04
	10	12.52 ±0.05	13.12 ±0.04	25.64 ±0.02	3.02 ±0.05	10.81 ±0.01	13.83 ±0.04
	12	15.37 ±0.03	15.81 ±0.02	31.18 ±0.08	4.02 ±0.04	13.03 ±0.04	17.05 ±0.06
15	6	5.03 ±0.01	5.21 ±0.06	10.24 ±0.05	1.21 ±0.02	4.88 ±0.06	6.09 ±0.04
	8	6.34 ±0.03	9.01 ±0.05	15.35 ±0.06	1.58 ±0.02	6.03 ±0.04	7.41 ±0.01
	10	9.22 ±0.05	10.01 ±0.02	19.23 +0.04	2.09 ±0.04	9.11 ±0.06	11.20 ±0.08
	12	12.55 ±0.05	13.83 ±0.03	26.38 ±0.06	2.88 ±0.08	9.61 ±0.08	12.49 ±0.07

Dust conc. (%)	Days after sowing (DAS)	Fresh weight (mg.)			Dry weight (mg.)		
		Shoot	Root	Seedling	Shoot	Root	Seedling
20	6	3.44 ±0.03	4.11 ±0.04	8.55 ±0.02	1.02 ±0.05	3.04 ±0.03	4.06 ±0.08
	8	4.01 ±0.04	6.02 ±0.03	10.03 ±0.01	1.62 ±0.05	4.05 ±0.08	5.67 ±0.07
	10	6.02 ±0.05	6.60 ±0.02	12.05 ±0.06	2.00 ±0.08	5.85 ±0.04	7.85 ±0.03
	12	7.02 ±0.04	7.18 ±0.06	14.20 ±0.07	2.33 ±0.04	6.11 ±0.03	8.44 ±0.08
25	6	2.02 ±0.03	2.13 ±0.04	4.65 ±0.02	0.72 ±0.06	2.32 ±0.05	3.04 ±0.02
	8	2.59 ±0.06	3.02 ±0.07	6.43 ±0.03	0.82 ±0.05	3.02 ±0.09	3.84 ±0.02
	10	3.01 ±0.02	4.46 ±0.04	7.47 ±0.05	1.11 ±0.06	3.38 ±0.05	4.49 ±0.03
	12	4.30 ±0.01	4.91 ±0.05	8.81 ±0.04	1.28 ±0.05	3.91 ±0.02	4.99 ±0.0

Table-X: *Effect of different concentrations of shoot dust of water hyacinth (E. crassipes) on fresh and dry weights of seedlings of Samba mahsuri cultivar of rice*

(Each value is mean of 10 samples ± SE)

Dust conc. (%)	Days after sowing (DAS)	Fresh weight (mg.)			Dry weight (mg.)		
		Shoot	Root	Seedling	Shoot	Root	Seedling
C	6	7.24 ±0.02	9.02 ±0.01	16.26 ±0.02	1.62 ±0.01	6.31 ±0.04	7.93 ±0.03
	8	9.62 ±0.04	11.52 ±0.02	21.14 ±0.03	2.11 ±0.02	9.14 ±0.06	11.25 ±0.05
	10	13.06 ±0.05	13.40 ±0.04	26.46 ±0.03	2.33 ±0.03	10.31 ±0.01	12.64 ±0.02
	12	16.08 ±0.05	16.13 ±0.02	32.21 ±0.02	3.15 ±0.01	13.01 ±0.03	16.16 ±0.02
5	6	8.42 ±0.02	9.94 ±0.01	18.36 ±0.01	1.96 ±0.04	7.30 ±0.02	9.26 ±0.02
	8	10.89 ±0.02	12.10 ±0.03	22.99 ±0.04	2.75 ±0.04	10.54 ±0.05	13.29 ±0.2
	10	14.28 ±0.06	14.79 ±0.02	29.07 ±0.05	3.20 ±0.04	12.35 ±0.03	15.55 ±0.01
	12	17.89 ±0.05	17.84 ±0.04	35.73 ±0.02	4.20 ±0.06	14.32 ±0.06	18.52 ±0.03
10	6	6.04 ±0.01	7.09 ±0.06	13.13 ±0.04	1.60 ±0.02	5.08 ±0.04	6.68 ±0.02
	8	8.71 ±0.05	10.00 ±0.02	18.71 ±0.06	2.02 ±0.02	8.02 ±0.06	10.04 ±0.02
	10	12.33 ±0.02	12.86 ±0.04	25.19 ±0.04	2.28 ±0.02	10.01 ±0.05	12.09 ±0.03
	12	15.07 ±0.02	15.51 ±0.03	30.58 ±0.06	3.01 ±0.03	12.33 ±0.02	15.34 ±0.05
15	6	4.00 ±0.06	05.11 ±0.04	9.11 ±0.01	0.54 ±0.05	4.49 ±0.02	5.03 ±0.01
	8	6.11 ±0.04	8.18 ±0.02	14.29 ±0.03	1.02 ±0.01	6.01 ±10.04	7.03 ±0.01
	10	9.01 ±0.06	9.05 ±0.06	18.06 ±0.04	2.00 ±0.05	8.48 ±0.04	10.48 ±0.06
	12	12.03 ±0.02	12.95 ±0.06	24.98 ±0.04	2.32 ±0.01	9.01 ±0.03	11.03 ±0.02

Dust conc. (%)	Days after sowing (DAS)	Fresh weight (mg.)			Dry weight (mg.)		
		Shoot	Root	Seedling	Shoot	Root	Seedling
20	6	3.01 ±0.02	4.09 ±0.06	7.10 ±0.05	0.63 ±0.04	3.00 ±0.02	3.63 ±0.01
	8	3.86 ±0.04	5.92 ±0.06	9.78 ±0.05	0.82 ±0.02	4.02 ±0.01	4.84 ±0.03
	10	6.01 ±0.02	6.50 ±0.04	12.01 ±0.01	1.51 ±0.04	5.44 ±0.06	6.95 ±0.03
	12	7.06 ±0.04	7.01 ±0.06	14.07 ±0.05	2.06 ±0.02	6.86 ±0.04	8.92 ±0.06
25	6	2.01 ±0.06	2.21 ±0.05	4.72 ±0.04	0.41 ±0.01	2.12 ±0.02	2.53 ±0.05
	8	2.99 ±0.04	3.00 ±0.03	5.99 ±0.06	0.52 ±0.04	2.46 ±0.02	3.15 ±0.01
	10	3.00 ±0.07	3.92 ±0.06	6.92 ±0.04	0.71 ±0.01	3.16 ±0.04	3.87 ±0.05
	12	3.71 ±0.04	4.22 ±0.07	7.93 ±0.06	1.01 ±0.05	3.50 ±0.01	4.51 ±0.03

Table-XI: *Effect of different concentrations of shoot dust of water hyacinth (E. crassipes) on fresh and dry weights of seedlings of Pratikshya cultivar of rice*

(Each value is mean of 10 samples ± SE)

Dust conc. (%)	Days after sowing (DAS)	Fresh weight (mg.)			Dry weight (mg.)		
		Shoot	Root	Seedling	Shoot	Root	Seedling
C	6	7.01 ±0.05	8.00 ±0.08	15.01 ±0.06	1.11 ±0.02	6.02 ±0.05	1.93 ±0.03
	8	9.12 ±0.04	10.04 ±0.06	19.16 ±0.04	1.36 ±0.03	8.01 ±0.05	9.37 ±0.03
	10	12.02 ±0.06	13.00 ±0.05	25.02 ±0.05	2.14 ±0.02	10.02 ±0.04	12.16 ±0.04
	12	15.01 ±0.05	15.71 ±0.08	30.72 ±0.06	2.88 ±0.01	12.78 ±0.02	15.66 ±0.05
5	6	7.80 ±0.01	8.99 ±0.08	16.79 ±0.08	1.65 ±0.03	7.05 ±0.04	8.70 ±0.07
	8	9.88 ±0.05	11.98 ±0.02	21.86 ±0.01	1.99 ±0.02	9.28 ±0.04	11.27 ±0.02
	10	13.99 ±0.04	14.65 ±0.01	28.64 ±0.03	2.90 ±0.01	11.99 ±0.04	14.89 ±0.01
	12	16.89 ±0.04	17.45 ±0.03	34.34 ±0.02	3.32 ±0.02	14.25 ±0.04	17.57 ±0.01
10	6	6.01 ±0.02	6.73 ±0.04	12.74 ±0.66	1.02 ±0.02	5.00 ±0.04	6.02 ±0.01
	8	7.01 ±0.01	8.74 ±0.06	15.75 ±0.02	1.33 ±0.01	7.08 ±0.08	8.31 ±0.08
	10	11.08 ±0.08	12.04 ±0.07	23.12 ±0.04	2.01 ±0.02	9.08 ±0.04	11.09 ±0.05
	12	14.02 ±0.02	15.05 ±0.08	29.07 ±0.04	2.69 ±0.01	12.0 ±0.03	14.76 ±0.02
15	6	3.29 ±0.04	4.85 ±0.04	8.14 ±0.05	0.85 ±0.02	3.66 ±0.03	4.51 ±0.01
	8	4.78 ±0.02	6.36 ±0.01	11.14 ±0.04	1.01 ±0.01	4.48 ±0.04	5.49 ±0.08
	10	7.22 ±0.08	7.59 ±0.07	14.81 ±0.05	1.59 ±0.01	5.28 ±0.04	6.87 ±0.02
	12	8.61 ±0.04	9.04 ±0.08	17.65 ±0.06	1.88 ±0.01	7.06 ±0.03	8.94 ±0.05

Dust conc. (%)	Days after sowing (DAS)	Fresh weight (mg.)			Dry weight (mg.)		
		Shoot	Root	Seedling	Shoot	Root	Seedling
20	6	2.55 ±0.02	3.08 ±0.03	5.63 ±0.08	0.59 ±0.06	2.05 ±0.07	3.14 ±0.02
	8	3.04 ±0.03	3.48 ±0.04	6.52 ±0.02	0.80 ±0.06	2.99 ±0.05	3.79 ±0.02
	10	4.21 ±0.02	4.72 ±0.02	8.93 ±0.02	1.01 ±0.04	3.46 ±0.02	4.17 ±0.03
	12	5.28 ±0.02	5.99 ±0.04	11.27 ±0.03	1.30 ±0.04	4.86 ±0.03	6.16 ±0.02
25	6	1.14 ±0.02	2.04 ±0.05	3.18 ±0.02	0.39 ±0.02	1.21 ±0.04	1.80 ±0.02
	8	1.85 ±0.08	2.48 ±0.05	4.53 ±0.04	0.58 ±0.02	1.64 ±0.03	2.22 ±0.02
	10	2.21 ±0.04	3.01 ±0.04	5.22 ±0.03	0.69 ±0.02	2.06 ±0.04	2.75 ±0.03
	12	3.01 ±0.02	3.25 ±0.04	6.26 ±0.03	1.00 ±0.06	2.28 ±0.01	3.28 ±0.04

Table-XII: *Effect of different concentrations of shoot dust of water hyacinth (E. crassipes) on fresh and dry weights of seedlings of Vijetha cultivar of rice*

(Each value is mean of 10 samples ± SE)

Dust conc. (%)	Days after sowing (DAS)	Fresh weight (mg.)			Dry weight (mg.)		
		Shoot	Root	Seedling	Shoot	Root	Seedling
C	6	7.89 ±0.02	9.68 ±0.04	17.57 ±0.01	2.25 ±0.02	7.24 ±0.06	9.49 ±0.04
	8	9.88 ±0.06	11.66 ±0.05	21.54 ±0.02	3.02 ±0.04	9.91 ±0.06	12.93 ±0.03
	10	13.64 ±0.07	13.72 ±0.08	27.36 ±0.04	3.22 ±0.01	10.99 ±0.04	14.21 ±0.02
	12	16.71 ±0.03	16.89 ±0.04	33.60 ±0.02	4.12 ±0.02	13.78 ±0.05	17.90 ±0.03
5	6	9.79 ±0.04	11.28 ±0.03	21.07 ±0.06	3.12 ±0.02	8.31 ±0.05	13.43 ±0.03
	8	12.22 ±0.04	13.61 ±0.03	25.83 ±0.06	3.62 ±0.04	11.51 ±0.05	15.13 ±0.07
	10	16.32 ±0.06	16.93 ±0.02	33.25 ±0.04	4.58 ±0.03	14.88 ±0.06	19.46 ±0.05
	12	19.22 ±0.04	19.91 ±0.03	39.93 ±0.02	5.32 ±0.08	16.85 ±0.04	22.17 ±0.06
10	6	7.61 ±0.02	8.78 ±0.01	16.39 ±0.03	2.21 ±0.05	7.21 ±0.04	9.42 ±0.06
	8	9.23 ±0.05	10.61 ±0.03	19.84 ±0.04	2.99 ±0.07	8.23 ±0.03	11.22 ±0.08
	10	12.69 ±0.04	13.61 ±0.06	26.30 ±0.09	3.32 ±0.02	10.91 ±0.08	14.03 ±0.06
	12	16.33 ±0.03	15.88 ±0.03	32.21 ±0.05	4.03 ±0.04	13.31 ±0.05	17.34 ±0.08
15	6	5.82 ±0.06	5.29 ±0.04	11.11 ±0.03	1.69 ±0.03	5.00 ±0.08	6.89 ±0.06
	8	6.68 ±0.05	9.11 ±0.02	15.79 ±0.06	1.98 ±0.02	6.11 ±0.05	8.09 ±0.09
	10	9.63 ±0.04	10.42 ±0.08	20.05 ±0.06	2.18 ±0.03	9.19 ±0.02	11.87 ±0.07
	12	12.61 ±0.07	13.77 ±0.06	26.38 ±0.02	2.94 ±0.03	9.71 ±0.05	12.65 ±0.08

Dust conc. (%)	Days after sowing (DAS)	Fresh weight (mg.)			Dry weight (mg.)		
		Shoot	Root	Seedling	Shoot	Root	Seedling
20	6	4.09 ±0.03	5.02 ±0.06	9.11 ±0.07	1.09 ±0.01	3.06 ±0.03	4.15 ±0.04
	8	5.03 ±0.04	6.33 ±0.05	11.36 ±0.02	1.80 ±0.05	4.21 ±0.06	6.01 ±0.03
	10	6.62 ±0.01	6.99 ±0.07	13.18 ±0.06	1.92 ±0.02	6.09 ±0.08	8.01 ±0.04
	12	7.66 ±0.05	7.79 ±0.05	15.45 ±0.08	2.77 ±0.05	6.69 ±0.01	9.46 ±0.03
25	6	2.08 ±0.02	2.71 ±0.05	4.79 ±0.04	0.61 ±0.02	2.87 ±0.03	3.68 ±0.06
	8	2.69 ±0.06	3.68 ±0.04	6.37 ±0.03	0.88 ±0.07	3.71 ±0.08	4.59 ±0.04
	10	3.11 ±0.02	4.66 ±0.07	7.77 ±0.05	1.42 ±0.02	4.16 ±0.05	5.28 ±0.04
	12	4.49 ±0.07	4.81 ±0.02	9.30 ±0.04	1.56 ±0.08	4.59 ±0.05	5.97 ±0.04

Table-XIII: *Effect of different concentrations of root dust of water hyacinth (E. crassipes) on fresh and dry weights of seedlings of Swarna mahsuri cultivar of rice*

(Each value is mean of 10 samples ± SE)

Dust conc. (%)	Days after sowing (DAS)	Fresh weight (mg.)			Dry weight (mg.)		
		Shoot	Root	Seedling	Shoot	Root	Seedling
C	6	7.82 ±0.02	9.65 ±0.05	17.47 ±0.02	2.45 ±0.01	7.08 ±0.05	9.53 ±0.03
	8	9.82 ±0.04	11.62 ±0.03	21.44 ±0.03	2.70 ±0.06	9.72 ±0.08	12.42 ±0.05
	10	13.62 ±0.02	13.66 ±0.04	27.28 ±0.02	3.06 ±0.05	10.91 ±0.07	13.97 ±0.04
	12	16.61 ±0.05	16.83 ±0.04	33.44 ±0.02	4.05 ±0.05	13.70 ±0.03	17.75 ±0.04
5	6	7.96 ±0.05	9.74 ±0.06	17.70 ±0.04	2.48 ±0.02	7.11 ±0.06	9.59 ±0.03
	8	9.90 ±0.01	11.99 ±0.02	21.89 ±0.01	2.72 ±0.03	9.82 ±0.04	12.54 ±0.02
	10	13.90 ±0.08	13.89 ±0.05	27.79 ±0.06	3.09 ±0.02	10.96 ±0.06	14.05 ±0.03
	12	16.81 ±0.05	16.96 ±0.07	33.77 ±0.03	4.11 ±0.06	13.81 ±0.04	17.92 ±0.03
10	6	5.81 ±0.05	7.91 ±0.02	13.72 ±0.03	0.82 ±0.01	4.92 ±0.05	5.73 ±0.02
	8	7.80 ±0.06	9.96 ±0.04	16.76 ±0.02	0.92 ±0.05	6.89 ±0.06	7.81 ±0.03
	10	9.91 ±0.06	11.74 ±0.07	21.65 ±0.05	1.80 ±0.01	8.79 ±0.04	10.59 ±0.02
	12	12.28 ±0.05	15.98 ±0.08	28.26 ±0.05	2.62 ±0.02	11.71 ±0.06	14.33 ±0.04
15	6	3.92 ±0.04	4.61 ±0.02	8.53 ±0.01	0.79 ±0.05	3.46 ±0.02	4.25 ±0.04
	8	4.82 ±0.06	5.82 ±0.08	10.64 ±0.02	0.91 ±0.06	4.81 ±0.04	5.72 ±0.05
	10	5.86 ±0.09	6.97 ±0.02	12.83 ±0.05	1.49 ±0.05	5.32 ±0.06	6.81 ±0.02
	12	7.33 ±0.06	8.43 ±0.08	15.76 ±0.02	1.87 ±0.01	6.86 ±0.05	8.73 ±0.03

Dust conc. (%)	Days after sowing (DAS)	Fresh weight (mg.)			Dry weight (mg.)		
		Shoot	Root	Seedling	Shoot	Root	Seedling
20	6	2.51 ±0.01	3.03 ±0.04	5.55 ±0.02	0.58 ±0.02	2.31 ±0.06	2.89 ±0.04
	8	3.28 ±0.02	3.85 ±0.06	7.13 ±0.03	0.71 ±0.04	3.22 ±0.05	3.83 ±0.03
	10	3.89 ±0.01	4.61 ±0.05	8.50 ±0.02	0.88 ±0.05	3.51 ±0.08	4.39 ±0.05
	12	4.84 ±0.05	5.71 ±0.04	10.55 ±0.03	1.20 ±0.05	4.08 ±0.05	5.28 ±0.03
25	6	1.08 ±0.05	1.45 ±0.02	2.43 ±0.02	0.26 ±0.01	1.01 ±0.08	1.27 ±0.05
	8	1.48 ±0.04	2.02 ±0.06	3.50 ±0.02	0.38 ±0.02	1.24 ±0.03	1.62 ±0.04
	10	2.11 ±0.04	2.61 ±0.07	4.42 ±0.03	0.51 ±0.02	2.00 ±0.01	2.51 ±0.01
	12	2.68 ±0.06	3.11 ±0.04	5.79 ±0.03	0.72 ±0.05	2.61 ±0.03	3.33 ±0.02

Table-XIV: *Effect of different concentrations of root dust of water hyacinth (E. crassipes) on fresh and dry weights of seedlings of Sambha mahsuri cultivar of rice*

(Each value is mean of 10 samples ± SE)

Dust conc. (%)	Days after sowing (DAS)	Fresh weight (mg.)			Dry weight (mg.)		
		Shoot	Root	Seedling	Shoot	Root	Seedling
C	6	7.24 ±0.02	9.02 ±0.01	16.26 ±0.02	1.62 ±0.01	6.31 ±0.04	7.93 ±0.03
	8	9.62 ±0.04	11.52 ±0.02	21.14 ±0.03	2.11 ±0.02	9.14 ±0.06	11.25 ±0.05
	10	13.06 ±0.05	13.40 ±0.04	26.46 ±0.03	2.33 ±0.03	10.31 ±0.01	12.64 ±0.02
	12	16.08 ±0.05	16.13 ±0.02	32.21 ±0.02	3.15 ±0.01	13.01 ±0.03	16.16 ±0.02
5	6	07.30 ±0.03	9.42 ±0.05	16.42 ±0.04	1.44 ±0.02	6.70 ±0.06	8.14 ±0.02
	8	9.76 ±0.02	11.63 ±0.05	21.39 ±0.02	1.78 ±0.05	9.27 ±0.05	11.05 ±0.06
	10	13.17 ±0.02	13.43 ±0.05	26.60 ±0.05	2.43 ±0.06	10.41 ±0.01	12.84 ±0.07
	12	16.18 ±0.02	16.44 ±0.05	33.62 ±0.06	3.20 ±0.01	13.04 ±0.06	16.24 ±0.04
10	6	5.01 ±0.07	7.01 ±0.02	12.02 ±0.02	0.81 ±0.04	4.05 ±0.02	4.86 ±0.03
	8	7.20 ±0.02	9.03 ±0.01	16.23 ±0.04	0.90 ±0.04	6.06 ±0.05	6.96 ±0.07
	10	9.47 ±0.02	11.43 ±0.01	20.90 ±0.03	1.50 ±0.01	8.07 ±0.05	9.57 ±0.04
	12	12.01 ±0.02	12.84 ±0.04	24.85 ±0.03	2.09 ±0.02	10.05 ±0.03	12.14 ±0.04
15	6	3.58 ±0.04	4.54 ±0.01	8.12 ±0.03	0.55 ±0.07	3.05 ±0.02	3.60 ±0.04
	8	4.57 ±0.05	5.55 ±0.02	10.12 ±0.01	0.70 ±0.03	4.07 ±10.04	4.77 ±0.02
	10	6.51 ±0.02	6.58 ±0.01	13.09 ±0.04	1.38 ±0.03	5.02 ±0.06	6.40 ±0.04
	12	7.01 ±0.01	8.11 ±0.02	15.22 ±0.04	1.51 ±0.02	6.41 ±0.01	7.92 ±0.03

Dust conc. (%)	Days after sowing (DAS)	Fresh weight (mg.)			Dry weight (mg.)		
		Shoot	Root	Seedling	Shoot	Root	Seedling
20	6	2.50 ±0.02	3.00 ±0.05	5.50 ±0.03	0.38 ±0.02	1.81 ±0.02	2.49 ±0.03
	8	3.13 ±0.02	3.77 ±0.03	6.90 ±0.04	0.57 ±0.06	2.18 ±0.07	2.75 ±0.05
	10	3.85 ±0.06	4.35 ±0.08	8.20 ±0.05	0.68 ±0.01	3.15 ±0.01	3.83 ±0.02
	12	4.27 ±0.06	5.48 ±0.02	9.75 ±0.03	1.08 ±0.08	4.01 ±0.07	5.09 ±0.05
25	6	0.73 ±0.02	1.63 ±0.03	2.16 ±0.01	0.21 ±0.06	0.77 ±0.04	0.88 ±0.03
	8	1.04 ±0.05	2.00 ±0.03	3.04 ±0.03	0.32 ±0.06	1.03 ±0.05	1.35 ±0.03
	10	2.01 ±0.02	2.51 ±0.02	4.22 ±0.01	0.45 ±0.05	1.25 ±0.04	1.70 ±0.02
	12	2.66 ±0.02	3.06 ±0.05	5.72 ±0.02	0.60 ±0.02	2.60 ±0.02	3.20 ±0.03

Table-XV: *Effect of different concentrations of root dust of water hyacinth (E. crassipes) on fresh and dry weights of seedlings of Pratikshya cultivar of rice*

(Each value is mean of 10 samples ± SE)

Dust conc. (%)	Days after sowing (DAS)	Fresh weight (mg.)			Dry weight (mg.)		
		Shoot	Root	Seedling	Shoot	Root	Seedling
C	6	7.01 ±0.05	8.00 ±0.08	15.01 ±0.06	1.11 ±0.02	6.02 ±0.05	1.93 ±0.03
	8	9.12 ±0.04	10.04 ±0.06	19.16 ±0.04	1.36 ±0.03	8.01 ±0.05	9.37 ±0.03
	10	12.02 ±0.06	13.00 ±0.05	25.02 ±0.05	2.14 ±0.02	10.02 ±0.04	12.16 ±0.04
	12	15.01 ±0.05	15.71 ±0.08	30.72 ±0.06	2.88 ±0.01	12.78 ±0.02	15.66 ±0.05
5	6	7.09 ±0.06	8.21 ±0.02	15.30 ±0.03	1.14 ±0.04	6.01 ±0.05	7.15 ±0.03
	8	9.16 ±0.06	10.37 ±0.08	19.53 ±0.04	1.38 ±0.02	8.27 ±0.05	9.65 ±0.03
	10	12.22 ±0.06	13.03 ±0.05	25.25 ±0.03	2.21 ±0.02	10.28 ±0.05	12.49 ±0.03
	12	15.02 ±0.08	15.81 ±0.08	30.83 ±0.06	3.01 ±0.02	12.88 ±0.04	15.89 ±0.02
10	6	5.00 ±0.06	7.00 ±0.07	12.00 ±0.02	0.72 ±0.01	4.00 ±0.06	4.72 ±0.04
	8	7.01 ±0.05	8.42 ±0.06	15.43 ±0.08	0.82 ±0.06	6.00 ±0.08	6.82 ±0.04
	10	9.22 ±0.06	10.03 ±0.09	19.25 ±0.07	1.31 ±0.01	8.00 ±0.02	9.31 ±0.02
	12	12.00 ±0.06	12.54 ±0.01	24.54 ±0.05	1.58 ±0.02	9.25 ±0.4	10.83 ±0.02
15	6	3.51 ±0.06	4.00 ±0.03	7.51 ±0.03	0.45 ±0.02	3.00 ±0.05	3.45 ±0.04
	8	4.12 ±0.06	5.13 ±0.08	9.25 ±0.06	0.52 ±0.02	4.01 ±0.05	4.53 ±0.04
	10	6.02 ±0.06	6.51 ±0.07	12.53 ±0.05	0.91 ±0.02	5.00 ±0.06	5.91 ±0.05
	12	7.00 ±0.08	7.81 ±0.02	14.81 ±0.06	1.44 ±0.02	6.21 ±0.04	7.65 ±0.03

Dust conc. (%)	Days after sowing (DAS)	Fresh weight (mg.)			Dry weight (mg.)		
		Shoot	Root	Seedling	Shoot	Root	Seedling
20	6	1.72 ±0.01	2.01 ±0.05	3.73 ±0.02	0.19 ±0.01	1.51 ±0.05	1.72 ±0.06
	8	2.21 ±0.05	2.55 ±0.08	4.76 ±0.04	0.26 ±0.02	2.02 ±0.08	2.28 ±0.05
	10	3.02 ±0.04	3.31 ±0.05	6.33 ±0.02	0.45 ±0.02	2.50 ±0.06	2.95 ±0.03
	12	3.61 ±0.01	3.96 ±0.05	7.57 ±0.02	0.77 ±0.01	3.11 ±0.06	3.88 ±0.04
25	6	0.71 ±0.02	1.21 ±0.09	2.22 ±0.05	0.11 ±0.02	0.75 ±0.06	0.77 ±0.04
	8	1.00 ±0.06	1.91 ±0.04	2.91 ±0.02	0.21 ±0.01	1.00 ±0.04	1.21 ±0.02
	10	2.00 ±0.05	2.55 ±0.03	4.05 ±0.02	0.31 ±0.01	1.51 ±0.04	2.52 ±0.02
	12	2.60 ±0.06	3.00 ±0.05	5.60 ±0.02	0.54 ±0.02	2.41 ±0.05	2.95 ±0.03

Table-XVI: *Effect of different concentrations of root dust of water hyacinth (E. crassipes) on fresh and dry weights of seedlings of Vijetha cultivar of rice*

(Each value is mean of 10 samples ± SE)

Dust conc. (%)	Days after sowing (DAS)	Fresh weight (mg.)			Dry weight (mg.)		
		Shoot	Root	Seedling	Shoot	Root	Seedling
C	6	7.89 ±0.02	9.68 ±0.04	17.57 ±0.01	2.25 ±0.02	7.24 ±0.06	9.49 ±0.04
	8	9.88 ±0.06	11.66 ±0.05	21.54 ±0.02	3.02 ±0.04	9.91 ±0.06	12.93 ±0.03
	10	13.64 ±0.07	13.72 ±0.08	27.36 ±0.04	3.22 ±0.01	10.99 ±0.04	14.21 ±0.02
	12	16.71 ±0.03	16.89 ±0.04	33.60 ±0.02	4.12 ±0.02	13.78 ±0.05	17.90 ±0.03
5	6	7.99 ±0.01	9.79 ±0.02	17.78 ±0.01	2.88 ±0.05	7.96 ±0.06	10.24 ±0.02
	8	9.92 ±0.06	12.02 ±0.02	21.94 ±0.03	3.07 ±0.02	9.96 ±0.02	13.03 ±0.01
	10	13.98 ±0.05	13.91 ±0.02	27.89 ±0.02	3.26 ±0.05	11.00 ±0.02	14.26 ±0.04
	12	16.82 ±0.02	16.99 ±0.02	33.81 ±0.01	4.19 ±0.01	13.88 ±0.03	18.07 ±0.02
10	6	5.88 ±0.05	7.98 ±0.05	13.86 ±0.03	1.05 ±0.02	4.98 ±0.05	6.03 ±0.04
	8	7.81 ±0.08	9.98 ±0.06	17.79 ±0.04	1.50 ±0.02	6.94 ±0.05	8.44 ±0.03
	10	9.92 ±0.05	11.85 ±0.06	21.77 ±0.04	2.08 ±.0.01	8.81 ±0.03	10.89 ±0.02
	12	12.99 ±0.05	15.99 ±0.07	28.98 ±0.04	3.05 ±0.08	11.89 ±0.09	14.94 ±0.06
15	6	3.95 ±0.04	4.80 ±0.02	8.75 ±0.03	0.82 ±0.01	3.48 ±0.05	4.30 ±0.03
	8	4.91 ±0.06	5.93 ±0.03	10.84 ±0.04	0.95 ±0.02	4.91 ±0.05	5.86 ±0.03
	10	6.31 ±0.05	6.98 ±0.08	13.29 ±0.06	1.64 ±0.02	5.40 ±0.04	7.04 ±0.03
	12	8.33 ±0.08	8.51 ±0.06	16.84 ±0.05	1.98 ±0.01	6.88 ±0.04	8.86 ±0.02

Dust conc. (%)	Days after sowing (DAS)	Fresh weight (mg.)			Dry weight (mg.)		
		Shoot	Root	Seedling	Shoot	Root	Seedling
20	6	2.65 ±0.05	3.21 ±0.08	5.86 ±0.05	0.42 ±0.03	2.41 ±0.05	3.03 ±0.04
	8	3.31 ±0.05	3.95 ±0.02	7.26 ±0.03	0.65 ±0.05	3.31 ±0.06	3.96 ±0.04
	10	4.22 ±0.06	4.62 ±0.07	8.84 ±0.05	0.91 ±0.03	3.58 ±0.08	4.49 ±0.06
	12	5.21 ±0.09	5.82 ±0.07	11.03 ±0.06	1.21 ±0.04	4.52 ±0.05	5.73 ±0.03
25	6	1.32 ±0.08	1.63 ±0.06	3.25 ±0.04	0.30 ±0.01	1.22 ±0.04	1.52 ±0.02
	8	1.91 ±0.08	2.10 ±0.05	4.01 ±0.04	0.39 ±0.02	1.74 ±0.05	2.13 ±0.04
	10	2.51 ±0.05	2.72 ±0.08	5.23 ±0.04	0.52 ±0.05	2.08 ±0.06	2.60 ±0.04
	12	3.01 ±0.08	3.21 ±0.06	6.22 ±0.03	0.88 ±0.02	2.66 ±0.05	3.54 ±0.03

Table-XVII: *Effect of different concentrations of shoot dust of water hyacinth (E.crassipes) on vegetative growth parameters of Swarna mahsuri cultivar of rice plants at different ages of development*

(Each datum is the mean of 20 replicates ± SE)

Dust conc. (%)	Age of the plants at the time of recording (days)	No. of tillers per plant	No. of green leaves on main shoot	Total No. of leaves per plant	Height of the plant (cm)
C	30	2.70 ± 0.01	4.05 ± 0.03	10.08 ± 0.05	40.02 ± 0.04
	40	3.88 ± 0.02	4.78 ± 0.04	15.41 ± 0.01	50.15 ± 0.05
	50	4.89 ± 0.06	4.98 ± 0.07	17.01 ± 0.02	60.12 ± 0.03
	60	5.11 ± 0.05	5.27 ± 0.03	17.55 ± 0.04	71.01 ± 0.02
	70	5.84 ± 0.07	5.92 ± 0.06	17.97 ± 0.02	87.54 ± 0.05
	F	6.00 ± 0.02	5.12 ± 0.04	18.16 ± 0.07	90.01 ± 0.01
5	30	2.75 ± 0.05	4.09 ± 0.06	10.91 ± 0.07	41.69 ± 0.02
	40	3.95 ± 0.02	4.82 ± 0.02	15.97 ± 0.05	51.22 ± 0.04
	50	4.96 ± 0.03	8.09 ± 0.08	17.12 ± 0.02	60.76 ± 0.06
	60	5.22 ± 0.05	5.48 ± 0.05	17.97 ± 0.04	71.36 ± 0.08
	70	5.89 ± 0.04	5.96 ± 0.02	18.64 ± 0.01	87.69 ± 0.02
	F	6.04 ± 0.04	5.30 ± 0.04	18.95 ± 0.06	99.68 ± 0.02

Dust conc. (%)	Age of the plants at the time of recording (days)	No. of tillers per plant	No. of green leaves on main shoot	Total No. of leaves per plant	Height of the plant (cm)
10	30	2.51 ± 0.05	3.82 ± 0.04	7.89 ± 0.03	30.98 ± 0.01
	40	3.60 ± 0.07	4.55 ± 0.06	12.25 ± 0.04	40.01 ± 0.05
	50	4.71 ± 0.05	4.73 0.02	14.08 ± 0.04	49.82 ± 0.04
	60	4.92 ± 0.03	5.35 ± 0.02	14.85 ± 0.08	62.01 ± 0.08
	70	5.61 ± 0.04	5.69 0.06	15.44 ± 0.07	80.22 ± 0.04
	F	5.79 ± 0.07	5.11 ± 0.01	16.03 ± 0.04	90.88 ± 0.06
15	30	2.09 ± 0.06	3.51 ± 0.06	5.55 ± 0.06	20.11 ± 0.05
	40	3.11 ± 0.09	4.03 0.02	9.12 ± 0.06	24.40 ± 0.07
	50	4.13 ± 0.03	4.50 ± 0.06	10.01 ± 0.09	32.14 ± 0.08
	60	4.49 ± 0.02	4.99 0.05	11.00 ± 0.02	40.85 ± 0.02
	70	5.10 ± 0.08	5.40 ± 0.01	12.40 ± 0.08	49.73 ± 0.03
	F	5.29 ± 0.04	4.70 ± 0.02	13.02 ± 0.05	62.59 ± 0.05
20	30	1.49 ± 0.05	3.02 ± 0.06	3.71 ± 0.04	12.98 ± 0.03
	40	2.01 ± 0.01	3.40 0.02	6.01 ± 0.05	17.06 ± 0.06
	50	2.51 ± 0.08	3.79 ± 0.05	6.91 ± 0.09	22.10 ± 0.09
	60	2.82 ± 0.05	4.44 0.09	7.82 ± 0.02	36.01 ± 0.08
	70	3.18 ± 0.05	4.76 ± 0.06	8.31 ± 0.06	44.06 ± 0.09
	F	3.33 ± 0.06	4.00 0.05	9.21 ± 0.04	51.13 ± 0.01

Dust conc. (%)	Age of the plants at the time of recording (days)	No. of tillers per plant	No. of green leaves on main shoot	Total No. of leaves per plant	Height of the plant (cm)
25	30	1.05 ± 0.08	2.03 ± 0.02	2.44 ± 0.07	6.03 ± 0.02
	40	1.68 ± 0.04	2.29 0.04	3.14 ± 0.05	9.15 ± 0.04
	50	1.89 ± 0.05	2.69 0.09	3.67 ± 0.02	12.22 ± 0.08
	60	2.01 ± 0.01	3.33 ± 0.05	4.91 ± 0.03	14.06 ± 0.06
	70	2.14 ± 0.08	3.43 0.02	5.88 ± 0.01	18.64 ± 0.02
	F	2.28 ± 0.07	3.00 ± 0.03	6.10 ± 0.09	22.74 ± 0.04

F = flowering stage

Table-XVIII: *Effect of different concentrations of shoot dust of water hyacinth (E.crassipes) on vegetative growth parameters of Samba mahsuri cultivar of rice plants at different ages of development*

(Each datum is the mean of 20 replicates ± SE)

Dust conc. (%)	Age of the plants at the time of recording (days)	No. of tillers per plant	No. of green leaves on main shoot	Total No. of leaves per plant	Height of the plant (cm)
C	30	2.61 ± 0.02	3.96 ± 0.03	9.92 ± 0.02	38.96 ± 0.03
	40	3.68 ± 0.08	4.24 ± 0.05	15.29 ± 0.05	49.02 ± 0.06
	50	4.61 ± 0.05	4.60 ± 0.08	16.88 ± 0.09	57.01 ± 0.05
	60	5.01 ± 0.02	5.19 ± 0.02	17.49 ± 0.09	70.08 ± 0.05
	70	5.69 ± 0.07	5.90 ± 0.09	17.88 ± 0.04	85.42 ± 0.03
	F	6.09 ± 0.05	4.96 ± 0.02	18.51 ± 0.03	92.07 ± 0.02
5	30	2.63 ± 0.04	3.99 ± 0.03	10.64 ± 0.04	39.54 ± 0.08
	40	3.73 ± 0.06	4.37 ± 0.04	15.91 ± 0.06	50.99 ± 0.05
	50	4.63 ± 0.02	4.70 ± 0.03	17.54 ± 0.02	58.89 ± 0.03
	60	5.04 ± 0.09	5.17 ± 0.08	18.22 ± 0.06	71.70 ± 0.02
	70	5.67 ± 0.02	5.93 ± 0.05	18.98 ± 0.02	86.94 ± 0.04
	F	6.99 ± 0.07	4.98 ± 0.04	19.25 ± 0.04	98.25 ± 0.08

Dust conc. (%)	Age of the plants at the time of recording (days)	No. of tillers per plant	No. of green leaves on main shoot	Total No. of leaves per plant	Height of the plant (cm)
10	30	2.48 ± 0.01	3.78 ± 0.05	17.88 ± 0.02	29.72 ± 0.06
	40	3.55 ± 0.08	4.00 ± 0.07	12.21 ± 0.05	39.30 ± 0.02
	50	4.52 ± 0.92	4.70 ± 0.02	14.02 ± 0.06	48.71 ± 0.08
	60	4.88 ± 0.04	5.00 ± 0.03	14.81 ± 0.01	60.91 ± 0.09
	70	5.20 ± 0.05	5.66 ± 0.06	15.42 ± 0.09	78.82 ± 0.07
	F	5.74 ± 0.06	4.77 ± 0.04	16.00 ± 0.04	88.54 ± 0.04
15	30	1.92 ± 0.04	3.48 ± 0.02	5.50 ± 0.08	19.18 ± 0.05
	40	3.01 ± 0.06	3.65 ± 0.05	9.01 ± 0.07	23.88 ± 0.02
	50	4.02 ± 0.01	3.98 ± 0.03	9.92 ± 0.02	31.01 ± 0.09
	60	4.39 ± 0.07	4.77 ± 0.09	10.86 ± 0.06	38.89 ± 0.05
	70	4.88 ± 0.02	5.33 ± 0.05	12.02 ± 0.06	47.73 ± 0.05
	F	5.28 ± 0.08	4.52 ± 0.06	12.88 ± 0.05	60.79 ± 0.09
20	30	1.44 ± 0.09	2.92 ± 0.02	3.63 ± 0.01	11.87 ± 0.02
	40	1.94 ± 0.08	3.22 ± 0.04	5.91 ± 0.09	17.02 ± 0.06
	50	2.42 ± 0.02	3.60 ± 0.01	6.88 ± 0.05	21.77 ± 0.02
	60	2.71 ± 0.03	4.12 ± 0.03	7.79 ± 0.08	34.99 ± 0.05
	70	3.11 ± 0.05	4.70 ± 0.08	8.31 ± 0.06	43.12 ± 0.08
	F	3.29 ± 0.04	3.91 ± 0.06	9.12 ± 0.02	48.02 ± 0.06

Dust conc. (%)	Age of the plants at the time of recording (days)	No. of tillers per plant	No. of green leaves on main shoot	Total No. of leaves per plant	Height of the plant (cm)
25	30	1.02 ± 0.06	1.80 ± 0.05	2.20 ± 0.08	5.21 ± 0.06
	40	1.50 ± 0.08	2.01 ± 0.06	3.02 ± 0.06	8.99 ± 0.02
	50	1.79 ± 0.05	2.39 ± 0.04	3.60 ± 0.02	13.03 ± 0.05
	60	1.99 ± 0.02	2.89 ± 0.05	4.81 ± 0.04	15.30 ± 0.09
	70	2.12 ± 0.04	3.28 ± 0.02	5.40 ± 0.02	18.12 ± 0.02
	F	2.22 ± 0.05	2.58 ± 0.05	6.09 ± 0.04	22.16 ± 0.03

F = flowering stage.

Table-XIX: *Effect of different concentrations of shoot dust of water hyacinth (E.crassipes) on vegetative growth parameters of Pratikshya cultivar of rice plants at different ages of development*

(Each datum is the mean of 20 replicates ± SE)

Dust conc. (%)	Age of the plants at the time of recording (days)	No. of tillers per plant	No. of green leaves on main shoot	Total No. of leaves per plant	Height of the plant (cm)
C	30	2.52 ± 0.04	3.90 ± 0.02	9.81 ± 0.02	42.01 ± 0.6
	40	3.70 ± 0.08	4.60 ± 0.05	15.21 ± 0.06	51.92 ± 0.01
	50	4.58 ± 0.04	4.85 ± 0.09	16.78 ± 0.08	62.01 ± 0.05
	60	4.92 ± 0.01	5.06 ± 0.07	17.40 ± 0.09	73.09 ± 0.09
	70	5.62 ± 0.09	5.81 ± 0.01	17.76 ± 0.02	88.99 ± 0.08
	F	5.96 ± 0.06	4.89 ± 0.03	17.98 ± 0.04	100.89 ± 0.05
5	30	2.61 ± 0.07	3.98 ± 0.01	10.53 ± 0.01	45.20 ± 0.03
	40	3.76 ± 0.03	4.64 ± 0.06	15.92 ± 0.07	54.90 ± 0.04
	50	4.60 ± 0.02	4.88 ± 0.09	16.98 ± 0.02	65.67 ± 0.02
	60	4.98 ± 0.05	5.11 ± 0.02	17.68 ± 0.05	78.23 ± 0.06
	70	5.65 ± 0.08	5.92 ± 0.09	18.12 ± 0.02	92.69 ± 0.08
	F	6.04 ± 0.02	4.96 ± 0.08	18.69 ± 0.06	105.72 ± 0.06

Dust conc. (%)	Age of the plants at the time of recording (days)	No. of tillers per plant	No. of green leaves on main shoot	Total No. of leaves per plant	Height of the plant (cm)
10	30	2.45 ± 0.01	3.76 ± 0.05	7.69 ± 0.05	31.99 ± 0.09
	40	3.51 ± 0.03	4.50 ± 0.06	12.04 ± 0.04	42.05 ± 0.07
	50	4.48 ± 0.09	4.66 ± 0.02	13.78 ± 0.08	50.09 ± 0.02
	60	4.86 ± 0.7	4.93 ± 0.06	14.52 ± 0.01	63.93 ± 0.02
	70	5.58 ± 0.06	5.63 ± 0.09	15.22 ± 0.09	81.99 ± 0.05
	F	5.72 ± 0.01	4.75 ± 0.02	15.90 ± 0.02	92.08 ± 0.08
15	30	1.90 ± 0.05	3.45 ± 0.08	5.45 ± 0.02	22.01 ± 0.06
	40	2.92 ± 0.02	3.90 ± 0.05	8.98 ± 0.07	24.69 ± 0.08
	50	3.94 ± 0.06	4.35 ± 0.02	9.90 ± 0.05	33.97 ± 0.02
	60	4.38 ± 0.02	4.74 ± 0.03	10.59 ± 0.06	42.62 ± 0.09
	70	4.88 ± 0.08	5.32 ± 0.05	11.91 ± 0.03	51.18 ± 0.02
	F	5.08 ± 0.05	4.51 ± 0.04	12.69 ± 0.07	64.66 ± 0.04
20	30	1.40 ± 0.01	2.90 ± 0.06	3.58 ± 0.09	13.24 ± 0.03
	40	1.90 ± 0.02	3.34 ± 0.02	5.82 ± 0.06	18.81 ± 0.05
	50	2.38 ± 0.05	3.66 ± 0.05	6.86 ± 0.04	24.17 ± 0.07
	60	2.55 ± 0.03	4.11 ± 0.06	7.75 ± 0.01	38.73 ± 0.06
	70	3.00 ± 0.06	4.66 ± 0.09	8.23 ± 0.02	45.62 ± 0.02
	F	3.18 ± 0.05	3.90 ± 0.07	9.08 ± 0.08	54.44 ± 0.08

Dust conc. (%)	Age of the plants at the time of recording (days)	No. of tillers per plant	No. of green leaves on main shoot	Total No. of leaves per plant	Height of the plant (cm)
25	30	1.01 ± 0.02	1.77 ± 0.05	2.26 ± 0.01	5.11 ± 0.05
	40	1.52 ± 0.01	2.00 ± 0.01	2.96 ± 0.04	9.13 ± 0.09
	50	1.70 ± 0.09	2.42 ± 0.09	3.53 ± 0.08	13.97 ± 0.07
	60	1.88 ± 0.08	2.88 ± 0.07	4.66 ± 0.08	15.46 ± 0.07
	70	2.01 ± 0.06	3.23 ± 0.02	5.75 ± 0.05	18.11 ± 0.66
	F	2.14 ± 0.09	2.78 ± 0.05	6.06 ± 0.09	22.15 ± 0.03

F = flowering stage

Table-XX: *Effect of different concentrations of shoot dust of water hyacinth (E.crassipes) on vegetative growth parameters of Vijetha cultivar of rice plants at different ages of development*

(Each datum is the mean of 20 replicates ± SE)

Dust conc. (%)	Age of the plants at the time of recording (days)	No. of tillers per plant	No. of green leaves on main shoot	Total No. of leaves per plant	Height of the plant (cm)
C	30	3.11 ± 0.01	4.49 ± 0.09	11.12 ± 0.02	43.05 ± 0.02
	40	4.08 ± 0.02	4.81 ± 0.05	16.49 ± 0.06	53.06 ± 0.05
	50	5.01 ± 0.09	4.98 ± 0.03	17.99 ± 0.05	62.99 ± 0.03
	60	5.66 ± 0.05	5.35 ± 0.02	18.73 ± 0.09	74.52 ± 0.09
	70	5.97 ± 0.06	6.19 ± 0.02	19.14 ± 0.02	90.55 ± 0.06
	F	6.19 ± 0.03	5.10 ± 0.06	20.08 ± 0.05	105.02 ± 0.03
5	30	3.15 ± 0.01	4.51 ± 0.02	11.84 ± 0.02	45.14 ± 0.02
	40	4.18 ± 0.09	4.84 ± 0.03	16.94 ± 0.06	64.23 ± 0.01
	50	5.11 ± 0.05	5.00 ± 0.08	18.41 ± 0.04	69.61 ± 0.02
	60	5.69 ± 0.06	5.56 0.07	18.94 ± 0.03	77.87 ± 0.09
	70	5.99 ± 0.02	6.21 ± 0.06	19.78 ± 0.03	95.92 ± 0.01
	F	6.41 ± 0.03	5.15 0.09	20.78 ± 0,04	118.77 ± 0.06

Dust conc. (%)	Age of the plants at the time of recording (days)	No. of tillers per plant	No. of green leaves on main shoot	Total No. of leaves per plant	Height of the plant (cm)
10	30	2.55 ± 0.06	3.83 ± 0.02	8.88 ± 0.07	33.11 ± 0.04
	40	3.68 ± 0.07	4.59 ± 0.06	13.15 ± 0.03	42.97 ± 0.07
	50	4.93 ± 0.02	4.75 ± 0.05	14.13 ± 0.03	51.02 ± 0.05
	60	5.15 ± 0.09	5.14 ± 0.03	15.04 ± 0.06	64.82 ± 0.04
	70	5.89 ± 0.02	5.70 ± 0.08	15.78 ± 0.07	83.01 ± 0.03
	F	5.15 ± 0.04	4.84 ± 0.02	16.41 ± 0.05	93.28 ± 0.09
15	30	2.28 ± 0.05	3.40 ± 0.02	5.69 ± 0.06	21.15 ± 0.05
	40	3.15 ± 0.06	4.01 ± 0.06	9.15 ± 0.03	26.10 ± 0.08
	50	4.38 ± 0.08	4.51 ± 0.05	10.19 ± 0.08	33.90 ± 0.09
	60	4.68 ± 0.03	5.08 ± 0.08	11.11 ± 0.07	42.11 ± 0.04
	70	5.43 ± 0.08	5.62 ± 0.07	12.61 ± 0.05	50.88 ± 0.03
	F	5.88 ± 0.07	4.78 ± 0.06	13.19 ± 0.09	63.61 ± 0.02
20	30	1.81 ± 0.02	3.09 ± 0.03	3.79 ± 0.02	13.32 ± 0.01
	40	2.18 ± 0.09	3.44 ± 0.02	6.11 ± 0.02	18.05 ± 0.09
	50	2.91 ± 0.05	3.83 ± 0.03	6.95 ± 0.04	23.11 ± 0.02
	60	3.72 ± 0.06	4.22 ± 0.04	7.88 ± 0.08	36.93 ± 0.04
	70	3.95 ± 0.02	4.79 ± 0.05	8.36 ± 0.09	44.99 ± 0.02
	F	4.10 ± 0.08	4.08 ± 0.04	9.39 ± 0.07	52.15 ± 0.06

Dust conc. (%)	Age of the plants at the time of recording (days)	No. of tillers per plant	No. of green leaves on main shoot	Total No. of leaves per plant	Height of the plant (cm)
25	30	1.51 ± 0.07	2.09 ± 0.02	2.49 ± 0.05	6.82 ± 0.05
	40	1.70 ± 0.01	2.38 0.02	3.21 ± 0.06	9.49 ± 0.07
	50	2.01 ± 0.03	2.72 ± 0.04	3.75 ± 0.02	12.39 ± 0.08
	60	2.19 ± 0.05	3.28 0.06	4.96 ± 0.05	15.89 ± 0.02
	70	2.37 ± 0.05	3.49 ± 0.08	5.55 ± 0.07	18.91 ± 0.06
	F	2.52 ± 0.03	3.02 ± 0.01	6.18 ± 0.09	23.98 ± 0.04

F = flowering stage.

Table-XXI: *Effect of different concentrations of root dust of water hyacinth (E.crassipes) on vegetative growth parameters of Swarna mahsuri cultivar of rice plants at different ages of development*

(Each datum is the mean of 20 replicates ± SE)

Dust conc. (%)	Age of the plants at the time of recording (days)	No. of tillers per plant	No. of green leaves on main shoot	Total No. of leaves per plant	Height of the plant (cm)
C	30	2.70 ± 0.01	4.05 ± 0.03	10.08 ± 0.05	40.02 ± 0.04
	40	3.88 ± 0.02	4.78 ± 0.04	15.41 ± 0.01	50.15 ± 0.05
	50	4.89 ± 0.06	4.98 ± 0.07	17.01 ± 0.02	60.12 ± 0.03
	60	5.11 ± 0.05	5.27 ± 0.03	17.55 ± 0.04	71.01 ± 0.02
	70	5.84 ± 0.07	5.92 ± 0.06	17.97 ± 0.02	87.54 ± 0.05
	F	6.00 ± 0.02	5.12 ± 0.04	18.16 ± 0.07	90.01 ± 0.01
5	30	2.73 ± 0.09	4.07 ± 0.04	10.65 ± 0.04	41.21 ± 0.09
	40	3.91 ± 0.02	4.80 ± 0.06	15.90 ± 0.03	51.00 ± 0.06
	50	4.93 ± 0.08	5.05 ± 0.08	17.51 ± 0.09	60.41 ± 0.03
	60	5.18 ± 0.02	5.30 ± 0.01	17.86 ± 0.08	71.20 ± 0.08
	70	5.88 ± 0.02	5.94 ± 0.02	18.22 ± 0.07	87.61 ± 0.09
	F	6.03 ± 0.09	5.17 ± 0.07	18.52 ± 0.04	99.44 ± 0.02

Dust conc. (%)	Age of the plants at the time of recording (days)	No. of tillers per plant	No. of green leaves on main shoot	Total No. of leaves per plant	Height of the plant (cm)
10	30	2.48 ± 0.03	3.52 ± 0.05	7.02 ± 0.04	30.12 ± 0.04
	40	3.30 ± 0.05	4.31 ± 0.05	11.04 ± 0.08	38.14 ± 0.03
	50	4.46 ± 0.08	4.59 ± 0.03	12.11 ± 0.05	48.13 ± 0.01
	60	4.90 ± 0.06	4.72 ± 0.05	13.03 ± 0.06	60.33 ± 0.09
	70	5.51 ± 0.03	5.13 ± 0.07	14.14 ± 0.09	77.18 ± 0.04
	F	5.77 ± 0.07	4.66 ± 0.09	14.89 ± 0.03	87.28 ± 0.07
15	30	2.00 ± 0.09	3.40 ± 0.02	5.29 ± 0.03	20.01 ± 0.01
	40	3.04 ± 0.07	3.82 ± 0.09	8.09 ± 0.09	24.08 ± 0.09
	50	4.02 ± 0.05	4.16 ± 0.04	9.08 ± 0.03	31.90 ± 0.04
	60	4.31 ± 0.03	4.60 ± 0.06	10.11 ± 0.04	40.62 ± 0.08
	70	5.00 ± 0.01	5.14 ± 0.03	11.21 ± 0.02	49.26 ± 0.03
	F	5.19 ± 0.06	4.45 ± 0.07	12.16 ± 0.03	62.29 ± 0.02
20	30	1.45 ± 0.02	3.42 ± 0.08	3.68 ± 0.07	12.70 ± 0.05
	40	1.92 ± 0.05	3.83 ± 0.09	5.88 ± 0.07	16.29 ± 0.05
	50	2.33 ± 0.09	4.17 ± 0.02	6.25 ± 0.01	22.02 ± 0.03
	60	2.65 ± 0.07	4.54 ± 0.09	7.52 ± 0.08	35.71 ± 0.05
	70	3.10 ± 0.03	5.10 ± 0.01	8.14 ± 0.06	43.93 ± 0.04
	F	3.28 ± 0.08	4.36 ± 0.05	9.12 ± 0.02	49.03 ± 0.07

Dust conc. (%)	Age of the plants at the time of recording (days)	No. of tillers per plant	No. of green leaves on main shoot	Total No. of leaves per plant	Height of the plant (cm)
25	30	1.03 ± 0.09	2.00 ± 0.05	2.12 ± 0.09	4.94 ± 0.03
	40	1.55 ± 0.03	2.22 ± 0.09	3.01 ± 0.05	8.29 ± 0.08
	50	1.79 ± 0.07	2.48 ± 0.08	3.52 ± 0.04	11.81 ± 0.06
	60	2.00 ± 0.08	2.91 ± 0.06	4.61 ± 0.06	14.02 ± 0.01
	70	2.13 ± 0.03	3.25 ± 0.03	5.36 ± 0.06	14.09 ± 0.09
	F	2.31 ± 0.07	2.76 ± 0.05	6.02 ± 0.09	22.70 ± 0.04

F = flowering stage.

Table-XXII: *Effect of different concentrations of root dust of water hyacinth (E.crassipes) on vegetative growth parameters of Samba mahsuri cultivar of rice plants at different ages of development*

(Each datum is the mean of 20 replicates ± SE)

Dust conc. (%)	Age of the plants at the time of recording (days)	No. of tillers per plant	No. of green leaves on main shoot	Total No. of leaves per plant	Height of the plant (cm)
C	30	2.61 ± 0.02	3.96 ± 0.03	9.92 ± 0.02	38.96 ± 0.03
	40	3.68 ± 0.08	4.24 ± 0.05	15.29 ± 0.05	49.02 ± 0.06
	50	4.61 ± 0.05	4.60 ± 0.08	16.88 ± 0.09	57.01 ± 0.05
	60	5.01 ± 0.02	5.19 ± 0.02	17.49 ± 0.09	70.08 ± 0.05
	70	5.69 ± 0.07	5.90 ± 0.09	17.88 ± 0.04	85.42 ± 0.03
	F	6.09 ± 0.05	4.96 ± 0.02	18.51 ± 0.03	92.07 ± 0.02
5	30	2.62 ± 0.02	3.97 ± 0.01	10.35 ± 0.01	39.21 ± 0.08
	40	3.70 ± 0.07	4.65 ± 0.09	15.72 ± 0.08	50.32 ± 0.09
	50	4.62 ± 0.02	4.88 ± 0.04	17.08 ± 0.07	57.22 ± 0.02
	60	5.02 ± 0.06	5.18 ± 0.03	17.72 ± 0.02	70.84 ± 0.01
	70	5.68 ± 0.08	5.92 ± 0.04	17.99 ± 0.09	85.55 ± 0.04
	F	5.99 ± 0.02	4.97 ± 0.06	18.66 ± 0.04	97.12 ± 0.03

Dust conc. (%)	Age of the plants at the time of recording (days)	No. of tillers per plant	No. of green leaves on main shoot	Total No. of leaves per plant	Height of the plant (cm)
10	30	2.46 ± 0.02	3.49 ± 0.01	7.81 ± 0.03	36.11 ± 0.07
	40	3.50 ± 0.01	4.30 ± 0.09	12.19 ± 0.06	46.72 ± 0.03
	50	4.50 ± 0.09	4.49 ± 0.02	13.95 ± 0.09	55.02 ± 0.05
	60	4.84 ± 0.08	4.97 ± 0.06	14.72 ± 0.05	66.79 ± 0.02
	70	5.51 ± 0.02	5.60 ± 0.09	15.25 ± 0.06	83.16 ± 0.01
	F	5.72 ± 0.06	4.68 ± 0.07	15.81 ± 0.01	92.92 ± 0.02
15	30	1.90 ± 0.05	3.45 ± 0.04	5.44 ± 0.06	19.01 ± 0.05
	40	3.00 ± 0.03	3.90 ± 0.02	8.88 ± 0.09	23.24 ± 0.02
	50	3.96 ± 0.01	4.31 ± 0.06	9.80 ± 0.01	30.86 ± 0.04
	60	4.31 ± 0.09	4.73 0.02	10.56 ± 0.02	38.18 ± 0.09
	70	5.04 ± 0.08	5.30 ± 0.06	11.69 ± 0.04	47.33 ± 0.02
	F	5.21 ± 0.06	4.48 ± 0.06	12.77 ± 0.06	60.12 ± 0.08
20	30	1.41 ± 0.02	2.46 ± 0.05	3.58 ± 0.09	11.37 ± 0.08
	40	1.91 ± 0.04	3.01 ± 0.06	5.76 ± 0.05	16.55 ± 0.01
	50	2.38 ± 0.07	3.38 ± 0.02	6.80 ± 0.06	21.75 ± 0.09
	60	2.70 ± 0.02	4.05 ± 0.08	7.68 ± 0.06	34.68 ± 0.03
	70	3.07 ± 0.05	4.32 ± 0.04	8.00 ± 0.04	43.02 + 0.07
	F	3.19 ± 0.08	3.49 ± 0.07	9.00 ± 0.03	47.91 ± 0.04

Dust conc. (%)	Age of the plants at the time of recording (days)	No. of tillers per plant	No. of green leaves on main shoot	Total No. of leaves per plant	Height of the plant (cm)
25	30	1.01 ± 0.05	1.61 ± 0.03	2.36 ± 0.07	5.11 ± 0.01
	40	1.52 ± 0.02	1.99 0.09	3.00 ± 0.01	8.77 ± 0.09
	50	1.72 ± 0.02	2.48 ± 0.08	3.49 ± 0.02	11.11 ± 0.08
	60	1.88 ± 0.06	2.82 ± 0.01	4.72 ± 0.06	14.36 ± 0.02
	70	2.01 ± 0.03	3.19 ± 0.05	5.60 ± 0.02	18.10 ± 0.04
	F	2.19 ± 0.07	2.75 ± 0.03	6.00 ± 0.01	22.50 ± 0.05

F = flowering stage.

Table-XXIII: *Effect of different concentrations of root dust of water hyacinth (E.crassipes) on vegetative growth parameters of Pratikshya cultivar of rice plants at different ages of development*

(Each datum is the mean of 20 replicates ± SE)

Dust conc. (%)	Age of the plants at the time of recording (days)	No. of tillers per plant	No. of green leaves on main shoot	Total No. of leaves per plant	Height of the plant (cm)
C	30	2.52 ± 0.04	3.90 ± 0.02	9.81 ± 0.02	42.01 ± 0.6
	40	3.70 ± 0.08	4.60 ± 0.05	15.21 ± 0.06	51.92 ± 0.01
	50	4.58 ± 0.04	4.75 ± 0.09	16.78 ± 0.08	62.01 ± 0.05
	60	4.84 ± 0.01	5.06 ± 0.07	17.40 ± 0.09	73.09 ± 0.09
	70	5.62 ± 0.09	5.81 ± 0.01	17.76 ± 0.02	88.99 ± 0.08
	F	5.96 ± 0.06	4.89 ± 0.03	17.98 ± 0.04	100.89 ± 0.05
5	30	2.55 ± 0.06	3.93 ± 0.08	9.92 ± 0.09	44.90 ± 0.03
	40	3.72 ± 0.08	4.62 ± 0.07	15.73 ± 0.02	52.63 ± 0.05
	50	4.59 ± 0.02	4.79 ± 0.06	16.85 ± 0.08	64.95 ± 0.08
	60	4.92 ± 0.04	5.09 ± 0.02	17.42 ± 0.04	77.89 ± 0.01
	70	5.64 ± 0.05	5.86 ± 0.01	17.84 ± 0.08	90.79 ± 0.06
	F	5.99 ± 0.02	4.90 ± 0.09	18.34 ± 0.01	104.67 ±0.05

Dust conc. (%)	Age of the plants at the time of recording (days)	No. of tillers per plant	No. of green leaves on main shoot	Total No. of leaves per plant	Height of the plant (cm)
10	30	2.00 ± 0.04	3.61 ± 0.06	6.99 ± 0.03	31.95 ± 0.07
	40	3.44 ± 0.05	4.12 ± 0.03	11.60 ± 0.05	41.96 ± 0.02
	50	4.08 ± 0.03	4.44 ± 0.05	12.65 ± 0.07	50.02 ± 0.05
	60	4.50 ± 0.07	4.71 ± 0.02	13.72 ± 0.03	63.80 ± 0.2
	70	5.00 ± 0.09	5.41 ± 0.08	14.79 ± 0.08	81.90 ± 0.01
	F	5.50 ± 0.07	4.58 ± 0.09	15.16 ± 0.03	92.01 ± 0.07
15	30	1.81 ± 0.05	3.36 ± 0.02	5.15 ± 0.04	21.86 ± 0.02
	40	2.88 ± 0.06	3.83 ± 0.05	8.76 ± 0.09	24.15 ± 0.01
	50	3.86 ± 0.09	4.21 ± 0.09	9.70 ± 0.06	33.29 ± 0.08
	60	4.19 ± 0.02	4.66 ± 0.05	10.29 ± 0.09	42.06 ± 0.06
	70	4.88 ± 0.01	5.19 ± 0.06	11.73 ± 0.01	50.80 ± 0.07
	F	4.93 ± 0.05	4.32 ± 0.09	12.41 ± 0.04	64.16 ± 0.03
20	30	1.32 ± 0.08	2.61 ± 0.07	3.27 ± 0.06	12.99 ± 0.03
	40	1.80 ± 0.09	2.79 0.08	5.18 ± 0.09	18.02 ± 0.01
	50	2.28 ± 0.07	3.12 ± 0.05	6.29 ± 0.04	23.96 ± 0.09
	60	2.49 ± 0.03	3.82 0.03	7.15 ± 0.06	38.04 ± 0.08
	70	2.91 ± 0.01	4.40 ± 0.01	7.60 ± 0.09	45.12 0.06
	F	3.01 ± 0.07	3.35 ± 0.06	8.77 ± 0.08	54.02 ± 0.02

Dust conc. (%)	Age of the plants at the time of recording (days)	No. of tillers per plant	No. of green leaves on main shoot	Total No. of leaves per plant	Height of the plant (cm)
25	30	1.00 ± 0.05	1.40 ± 0.08	2.03 ± 0.02	5.97 ± 0.01
	40	1.40 ± 0.02	1.82 ± 0.04	2.59 ± 0.06	10.93 ± 0.06
	50	1.74 ± 0.09	2.02 ± 0.01	3.01 ± 0.07	13.17 ± 0.08
	60	1.85 ± 0.08	2.43 ± 0.02	3.82 ± 0.08	15.15 ± 0.04
	70	2.00 ± 0.06	2.90 ± 0.08	4.87 ± 0.02	18.00 ± 0.01
	F	2.17 ± 0.06	2.20 ± 0.07	5.49 ± 0.06	22.32 ± 0.09

F = flowering stage.

Table-XXIV: *Effect of different concentrations of root dust of water hyacinth (E.crassipes) on vegetative growth parameters of Vijetha cultivar of rice plants at different ages of development*

(Each datum is the mean of 20 replicates ± SE)

Dust conc. (%)	Age of the plants at the time of recording (days)	No. of tillers per plant	No. of green leaves on main shoot	Total No. of leaves per plant	Height of the plant (cm)
C	30	3.11 ± 0.01	4.49 ± 0.09	11.12 ± 0.02	43.05 ± 0.02
	40	4.08 ± 0.02	4.81 ± 0.05	16.49 ± 0.06	53.06 ± 0.05
	50	5.01 ± 0.09	4.98 ± 0.03	17.99 ± 0.05	62.99 ± 0.03
	60	5.66 ± 0.05	5.35 ± 0.02	18.73 ± 0.09	74.52 ± 0.09
	70	5.97 ± 0.06	6.19 ± 0.02	19.14 ± 0.02	90.55 ± 0.06
	F	6.19 ± 0.03	5.10 ± 0.06	20.08 ± 0.05	105.02 ± 0.03
5	30	3.05 ± 0.03	4.50 ± 0.09	11.65 ± 0.09	47.79 ± 0.04
	40	4.02 ± 0.02	4.83 ± 0.04	16.66 ± 0.06	58.64 ± 0.07
	50	4.96 ± 0.08	5.17 ± 0.01	18.05 ± 0.04	65.17 ± 0.02
	60	5.60 ± 0.04	5.48 ± 0.02	18.65 ± 0.08	75.28 ± 0.02
	70	5.93 ± 0.08	6.20 ± 0.08	19.65 ± 0.01	92.17 ± 0.06
	F	6.13 ± 0.05	5.30 ± 0.02	20.25 ± 0.09	105.99 ±0.09

Dust conc. (%)	Age of the plants at the time of recording (days)	No. of tillers per plant	No. of green leaves on main shoot	Total No. of leaves per plant	Height of the plant (cm)
10	30	2.50 ± 0.01	3.80 ± 0.05	8.18 ± 0.06	32.04 ± 0.09
	40	3.60 ± 0.03	4.19 ± 0.07	12.62 ± 0.02	42.07 ± 0.04
	50	4.61 ± 0.06	4.39 ± 0.07	14.13 ± 0.05	50.29 ± 0.07
	60	4.82 ± 0.08	5.01 ± 0.02	14.91 ± 0.02	64.22 ± 0.03
	70	5.72 ± 0.07	5.45 ± 0.05	15.29 ± 0.06	82.71 ± 0.04
	F	5.90 ± 0.03	4.71 ± 0.09	15.89 ± 0.04	92.88 ± 0.06
15	30	2.26 ± 0.02	3.78 ± 0.02	7.11 ± 0.01	20.10 ± 0.05
	40	3.10 ± 0.06	4.26 ± 0.05	9.00 ± 0.08	25.15 ± 0.02
	50	4.12 ± 0.01	4.59 ± 0.02	9.99 ± 0.02	33.70 ± 0.01
	60	4.42 ± 0.08	4.84 ± 0.02	11.01 ± 0.04	41.90 ± 0.09
	70	5.13 ± 0.09	5.40 ± 0.08	12.09 ± 0.08	50.28 ± 0.07
	F	5.61 ± 0.04	4.66 ± 0.06	13.02 ± 0.03	63.01 ± 0.04
20	30	1.62 ± 0.03	2.71 ± 0.04	3.62 ± 0.05	12.90 ± 0.08
	40	2.16 ± 0.06	3.11 ± 0.05	4.91 ± 0.06	17.91 ± 0.02
	50	2.70 ± 0.08	3.49 ± 0.06	6.02 ± 0.02	23.00 ± 0.04
	60	3.11 ± 0.02	4.02 ± 0.09	7.16 ± 0.01	36.70 ± 0.03
	70	3.62 ± 0.02	4.44 ± 0.05	8.02 ± 0.09	44.68 ± 0.02
	F	3.91 ± 0.08	3.86 ± 0.07	9.10 ± 0.06	51.89 ± 0.09

Dust conc. (%)	Age of the plants at the time of recording (days)	No. of tillers per plant	No. of green leaves on main shoot	Total No. of leaves per plant	Height of the plant (cm)
25	30	1.21 ± 0.06	1.92 ± 0.02	2.21 ± 0.08	5.50 ± 0.05
	40	1.46 ± 0.02	2.11 ± 0.04	3.01 ± 0.06	9.02 ± 0.04
	50	1.88 ± 0.03	2.41 ± 0.02	3.75 ± 0.07	12.00 ± 0.06
	60	2.07 ± 0.08	2.66 ± 0.01	4.56 ± 0.04	14.58 ± 0.04
	70	2.31 ± 0.09	3.04 ± 0.06	5.77 ± 0.02	19.00 ± 0.02
	F	2.51 ± 0.06	2.52 ± 0.09	5.91 ± 0.03	23.00 ± 0.07

F = flowering stage.

Table-XXV: *Effect of different concentrations of shoot (a) and root (b) dust of water hyacinth (E. crassipes) on yield and components of yield of Swarna mahsuri cultivar of rice plant*

(Each datum is the mean of 20 replicates ± SE)

Parameters studied	Dust concentration (%)					
	C	5	10	15	20	25
(a) Shoot dust						
No. of panicles per plant	5.32 ±0.02	5.85 ±0.09	3.88 ±0.02	2.62 ±0.08	1.90 ±0.04	1.25 ±0.09
Length of panicle (cm)	22.82 ±0.09	25.85 ±0.06	18.44 ±0.02	13.01 ±0.08	11.11 ±0.05	8.62 ±0.06
No. of spikelets per panicle	169.29 ±0.06	169.32 ±0.04	100.14 ±0.05	85.06 ±0.07	56.09 ±0.02	28.92 ±0.01
No. of fertile grains/ panicle	127.25 ±0.08	127.41 ±0.01	52.09 ±0.04	31.60 ±0.07	13.91 ±0.06	3.98 ±0.01
% of seed setting	75.17 ±0.09	75.20 ±0.01	52.02 ±0.05	37.16 ±0.03	24.81 ±0.05	13.77 ±0.02
Wt. of 1000 grains (gm)	18.511 ±0.05	18.522 ±0.09	13.893 ±0.05	9.501 ±0.08	6.612 ±06	3.882 ±0.03
Yield/plant (gm)	12.531 ±0.05	13.805 ±0.09	2.808 ±0.07	0.786 ±0.06	0.174 ±0.08	0.019 ±0.002
(b) Root dust						
No. of panicles per plant	5.32 ±0.02	5.54 ±0.05	3.85 ±0.03	2.52 ±0.08	1.72 ±0.06	1.02 ±0.01
Length of panicle (cm)	22.82 ±0.09	25.83 ±0.04	18.38 ±0.08	12.75 ±0.02	9.01 ±0.01	7.42 ±0.06
No. of spikelets per panicle	169.29 ±0.06	169.31 ±0.02	99.11 ±0.01	84.05 ±0.07	55.11 ±0.03	28.09 ±0.04
No. of fertile grains/ panicle	127.25 ±0.08	127.28 ±0.02	48.38 ±0.04	30.77 ±0.01	13.25 ±0.07	3.67 ±0.04
% of seed setting	75.17 ±0.09	75.18 ±0.07	51.41 ±0.06	36.62 ±0.03	24.06 ±0.01	13.07 ±0.02
Wt. of 1000 grains (gm)	18.511 ±0.05	18.518 ±0.02	12.346 ±0.08	8.731 ±0.04	6.004 ±0.04	3.009 ±0.05
Yield/plant (gm)	12.531 ±0.05	13.058 ±0.08	2.299 ±0.02	0.677 ±0.06	0.136 ±0.01	0.011 ±0.005

Table-XXVI: *Effect of different concentrations of shoot (a) and root (b) dust of water hyacinth (E.crassipes) on yield and components of yield of Samba mahsuri cultivar of rice plant*

(Each datum is the mean of 20 replicates ± SE)

Parameters studied	Dust concentration (%)					
	C	5	10	15	20	25
(a) Shoot dust						
No. of panicles per plant	5.18 ±0.04	5.22 ±0.05	3.54 ±0.04	2.35 ±0.01	1.65 ±0.05	1.08 ±0.07
Length of panicle (cm)	22.05 ±0.02	25.07 ±0.06	17.12 ±0.08	12.22 ±0.05	10.51 ±0.01	7.94 ±0.06
No. of spikelets per panicle	160.82 ±0.09	160.84 ±0.02	96.05 ±0.01	78.44 ±0.08	50.50 ±0.05	24.56 ±0.04
No. of fertile grains/ panicle	113.71 ±0.05	114.06 ±0.09	43.62 ±0.05	25.19 ±0.02	10.70 ±0.01	2.45 ±0.08
% of seed setting	70.71 ±0.05	70.92 ±0.08	45.42 ±0.03	32.12 ±0.06	21.19 ±0.07	10.01 ±0.05
Wt. of 1000 grains (gm)	17.821 ±0.02	17.916 ±0.09	13.101 ±0.05	8.812 ±0.08	6.005 ±0.02	3.053 ±0.01
Yield/plant (gm)	10.497 ±0.01	10.667 ±0.08	2.023 ±.06	0.521 ±0.04	0.106 ±0.06	0.008 ±0.003
(b) Root dust						
No. of panicles per plant	5.18 ±0.04	5.20 ±0.07	3.06 ±0.07	2.13 ±0.04	1.41 ±0.05	0.91 ±0.03
Length of panicle (cm)	22.05 ±0.02	25.06 ±0.06	16.16 ±0.08	11.61 ±0.01	7.05 ±0.09	6.81 ±0.02
No. of spikelets per panicle	160.82 ±0.09	160.83 ±0.05	95.44 ±0.02	76.26 ±0.02	50.08 ±0.05	24.16 ±0.08
No. of fertile grains/ panicle	113.71 ±0.05	113.86 ±0.06	88.77 ±0.02	23.41 ±0.09	10.26 ±0.07	2.31 ±0.03
% of seed setting	70.71 ±0.05	70.80 ±0.02	40.63 ±0.09	30.70 ±0.08	20.49 ±0.03	9.58 ±0.04
Wt. of 1000 grains (gm)	17.821 ±0.02	17.830 ±0.09	11.867 ±0.08	8.004 ±0.04	5.518 ±0.02	2.519 ±0.07
Yield/plant (gm)	10.497 ±0.01	10.656 ±0.05	1.408 ±0.09	0.399 ±0.07	0.079 ±0.05	0.005 ±0.002

Table-XXVII: *Effect of different concentrations of shoot (a) and root (b) dust of water hyacinth (E.crassipes) on yield and components of yield of Pratikshya cultivar of rice plant*

(Each datum is the mean of 20 replicates ± SE)

Parameters studied	Dust concentration (%)					
	C	5	10	15	20	25
(a) Shoot dust						
No. of panicles per plant	5.02 ±0.06	5.05 ±0.05	3.02 ±0.09	2.11 ±0.01	1.32 ±0.03	1.08 ±0.04
Length of panicle (cm)	20.00 ±0.02	23.11 ±0.05	16.01 ±0.07	11.05 ±0.02	8.25 ±0.07	6.01 ±0.08
No. of spikelets per panicle	154.88 ±0.05	159.92 ±0.08	98.02 ±0.04	76.18 ±0.02	48.85 ±0.01	22.11 ±0.03
No. of fertile grains/ panicle	101.35 ±0.06	111.12 ±0.02	47.10 ±0.08	22.05 ±0.05	9.30 ±0.09	2.61 ±0.05
% of seed setting	65.44 ±0.08	69.49 ±0.06	48.06 ±0.03	28.95 ±0.02	19.04 ±0.09	11.82 ±0.01
Wt. of 1000 grains (gm)	17.163 ±0.09	17.166 ±0.05	12.003 ±0.009	8.115 ±0.06	4.823 ±0.04	2.511 ±0.02
Yield/plant (gm)	8.732 ±0.05	9.633 ±0.05	1.707 ±0.02	0.377 ±0.06	0.059 ±0.04	0.007 ±0.002
(b) Root dust						
No. of panicles per plant	5.02 ±0.06	5.03 ±0.08	2.82 ±0.08	2.01 ±0.09	1.13 ±0.03	1.00 ±0.04
Length of panicle (cm)	20.00 ±0.02	22.02 ±0.06	15.46 ±0.01	10.69 ±0.04	7.03 ±0.05	5.78 ±0.01
No. of spikelets per panicle	154.88 ±0.05	157.99 ±0.09	90.11 ±0.04	75.19 ±0.08	47.13 ±0.01	20.26 ±0.09
No. of fertile grains/ panicle	101.35 ±0.06	108.14 ±0.05	41.88 ±0.01	18.98 ±0.02	8.65 ±0.05	2.04 ±0.08
% of seed setting	65.44 ±0.08	68.45 ±0.05	46.48 ±0.06	25.25 ±0.08	18.36 ±0.03	10.09 ±0.09
Wt. of 1000 grains (gm)	17.163 ±0.09	17.164 ±0.06	10.397 ±0.01	6.896 ±0.06	5.007 ±0.04	2.011 ±0.05
Yield/plant (gm)	7.732 ±0.05	9.336 ±0.09	1.227 ±0.02	0.263 ±0.04	0.048 ±0.03	0.004 ±0.001

Table-XXVIII: *Effect of different concentrations of shoot (a) and root (b) dust of water hyacinth (E.crassipes) on yield and components of yield of Vijetha cultivar of rice plant*

(Each datum is the mean of 20 replicates ± SE)

Parameters studied	Dust concentration (%)					
	C	5	10	15	20	25
(a) Shoot dust						
No. of panicles per plant	6.02 ±0.02	6.05 ±0.01	4.10 ±0.04	2.75 ±0.05	2.11 ±0.02	1.51 ±0.06
Length of panicle (cm)	27.20 ±0.06	28.36 ±0.09	19.82 ±0.07	14.46 ±0.02	11.82 ±0.03	9.89 ±0.06
No. of spikelets per panicle	172.92 ±0.01	172.98 ±0.05	105.95 ±0.09	88.86 ±0.07	59.66 ±0.05	36.42 ±0.02
No. of fertile grains/ panicle	134.46 ±0.02	134.78 ±.05	59.18 ±0.08	36.18 ±0.07	16.20 ±0.04	6.18 ±0.09
% of seed setting	77.76 ±0.06	77.92 ±0.05	55.86 ±0.03	40.72 ±0.02	27.16 ±0.05	16.98 ±0.09
Wt. of 1000 grains (gm)	18.866 ±0.09	18.951 ±0.07	14.996 ±0.05	10.499 ±0.01	7.913 ±0.02	4.912 ±0.04
Yield/plant (gm)	15.271 ±0.02	15.453 ±0.06	3.638 ±0.09	1.044 ±0.01	0.270 ±0.03	0.045 ±0.005
(b) Root dust						
No. of panicles per plant	6.02 ±0.02	6.03 ±0.08	4.01 ±0.03	2.73 ±0.06	1.92 ±0.05	1.22 ±0.07
Length of panicle (cm)	27.20 ±0.06	28.01 ±0.02	19.45 ±0.01	13.61 ±0.09	10.99 ±0.06	8.14 ±0.09
No. of spikelets per panicle	172.92 ±0.01	173.92 ±0.06	111.35 ±0.04	88.16 ±0.01	61.52 ±0.03	35.21 ±0.07
No. of fertile grains/ panicle	134.46 ±0.02	135.30 ±0.07	60.63 ±0.08	34.96 ±0.04	16.11 ±0.02	5.34 ±0.03
% of seed setting	77.76 ±0.06	77.80 ±0.05	54.45 ±0.03	39.66 ±0.02	26.19 ±0.01	15.18 ±0.08
Wt. of 1000 grains (gm)	18.866 ±0.09	18.871 ±0.02	13.491 ±0.04	9.823 ±0.05	6.692 ±0.01	3.572 ±0.08
Yield/plant (gm)	15.271 ±0.02	15.397 ±0.05	3.280 ±0.01	0.937 ±0.09	0.207 ±0.06	0.023 ±0.001

Bibliography

Abbas, Z.M.; M.M. Samiullha; R.K. Afridi; A. Inam and N. Ashfaq (1983). Response of *Triticale* varieties varying plant densities, yield components and yield. *Acta. Bot. indica,* **11** : 83-85.

Acharya, B. (1994). Studies on the effect of certain agro-chemicals on seed germination, growth and yield of ragi (*Eleusine coracana* Gaert.): Ph.D. Thesis, Berhampur University, Berhampur, Odisha, India.

Asana, R.D., P.K. Ramaiha and M.V.K.Rao (1966). The Uptake of nitrogen, phosphorous and potassium by three cultivars of wheat in relation to growth and development. *J. Pl. Physiol.,* **9** : 95-107.

Aspinal, D (1961). The control of tillering in the barley plant. I. The pattern of tillering and its relation to nutrient supply. *Aust. J. Biol. Sci.,* **14** : 493-505.

Ayaz, S.; F.Hussain; I. Ilahi and Bong-seop kill (1989). Allelopathic potential of *Adhatoda vasica* Ness. *Korean J. Botany,* **32** (2) : 109-119.

Barley, K.P. and N. A. Naidu (1964). The performance of three Australian wheat varieties at high levels of nitrogen supply. *Aust. J. Exp. Agric. Anim. Husb.*, **4** : 39-48.

Basu, P.K. Kapoor; S. Nath and S.K. Banerjee (1987). Allelopathic influence : An assessment on the response of agricultural crops growing near *Eucalyptus tereticornis*. *Indian J. Forestry*, **10** (4): 267-271.

Bhattacharjee, D. P.; G. Ramakrishnaya and A. K. Ghosh (1973). Analysis of yield components and productive efficiency of rice varieties under soil moisture deficiency. *Oryza*, **10** (2): 17-28.

Bokhari, U.G. (1978). Allelopathy among prairie grasses and its possible ecological significance. *Annal. of Bot.*, **42**: 127-36

Bonner, J. (1950). The role of toxic substances in the interaction of higher plants. *Botanical Review,* **16:** 51-65

Brar, D.S. and, G.S. Khush (2002). Transferring genes from wild species into rice. In: *Quantitative genetics, Genemic and plant breeding* (Ed. MS Kang). CAB, Wallingford, UK

Bremner, P.M. (1969a). Effect of time and rate of nitrogen application on tillering. "Sharp eye spot" and in winter wheat. *J. Agric. Sci. Camb.*, **72** : 273-280.

Bremner, P.M. (1969b). Growth and yield of three varieties of wheat with particular reference to the influcne of unproductive tillers. *J. Agric. Sci.*, **72** : 281-287.

Carnel, R.Q. (1969). The tillering pattern in barley varieties. I . production, survival and contribution of yield by component tillers. *J. Agric. Sci. Camb.*, **72** : 405-422.

Chakraverty, R.K.(1983). Mode of action of hadacidin in plants. *Acta Bot. Ind.,* **11**: 53-56.

Chakravorty, S.C.; S.Dutta and S. Banerjee (1991). Environment and Ecology: An ecological perspective. *Ind. J. Animal Nutri.,* **61:** 1245.

Chang, T.T. (1976). The origin and evolution, cultivation, dissemination and diversification of Asian African rices. *Euphytica,* **25:** 435-441.

Chaturvedi, S.N. and G.G. Zabka (1969). Interaction of water stress conditions and photoperiod in dark CO_2 fixation in *Kalanchoe blossfeldiana. Plant Physiol.* **442** (Suppl.) : 24.

Chetty, K.M. (1988). Medicinal chemical importance of some angiospermic weeds used by the rural people of Chittor district of Andhra Pradesh. *Indian Vegetos,* **1**:160.

Ching, Te may (1972). Metabolism of germinating seeds. In : *Seed biology,* (Ed. Kazlowski, T.T.). Academic press, N.Y., Vol. II, PP. 103-105.

Choe, H.T. (1972). Effect of pre-soaking seeds of *Pisum sativum* L. in GA_3, IAA and Kinetin solution on seedling growth. *Hort. Sci.,* **7**: 467-478.

Cleland, R. (1964). The role of endogenous auxins in the elongation of *Avena* leaf section. *Physiol. Plant.,* **17** : 126-135.

Cooper, J.P. (1956). Development analysis of population in the cereals and herbage grasses methods and techniques. *Agric. Sci. Camb.,* **47** : 262-279.

Dabadghao, P.M.; R.D. Roy and S.P Marwaha (1973). The effect of interval and intensity of some important grass species of western Rajasthan. *Ann. Arid Zone.*, **12** : 1-8.

Dai, Q.H.; Q.Y. Zheng and Z.Y. Wang (1992). Quantitative explanation on structure, carcinogenic activity relationship of aromatic amines by di-region theory. *Chin. Sci. Bull.*, **37**: 1028

Das, T.K. (1999). "Studies on impact of certain industrial effluents on rice crop." Ph.D Thesis, Berhampur university, Berahmpur, Odisha, India.

Das, P.K. and S.K. Sinha (1986). Relation of a seedling character to yield and yield components in fingure millet. *J. Orissa Bot. Sco.*, **8** (1) : 49-50.

Davidson, J.L. (1964). Some effects of leaf area control on the yield of wheat. *Aust. J. Agric. Res.,* **16** : 721-731.

De puit, J.E. and M.M.Caldwell (1975). Gas exchange of three cool semi-desert species in relation to temperature and water stress. *J. Ecol.,* **63** : 835-586.

Del moral, R. and C.H.Huller (1970). The Allelopathic effect of *E. camaldulensis.* Amer. Midland Naturalist, **83** : 254-82.

Del Moral, R. and R.G. Cates (1971). Allelopathic potential of the dominant vegetation of Western Washington. *Ecology,* **52**: 1030-1037.

Einhelling, F.A. (1985) Allelopathy-A natural protection allelochemicals. In: *Hand book of natural pesticides.* (Eds. N. D. Mandava and B. Bhusan), CRC press, Boca Raton FL., USA., **1**: 161-200.

Evans, L.T. (1960). Inflorescence initiation in *Lolium temulentum* L. I. effect of plant age and leaf area on sensitivity to photoperiodic induction. *Aust. J. Biol. Sci.,* **13** : 123-131.

Evenary, M. (1961). A survey of the work done in seed physiology by the department of Botany, Berhampur univ, Jerusalem, Israel. In : *Proc. of International Seed Test Asso.,* **26** : 597-658.

Feng-min, Li. And Hu. Hong-Yang(2005). Isolation and characterization of Novel antialgal allelochemicals from weeds. *Appl. Environ. Microbiol.* **71(II):** 6545.

Fisher, J.E. (1973) Development morphology of the inflorescence in hexaploid cultivars with and without the cultivar Norin 10 in their ancestry. *Can. J. Pl. Sci.,* **53** : 7-15.

Fisher, R.F. (1979) In: Plant disease. *Treatise* (F.G. Horr fall and E.B. Cawling, Eds.), Academic Press, New York, PP-313.

Ganguly, S. and S.M. Sircar (1954). Cell growth and metabolism of pea *(Pisum sativum L.)* Internode as affected by the growth substances from the root of water hyacinth (*Eichhornia crassipes* Solms). *Bull. Bot. Soc. Bengal,* **18**(1 & 2): 83-86.

Gantayat, P.K. (2001). Impact of leaf litter leachate of *Eucalyptus* on germination and seedling growth of some gram seeds. M.Phil. dissertation, Berhampur, University, Berhampur, Odisha, India.

Gaonkar, S.M.; P.R. Kulkarni (1987). Physical and mechanical properties of micro-crystalline cellulose (MCC) prepared from local agricultural residues, *Res. Ind.,* **32**:90.

Gelmond, H. (1991). Problems in crop seed germination. In : *Crop physiology* (Ed. Gupta, U.S.) Oxford and IBIT Publ.co. New Delhi, PP 1-64.

Gerakis, P.A.; E.P. Gurrero and W.A. willams (1975). Growth, water relation and nutrition of three grass land annuals affected by drought. *J. APP. Ecol.,* **12** : 125-135.

Gopal, B. (1987). *Water hyacinth.* Elsevier Science Publisher, Amsterdam. P-471.

Gopal, B. and U. Goel (1993). Competition and allelopathy in aquatic plant communities. *The Botanical Review,* **59**: 155-210.

Grummer, G and H. Bayer (1960). The influenced exerted by species of *Camlina* on flex by means of toxic substances. In: *The Biology of Weeds* (Ed. J.L. Merper) Blackwell; Oxford, PP : 153-157

*Gupta, O.P. and P.S. Lamba (1978). *Modern Weed Science:* Today and tomorrows Publisher, New Delhi, P-421.

*Holm, L.G.; D.L. Plucknett; J.V. Pancho and J.P. Herberger (1977). *The World's Worst Weeds: Distribution and Biology.* Honolulu; University press of Hawai, PP-609.

Horiuchi,T. (1977). Effect of shading treatment on yield components of rice plant in the double cropping area. *Res. bull .Fac gill University,* **40** : 1-5.

---

*Original not seen.

Hussain F.; M.I. Zaidi and S.R. Chaghtai (1984). Allelopathic effects of Pakistani weeds, *Eragrostis poacoides* P. Beauv. *Pak. J. Sci. Ind. Res.*, **27** : 159-164.

Jain, J.and V.K. Khana (1987). Role of alpha and beta amylase during seedling growth and grain formation in Triticales. *Acta. Bot. Ind.*, **15** : 270-273.

Jamil, K. and U.Rani (1988). Chemosensory response of cowpea weevil (*Callosobruchus chinesis*) to aquatic weed water hyacinth (*Eichhornia crassipes* (mart) Solm. *Curr. Sci.*, **57**:1002.

Jayakumar, M.; M.Eyini and S.Pannirselvam (1990). Allelopathic effect of *Eucalyptus globulus Labill.* in ground nut and corn. *Comp. Physol. Eco.*, **15** (3) : 109 -113.

Khan., P.A.; U.K.Sabat and B.Padhy (1987). Chemical regulation of vegetative growth in rice plants. *J. Berhampur University*, **8** : 21-25.

Kibria, S.S.; M.R. Islam and C.K. Saha (1990). *Development of straw based ration for feeding ruminants.* Bangladesh Livestock research institute, Sarar, Dhaka-1341, Bangladesh, **4** (3): 235-240.

Kid, B.S. and Y.J. Yim (1983). Allelopathic effect of *Pinus densiflora* on under growth of red pine forest. *J. Chemical Ecol.*, **9**: 1135-1151.

Kohli, R.K. K.Kaur and A. Kumari (1988). Inhibition of seed germination of *Vigna ambelata* in response to *Eucalyptus globulus* allelochemicals. In : *Proceedings of intl. cong., plant physiol.*, Society of plant physiol. and biochem., New Delhi, P 15-50.

Kolykhamatov, V. (1985). Flowering plants which attack economic crops. In: *Rice growing* (Ed. by V. Konokhova) Mir Publisher Moscow Kumar, L.S.S (1992). 11, Orobanche.

Langeland, K.A. and K.C. Burks (1998). Identification and Biology of Non-native plants in Florida's Natural Areas. 4F/IFAS 165 PP.

Langer, R.H.M. (1963). Tillering in herbage grasses. *Herb Abstr.*, **33** : 141-148.

Levin, D.A. (1976). The Chemical defences of plants to pathogen and herbivores. *Annual Rev. Ecol. Systematics*, **7**:121-59.

Lisanwork, N. and A. Michelsen (1993). Allelopathy in agro - forestry systems: the effects of leaf extracts of *Cupressus lustarica* and three eucalyptus species on four ethopian crops. *Agro forestry systems,* **21** : 63-74.

Lodhi, M.A.K. (1970). Role of allelopathy as expressed by dominating trees in a low land forest in controlling the productivity and pattern of herbaceous growth. *Amer. J. Bot.,* **63:** 1 – 8.

Lodhi, M.A.K. (1978). Allelopathic effects of decaying litter of dominate trees and their associated soil in a low land forest community. *Amer. J. Bot.,* **65** : 340-344.

Lovett, J.V. (1982). The effects of allolochemicals on crop growth and development. In: *Chemical manipulation of crop growth and development*; (Ed. J.S. Melaven) Butterworths, London, p-93-110.

Lovett, J.V. and M.D. Speak (1979). Morphology and anatomy of leaves of *Salvia reflexa* (Mint weed) a strongly scented weed. *Proc. 7th Asian-Pacific Weed. Sci. Soc. Conf.* (Suppl.), 79.

Low, K.S. and C.K. Lee (1990). Removal of Arsenic from solution by water hyacinth [*Eichhorria crassipes* (mart.)Solms.] *Quart. Rev. Biol.,* **48:** 3-15.

Majid, E.; K.B. Male and J.H.T. Lyong (1992). New crops and uses: Their growth and role in rapidly changing world, *Bangladesh, J. Sci. Ind.* Res., **27**: 3 – 4.

Malik, C.P. (1981). The physiology of seeds development and germination. In : *Plant Physiology* (Ed. C.P. Malik,) Kalyani Publishers, New Delhi, pp-572-582.

Martin, P. and B. Rademacher (1960). Studies on the mutual influence of weed and crops. *Symp. of British Ecological Soc.,* **1:** 143-152.

Mathur, P.N., N.C., Sinha ad R.P. Singh (1982). Effect of seeds size on germination and seed vigour in oat (*Avena sativa* L.). *Seed Res.,* **10** : 109-113.

Mishra, M.K. and A. Panda (2008). *Wetlands. Status, utilization and protection*; Dept. of Bot. Berhampur University, Odisha, P-08-10.

Mohanty, A. and M. Nagaraju (2003). Quantitative analysis for inheritance of bacterial blight resistance in Rice. *Oryza,* **40** (3&4): 57-60.

Mohanty, B.C. (1995). Studies on allelopathic effect of water hyacinth *(Eichhorria crassipes)* on some crop plants. M.Phil dissertation, Berhampur University, Odisha, India.

Mohapatra, I.C. (2002). Multi disciplinary problem solving demand driven location and ecosystem, specific participatory rice research and development in eastern India; *Oryza*, **39** (1-4): 1 – 13

*Molish, H (1937). Uberder Einfluss einer pflanze aurdie. Ander – Allelopathic, Gustav Fischer Verlag Jena, PP 106.

*Muenscher, W.C. (1946). Weeds. The McMillan Co., New York, PP.-577.

Mukherji and R.K.Chakroverty (1970). Hadacidin induced changes in á-amylase production in germinating rice seeds. *Sci. Cult.*, **36**: 290-291.

Muller, C.H. (1969). Allelopathy as a factor in ecological process *Vegetation*, **18**: 348-57.

Muller, C.H. (1970). Phytotoxins as plant habit variables. *Recent advances in phytochem.*, **3** :106-121.

Muller, C.H. and C. Choe (1971). Phytotoxins : An Ecological phase of Phytotoxicity In : *Phytochemcial ecology*, (Ed. J.B.Harbourne), Academic press, London, PP-201-216.

Muralikrishan, S. and O.P. Saxena (1981). Germination behavior of wheat seeds as influenced by different moisture regimes, soaking duration and temperatures. *Proc. Intnl. Seed Symp., Jodhpur,* PP.-299-302.

Murty, K.S. and G.,Sahu (1977). Variability in the harvest index of late duration high yielding rice cultures. *Ind. J. Pl. Physiol.*, **20** (2) : 115 -118.

Narsaiah, A.V.; P. Narsimha and G. Navitha (1989). A simple and straight forward synthesis of antihistaminic drug and application to plants, *Indian J. Exp.* Biol., **27**: 62.

Narwal, S.S. (1994c). Future prospects of allelopathic research. In : *Allelopathy in crop production*. (Ed. S.S. Narwal), Scientific Publishers, Jodhpur, India, PP-221-223.

Ninawe, A.S. (1997). Ecological approach in sustaining agricultural food production and malnutrition. The Employment News, Ministry of Information and broad casting, Govt. of India, New Delhi Vol. **XXII**, 28:1

Padhy, B. (1980). "Impact of photo-period and seasonal sowing in rice with some studies on biochemical and histological aspects." Ph.D. Thesis, Berhampur University, Odisha, India.

Padhy, B.; P.K. Gantayat; S.K. Padhy and M.D.Sahu (2006a). A rapid bioassay method for allelopathic studies. *Allelopthy Journal*, **17** (1): 105-112.

Padhy, B.; P.A. Khan; B.Achary and N.P.Buxipatra (1992). Allelopathic effects of *Eucalyptus* leaves on seeds germination and seedlings growth of finger millet. In : *Proc. First National symposium "Allelopathy in agro-ecosystem"* (Eds. P.Tauro and S.S. Narwal), Indian Society of allelopathy, Hisar, India, PP-102-104.

Paleg, L.G. (1960a). Physiological effect of gibberellic acid. I. On carbohydrate metabolism of amylase activity of barely endosperm. *Plant physiol.*, **35** : 293-299.

Paleg, L.G. (1961) Physiological effects of gibberllic acid. III. Observations on its mode of action on barley endosperm. *Plant Physiol.*, **36** : 829-837.

Palit, P.; A. Kundu; R.K.Mandal and S.M.Sircar (1976). Varietal and seasonal difference in growth and grown with constants doses of fertilizers. *Ind. J. Agric. Sci.*, **46** (7): 327-337.

Paroda, R.S. (2006). Strategy for increasing productivity growth rate in agriculture. *Farmers Forum*, **6**(8): 2-6.

Patanaik, P.K. (1998). "Studies on allelopathic effects of *Eucalyptus* leaves on ragi (finger millet) crop." Ph.D. Thesis, Berhampur University, Berhampur, Odisha, India.

Patrick, Z.A. and L.W. Koch (1958). Inhabitation of respiration, germination and growth by substances arising during the decomposition of certain plant residues in soil. *Can. J. Bot.*, **36** : 621-647.

Pearman. I., S.M. Thomas and G.N.Thorne (1978). Effect of nitrogen fertilizer on growth and yield of semi dwarf tall verities of winter wheat. *J. Agr. Sci.*, **91** : 31-45.

Philips, I.D.J. and R.L. Jones (1964). Gibberellins like activity in bleeding sap of root systems of *Helianthus Annus* detached by a new pea epicotyls assay and other methods. *Planta*, **63** : 269-278.

Poddar, A.K.; D.S. Poddar and R.N. Mandal (1991). NEIST (North East Institute of Science & Technology) activities for environmental protection and restoration; Jorhat, Assam; *Indian Journal of Biosciences*, **61**:452.

Putnam, A.R. (1985). Allelopathic research in agriculture past highlights and potential. In: *The chemistry of allelopathy*. (Ed. A.C. Thompson), Washington; D.C. American Chemical Society, P - 1-8.

Putnam, A.R. and W.B. Duke (1978). Allelopathy in agroecosystems. *Annual Rev. Phytopathol.*, **6**: 431-51.

Qaseem, S.M; M.M.R.K. Afridi and Samiullah (1978). Effect of leaf applied phosphorus on the yield characteristics of ten barely varieties. *Ind. J. Agr. Sci.*, **48** : 215-217.

Ramey, V. (2001). Non Native Invasive Aquatic Plants in the United States: *Eichhornia crassipes*. Centre for aquatic and invasive plants, University of Florida, Florida's Natural areas, p-210.

Rao, K.S. and B.T.S. Moorthy (1993). Effect of different area formulations on the yield of medium and long duration varieties of rice. *Oryza*, **30** : 129-132.

Rawson, H.M. (1967). "Competition within the wheat plant and the plasticity of response." Ph.D Thesis, University of Adelaide.

Rawson, H.M. (1970). Spikelet number, its control and relation to yield per year in wheat. *Aust. J.Biol., Sci.*, **23** : 1-15

Rawson, H.M. and P.M. Bremner (1981). Development relation to grain yield in temperate cereals. In : Crop Physiology, (Ed. Gupta, U.S.), Oxford and IBH Pub. C. pp-238 -261.

*Reesse, J.C. (1979). Interaction of allelochemicals with nutrients in herbivore food. In: *Herbivorous; their interactions with secondary plant metabolites* (Eds. G.A. Resenthal and D.H. Janzen)

Rice, E.L. (1979). Allelopathy; An update. *Bot. Rev.*, **45**: 15-109.

Rice, E.L. (1984). *Allelopathy*. Second ed., New York; Academic Press, PP-422.

*Robbins, W.W.; A.S. Crafts and R.N. Raynor (1942). Phyto Chemicals. In : *Weed Control*. McGraw Hill Book Co., New York, PP-543.

*Robinson, T. (1963) In: The organic constituents of higher plants, (Ed. T. Robinson), Burgess Publi. Minneapolis, Minnesota, USA, PP 306.

Sabat, S.N. (2008). "Studies on allelopathic effect of Cocklebur (*Xanthium indicum*) on some Legume cultivars." Ph.D. Thesis, Berhampur University, Berhampur, Odisha, India.

Sahu, G. and K.S.Murty (1978). Productivity efficiency and nitrogen utilization in semidwarf rice cultures derived from different gene sources. *Oryza*, **15** (1) : 39-45.

Saxena O.P. and G.Singh (1987). Osmotic priming studies in some vegetable seeds. *Acta Hort.*, **215** : 201-207.

Sen, A. (1999). Hunger and Public action, *Journal of Democracy*, **10** (3) :3 – 17.

Sharma, H.C. and I. Habib (1994). Water hyacinth – use, abuse and control. In : *Ever. Sci.*, **XXIX** (2) : 38-40.

Shinoty, N.W. and R.J.Waver (1970). Export of photosynthate affected when leaves are pretreated with growth substances. *Nature*, **227** : 301-302.

Shivanna, L.R.; K.T. Prasanna and J. Mumtaz (1992). Allelopathic effects of *Eucalyptus* : An assessment on the response of agricultural crops.

In : *Proc. First National Symposium on "Allelopathy in Agro-ecosystems"*, (Eds. P. Tauro and S.S. Narwal), Indian society of allelopathy", Hisar, India, pp-108-110.

Shukla, L. M and R.D. Tripathi (1989). Role of antioxidant enzymes and anti-oxidant substances an algal plants, *Sci. Cult.*, **55**: 209.

Sing, G. and O.P. Saxena (1991). Physiological and biochemical studies associated with instant germination in tomato. In: *Int. Seed Symp,* (Eds. David N. Sen and S. Mohammed), Jodhpur, India, 313-317.

Singh, R. and R.Bawa (1982). Effect of leaf leachates from *Eucalyptus indica* Coleor. on germination of *Glaueium flavum* Crantz. *Indian J. Ecol.,* **9** : 21-28.

Singh, R.P. and D.P.S. Nandal (1993). Allelopathic effects of *eucalyptus* and *leucaena* leaf-liter on germination and seedling growth of fodder crops. *Forage Res.*, **19** : 13-16.

Sinha, S.K. and M.N. Swain (1978). Chemically aided selection in two EMS derived populations on Ragi. In : *Proc. 66th Ind. Sc. Cogr.* pp-3.

*Sircar, S.M. (1967). *Proceedings of the International symposion plant growth substances.* Department of Botany, Calcutta University, Calcutta (India).

Sircar, P.K.; S. Banerjee and S.M. Sircar (1973). Gibberllin Like activity in the shoot extract of water hyacinth (*Eichhornia crassipes* Solms.). *Indian J. Agric. Sci.,* **43** (1) 1-8.

Sircar, S.M. and M. Kundu (1959). Effect of root extract of water hyacinth on the growth and flowering of rice. *Sci. and Cult.,* **24**: 332.

Sircar, S.M and M. Kundu (1960). Growth regulating properties of the root extract of water hyacinth. *Physiologica planta.,* **13**: 56-63.

Sircar, S.M. and S.C. Chakravorthy (1961). The effect of gibberlic acid and growth substances of the root extracts of water hyacinth [*E. crassipes* (mort) Solms.] on Jute (*Corchorus capsularies* Lin.) *Curr. Sci.,* **30:** 428-431.

Srivastava, A.K. (1990). Floating aquatic macrophytes – water hyacinths. *Indian Farming,* **40** (8): 20.

Stowe, L.G. (1979). Allelopathy and its influence on the distribution of plants in an illinois field. *J. Ecol.,* **67:** 1065-1085.

Subani, S.M. (1983). "Effect of photoperiodic treatments on growth and development of rice in relation to its yield." PhD. Thesis, Berhampur University, Berhampur, Odisha, India

Sundaram, R.M. and J.S. Bentur (2006). Rice Genetics. *Curr. Sci.,* **90** (7): 901-903.

Toki, K.; N. Saito; K. Limura; T. Suzuki and T. Honda (1994 a). Delphinidin 3-gentiobiosyl (apigen in 7-glucosyl) Malonate from the flower of *Eichhorria crassipes. Phytochemistry,* **36**: 1181-1183.

Toki, K.; N. Saito; K. Kawano; T.S. Lu; Shigihara and T. Honda (1994 b). An analytical delphinidin glycoside in the blue flowers of *Evolvulus pilosus. Phytochemistry,* **36**: 609-612.

Tripathy, A.K. (2000) "Studies on the allelopathic effect of *Acacia* species on some rice (*Oryza sativa* L.) cultivars." Ph.D Thesis, Berhampur University., Berhampur, Odisha, India.

Vaughan, W.L. (1989). The evolving story of rice evolution. *Plant Sci.,* **174** (4): 394-408.

---

*Original not seen.

Vergara, B.S.; A.Tanaka; R.Lilis and S. Puranabhavung (1966). Relationship between growth duration and grain yield of rice plants. *Soil Sci. and Pl. Nutr.,* **12** : 31-39.

Vergara, B.S.; R. Lilis and A.Tanaka (1964). Relationship between length of growing period and yield of rice plants under a limited nitrogen supply. *Soil Sci. and Pl. Nutr.,* **10** : 59-65.

Waller, G.R. (1988). Biochemical frontiers of allelopathy. *Biologia plantarum,* **31** (6): 418-447.

Winter, A.G. (1961). New physiological and biological aspects in the inter-relationship between higher plants. In: *Mechanisms in biological competition.* (Ed. F.L. Milthorpe), Cambridge University Press, Cambridge, P-228-244.

Wu, H.: Zhou, HQ.; Huang, SY.; Ma, K. and Lao, XF. (1991). A Novel Steroid from *Eichhornia crassipes. Chinese Chemical Letters,* **2** (7): 509.

Yang, SY.; Yu, ZW.; Sun, WH.; Zhao, BW.; Wu, H.; Huang, SY.; Zhou, HQ.; Ma, K. and Lao, XF. (1992). Isolation and identification of antialgal compounds from root system of water hyacinth. *Acta. Phytophysiologica,* **18** (4): 399.

*Yomo, H (1960). Studies on the amylase activity substance. IV. On the amylase activating action of gibberellins. *Hakko Kyokaishi,* **18** : 600-602.

Yoshida, S. (1972). Physological aspects of grain yield. *Ann. Rev. Pl. Physiol.,* **23** : 437-464.

Yoshida, S.; F.T. Parao and H.M. Beachell (1972). A maximum annual rice production trial in the tropics. *Int. Rice common. Newsl.,* **21**: 27-32.

❑❑❑

*Original not seen.

Index